T0328442

Ricardo's Economics

**A general equilibrium theory
of distribution and growth**

Michio Morishima

Ricardo's Economics

A general equilibrium theory of distribution and growth

The right of the
University of Cambridge
to print and sell
all manner of books
was granted by
Henry VIII in 1534.
The University has printed
and published continuously
since 1584.

Cambridge University Press

Cambridge
New York   Port Chester
Melbourne   Sydney

CAMBRIDGE UNIVERSITY PRESS
Cambridge, New York, Melbourne, Madrid, Cape Town, Singapore,
São Paulo, Delhi, Dubai, Tokyo, Mexico City

Cambridge University Press
The Edinburgh Building, Cambridge CB2 8RU, UK

Published in the United States of America by
Cambridge University Press, New York

www.cambridge.org
Information on this title: www.cambridge.org/9780521396882

First published 1989
First paperback edition 1990

A catalogue record for this publication is available from the British Library

Library of Congress Cataloguing in Publication Data

Morishima, Michio, 1923—
Ricardo's economics: a general equilibrium theory of distribution
and growth/Michio Morishima.
          p.   cm.
Includes index.
ISBN 0-521-36630-5
1. Ricardo, David, 1772–1823. 2. Equilibrium (Economics)
3. Classical school of economics. I. Title.
HB103.R5M67   1989
330.15′3 – dc19   88-38760 CIP

ISBN 978-0-521-36630-4 Hardback
ISBN 978-0-521-39688-2 Paperback

Contents

Preface   *page* vii

Introduction   1

Part I Prices and rent

1   Prices and the Ricardian marginalism   17

2   Differential rent   36

Part II Wages and profits

3   Wages, profits and general equilibrium   59

4   The equal rate of profit and exploitation   81

Part III Growth

5   Ricardian growth   103

6   International trade   126

Part IV Say's law

7   Say's law of markets   149

8   Machinery   168

Part V Three paradigms compared

9   Towards an anti-Say's law regime   189

10 Ricardo, Walras and Keynes   209

11 The epoch of Ricardo's economics   233

Index   252

Preface

For nearly ten years I have given, at London School of Economics, a course entitled 'Marx, Walras and Keynes in the light of Contemporary Economic Analysis'. Its first two parts have already produced books on Marx and Walras, respectively, while the final part has yet remained to be written. During the time when I was writing these books, I became more and more convinced by a somewhat surprising new view that Marx and Walras might not have been diagonally opposed to each other. We can clearly observe in Marx's examinations of the so-called 'transformation' problems and his analysis of the reproduction schemes the discussion which is equivalent or, at least, corresponds with what Walras called the general equilibrium analysis. Moreover, more microscopically, we may say that these two scholars used a number of the same 'parts' in their respective systems analysis, especially the dual adjustment rules of prices and quantities.

These findings have directed my interest to Marx's and Walras' common guru, David Ricardo. As will become clear in this volume, at the time of Ricardo, Marx and Walras, the economic discipline had a core which might deserve the name of the old general equilibrium theory. This theory, being spanned by these three great names, is very much, if not entirely, different from the contemporary one represented by such economists as Hicks, Arrow, Debreu, Hahn, Malinvaud and others. Although this volume is not primarily a book on history of economic analysis but a reappraisal of past great economists from the viewpoint of contemporary economic theory, I hope it will be able to offer some new material for reconsideration to those historians who have so far been accustomed to simply regarding Marx as an offspring of Ricardo who founded Marxian economics and Walras as the first economist who formulated the general equilibrium analysis based on marginal concepts.

Such being the case, I have given up my original idea to conclude the triology with Keynes. I have instead been concerned, in this volume, with transition from Ricardo (who highly appraises Say's law of markets as a 'very important' principle) to Keynes (who rejects the law). Via this channel, a number of Keynesian problems, especially the problems of effective demand and unemployment, are introduced and discussed particularly in the last part of the volume. Also, I try and identify the epoch of Ricardian economics and those of Walrasian and Keynesian economics, in parallel with this transition.

Naturally, Sraffa is taken as a focal figure in one of the chapters of the book. I do not, however, discuss his distribution formula for its own sake but construe it as an indispensable 'part' of the Ricardian general equilibrium system. This does not mean that I accept it whole in lumps without any correction. Ricardo's own distribution formula is dynamic and shifts downwards in a progressive economy, so that it differs remarkably from Sraffa's static formula. In its construction the idea of Ricardian marginalism based on the limitation of land of various qualities plays an essential role. Furthermore, unlike Sraffa's, Ricardo's formula is linked with other 'parts' of Ricardian economics, such as the opportunity of international trade, the introduction of machinery and so on. Also Ricardo's *marginal* labour theory of value is compared with Marx's average or linear labour theory and its significance for Ricardo is identified. In his *Principles* I take Chapter XXI entitled 'Effects of Accumulation on Profits and Interest' as the most important chapter; all parts carefully produced and tested in other places are gathered and assembled there to form a general equilibrium system which is examined in order to confirm a pattern of economic growth which I call Ricardian growth. From this point of view I review recent macroeconomic interpretations of Ricardo, particularly Samuelson's and Casarosa's.

Finally, it is acknowledged that my essay, 'Anti-Say's Law versus Say's Law: A Change in Paradigm' which I wrote with G. Catephores for *Evolutionary Economics: Application of Schumpeter's Ideas,* edited by H. Hanusch, Cambridge University Press, 1988, is contained in Chapters 7 and 9 after some modifications, revisions and rearrangements. Also my acknowledgement is due to Miss Rachel Hall for her great help.

January 1989   Michio Morishima

Introduction

1 This volume, together with my previous works, *Marx's Economics* and *Walras's Economics*,[1] forms a trilogy on the first-generation of scientific economists – Ricardo, Marx and Walras. Whilst many of us have little objection to regarding Marx as a Ricardian, some, perhaps many, would reject the view that Walras tried and provided, in his *Elements of Pure Economics*, a microeconomic foundation to Ricardo's economics. In fact, William Jaffé, the translator of Walras' *Éléments*, insists that there was 'no room for growth' in Walras' economics,[2] whereas growth was Ricardo's central subject. However, Jaffé's conclusion completely contradicts the facts. In Part VII (of the *Elements*) entitled 'Conditions and Consequences of Economic Progress: Critique of Systems of Pure Economics', Walras used the general equilibrium models developed in Parts II–VI to derive *'the laws of the variation of prices in a progressive economy'*.[3] This means that his general equilibrium theory is nothing else but the groundwork for those laws which are summarized as:

1 'In a progressive economy, the price of labour (wages) remaining substantially unchanged, the price of land-services (rent) will rise appreciably and the price of capital-services (the interest charge) will fall appreciably.'
2 'In a progressive economy, the rate of net income will fall appreciably.'
3 'In a progressive economy, the price of capital goods proper remaining constant, the price of personal faculties will rise in proportion to the fall in the rate of net income, and the price of land will rise both by reasons of the fall in the rate of income and by reason of the rise in rent.'[4]

---

[1] *Marx's Economics* and *Walras' Economics*, Cambridge University Press, 1973 and 1977, respectively.
[2] W. Jaffé, 'Walras's Economics As Others See It', *Journal of Economic Literature*, Vol. XVIII, June, 1980, pp. 528–49. See also my reply: M. Morishima, 'W. Jaffé on Leon Walras: A Comment', *Journal of Economic Literature*, pp. 550–8.
[3] L. Walras, *Elements of Pure Economics*, Richard D. Irwin, Inc., 1954, p. 382, Walras' italics.
[4] Walras, *Elements*, pp. 390–1.

These are obviously very similar to, though not identical with, the laws which Ricardo wanted to establish in his *Principles*.[5] They are the laws which regulate what proportion of the whole produce of the earth (or the GNP according to contemporary terminology) will be allotted to each of the three classes of the community, landowners, capitalists and workers, under the names of rent, profit and wages, respectively. They show how the distribution will change at different stages of society and, according to Ricardo, this dynamic law of distribution is the principal problem of political economy.[6] In spite of Jaffé's insistence on the interpretation that 'the *Elements*, instead of aiming to delineate a theory of the working of any real capitalistic system, was designed to portray how an imaginary system *might* work in conformity with principles of "justice" rooted in the traditional natural law philosophy',[7] it cannot be denied that Walras constructed a model, from which he derived the three Ricardo-like laws of the workings of the progressive economy. It should be emphasized that the section in which the laws are derived is followed directly by four chapters which examine various systems of pure economics, especially that of Ricardo. Walras carefully reformulated Ricardo's theory of rent and critically examined English (Ricardo's and J. S. Mill's) theories of prices, wages and interest. This suggests that Walras did not derive these laws, independently of, or without knowing, Ricardo but with a clear consciousness of his existence. Moreover, there is no other major economic conclusion to be found in the *Elements*; this is the reason why I regard Walras as a Ricardian.

Rejecting this view, Jaffé insists that Part VII of the *Elements* should be regarded as its 'coda' and, therefore, it should be neglected when one discusses Walras' economics. On the other hand, Jaffé accuses me of focussing attention exclusively on the *Elements* with no reference to Walras' other writings. If such an arbitrary selection – deletion and inclusion – of an economist's works is permitted, anything can be said of him. In fact Jaffé contradicts himself by

[5] D. Ricardo, *The Principles of Political Economy, and Taxation*, Cambridge University Press, 1953. Throughout the present volume, a quotation from the *Principles* is referred to only by the page number where it appears, without mentioning the title of the book.
[6] Ricardo, *Principles*, p. 5.
[7] Jaffé, *Walras' Economics*, p. 530. He also writes: 'The *Elements* was intended to be and is ... a realistic utopia, i.e. a delineation of a state of affairs nowhere to be found in the actual world, ... ideally perfect in certain respects ...' (p. 530). This view may be adequate of Debreu and Arrow–Hahn, but not of Walras.

recognizing, in other places, growth theoretic elements in Walras. As he points out, the correspondence of Walras with such scholars as Lexis and Loria evidences that Walras' idea of nationalization of land ownership was based on the very principle of constant rise of rent which was evidently due to his Ricardo-like growth theory.

In this volume entitled *Ricardo's Economics*, I concentrate on his main work, the *Principles of Political Economy, and Taxation*, with no reference to other works; I have already followed the same policy in the case of Marx, as well as Walras. What I want to examine in this trilogy is the classical paradigm formed by the three major works, the *Principles*, the three volumes of *Capital* and the *Elements*, but not a full restoration of the three giants, Ricardo, Marx and Walras, in their entirety including their secondary books, articles, pamphlets and private correspondence. I have never been a historian of economic thought but have been an economic theorist throughout my life. With such a specialty, I believe, I am allowed to concentrate solely on their main works; and by making this constraint I am able to read these works more deeply and more rigorously than specialists in the history of economic thought, so that present-day economists can learn from them.

It is evident that Ricardo was the classical economist most highly respected by Marx who noted 'the scientific impartiality and love of truth characteristic of him'.[8] Walras too respected him as 'the founder of pure economics in England'.[9] These attributes are mainly due to the methodology adopted by Ricardo. On the basis of clearly defined concepts, he logically examined relationships and rigorously deduced economic laws (propositions) from the explicitly postulated hypotheses (axioms) concerning free competition and rational behaviour. (If the axiom is deemed to be incorrect it must be modified or replaced by a correct axiom, though this second phase of scientific activity, that is, the correction of theories in the face of observations, was not yet on the actual agenda of investigation at the time of Ricardo, a first-generation theorist.)

In fact, his political economy is nothing other than mathematical economics without mathematical symbols and formulas. It can easily be translated into mathematical language and one may find, as we shall do in this book, a general equilibrium system (that is very similar to Walras') concealed within. In comparison to this

---

[8] K. Marx, *Capital*, Vol. I, Progress Publishers, Moscow, 1965, p. 438.
[9] Walras, *Elements*, p. 398.

similarity, the dissimilarity usually emphasized by historians of economic thought – that is the labour theory of value supported by Ricardo and Marx versus the scarcity theory of value by Walras – is of minor or secondary importance. We may thus conclude that Ricardo, Marx and Walras constitute a trio. The first developed a general-equilibrium model of economic growth verbally, logically, and the second extended it in a number of directions and examined interesting novel mathematical properties that were concealed within it, again with no explicit use of mathematical formulas,[10] while the third put the model into a rigorous mathematical form and, by doing so, made it operationally more workable.

In this volume I shall discuss Ricardo's *Principles* from this point of view; I shall, moreover, neglect the chapters on taxation entirely. Although the title of the book is usually understood as signifying that it is a book on the principles of both economics and taxation, it is found that it is a book on the principles of economics, and taxation, if the title is more carefully read. This may be seen by the fact that, for all editions published while Ricardo was alive, there was a comma between 'political economy' and 'and taxation' in the title.[11] Thus the taxation chapters are not the chapters where the theory of taxes is expounded but where economic theory is applied to the problem of taxation. This was known to Marx as he wrote: 'The whole work consists of thirty-two chapters (in the third edition). Of this, fourteen chapters deal with *taxes*, thus dealing only with the application of the theoretical principles.'[12] Since we concentrate, in this volume, on Ricardo's economic theory, we shall totally neglect all the taxation chapters.

It is noted that selected works on Ricardo by contemporary economists are to be examined in this volume; this has been done with the intention of contrasting them with my own formulation of Ricardo's theory. This volume also discusses such problems as the 'fundamental Marxian theorem' and the 'Say's law versus anti-Say's law' controversy. Although one might consider them as unrelated with Ricardo, I do consider that they are really necessary in order to clarify some aspects of Ricardo in comparison with Marx and

[10] See my 'Marx in the Light of Modern Economic Theory', *Econometrica*, Vol. 42, 1974.

[11] This fact has been pointed out by T. Hatori, a co-translator of Ricardo's *Principles* into Japanese.

[12] Marx, *Theories of Surplus Value*, Part II, Lawrence and Wishart, London, 1969, pp. 166–7.

Walras. It is emphasized that this is primarily a book on Ricardo's economics rather than a work on Ricardian economics. In exactly the same way as I ignored most of the works by Marxists and Walrasians in the previous volumes on Marx and Walras, many contributions of Ricardian (or neo-Ricardian) economists are neglected in this book.

2 Ricardo's world consisted of agriculture and industry. While the former makes use of land of various grades, No. 1, No. 2, etc., the latter, which produces non-food necessaries for subsistence, luxuries and capital goods, is assumed to need no land. The availability of land is fixed, so that diminishing returns prevail in agriculture, while returns are constant with respect to scale in industry. In a progressive economy with a growing population, food will become dearer and dearer, so that real wages (the wages in terms of food) will decline, eventually reaching subsistence level, at which point the population will cease to grow and economic progress will be stopped. To avoid this classical stationary state Ricardo advocated a theory of an international division of labour based on free trade. At some stage of development, the progressing country will lose its comparative advantage in agriculture over less developed countries; cheap corn will then be imported from the latter, agricultural countries and colonies. Land is vast in these and diminishing returns are, therefore, negligible, so that real wages will not decline. The population will continue to grow and the stationary state will be thus avoided.

This may be considered as a success brought about by Ricardian policy. But while the population expands, the country must import more and more food, and to finance ever increasing imports it has to export industrial products in an ever increasing amount. So far as the country is able to do so, Ricardo's programme may be viable; but, once the country's monopoly in international markets of industrial products is shaken by some late coming nations, the Ricardian doctrine will become unworkable. Moreover, it will be more and more difficult to maintain full employment of labour and capital, because Say's law (accepted by Ricardo) will become an even more unrealistic supposition. In fact, as will be discussed later in this volume, full employment is not automatic in a non- or anti-Say's law economy, and the full employment equilibrium is a saddle point; that is to say, if the economy is placed at a point where labour and capital are not fully employed, it will, generally speaking, increasingly diverge from the equilibrium with the lapse of time. Due to the achievements of its doctrine and policy Ricardo's economics was eventually replaced by Keynes' economics.

Being a supporter of free trade and free enterprise, Walras, like Ricardo, was concerned with diminishing returns due to the limited availability of land. In his words:

> In general it is possible to employ smaller and smaller quantities of land-services per unit of output of consumers' goods and new capital goods provided that larger and larger quantities of the services of capital good proper are used. Whence the possibility of indefinite progress.[13] (Walras, *Elements*, p. 383)

> Since the quantity of land does not increase in a progressive state, we are faced with the problem of obtaining more products with the same, or very nearly the same, total quantity of land-services. Population, on the other hand, does increase, for such an increase is implicit in our definition of progress; and thus additional labour, naturally proportional to the additional future output, is assured. What else is needed? It is necessary that the quantity of capital goods be increased in order to furnish the required additional amounts of capital-services. (*Ibid.*, p. 386)

> *Consequently: Progress . . . is possible, in spite of the failure of the quantity of land to increase, thanks to the increase in the quantity of capital goods proper, provided, however, that this increase in the quantity of capital goods proper precedes and is proportionately greater than the increase in population.* (*Ibid.*, Walras' italics)

> The truth is that a progressive rise in the value of land and its services . . . is, along with the expansion of capital and population, the essential characteristic of economic progress. (*Ibid.*, p. 392)

All these are extracts from a chapter of the *Elements*, entitled 'The Marginal Productivity Theorem', where Walras used the theorem to derive the three Ricardo-like laws of general price movements in a progressive economy, referred to in Section 1 above. In view of this we find it natural that he examined Ricardo seriously and critically in the three chapters following his discussion of the marginal productivity theorem. In fact, expressing his highest respect of

---

[13] To the same effect, he also writes: 'The infinite multiplication of products can only take place to the extent that capital-services can be substituted more and more for land-services though never wholly replacing them' (Walras, *Elements*, p. 383), 'its services . . . is, along with the expansion of capital and population, the essential characteristic of economic progress' (Walras, *Elements*, p. 392).

Ricardo as 'the founder of pure economics in England', he wrote:

> The efforts of the English School to develop a theory of rent, wages and interest were far more sustained and thorough than those of the various French schools that came into existence after the Physiocrats. We must turn, therefore, to a critical examination of the English theory. That is the purpose of this and the following two Lessons. (*Ibid.*, p. 398)

Then in one of these Lessons he stated:

> The need for restating Ricardo's reasoning in terms of infinitesimals is so imperative that a number of authors have succumbed to it even though they continued to use ordinary language. Hence the rigorous formation which we have just given to this reasoning is the true formulation of the English theory of rent. (*Ibid.*, p. 411)

Afterwards he criticized Ricardo for being unsuccessful in formulating a general equilibrium system to determine the prices of services, i.e., rent, wages and interest charges, as well as the prices of products, simultaneously.[14] Finally he wrote:

> Now, in order to demonstrate that commodity prices ... result effectively from such and such givens or conditions, it is absolutely indispensable, as I see it: (1) to formulate, in conformance with these givens or conditions, a system of conditions which will be exactly equal in number to the unknowns, and of which the unknowns are the roots; and (2) to show that the sequence of actual events gives us, in fact, an empirical solution of this system of equations. This is what I have done first with regard to exchange, then with regard to production and finally with regard to capital formation. The use of the language and method of mathematics has thus enabled me to demonstrate not only the laws of the establishment of current equilibrium prices but also the laws of change in these prices. It has made it possible for me to analyse the facts, and thus to set the principle of free competition on firm foundations. (*Ibid.*, p. 427)

From this we may now conclusively say that the aim (or one of the aims) of Walras' *Elements* was to give Ricardo's economics a true formulation and to establish it on rigorously mathematical foundations. In doing so, Walras used both general equilibrium analysis and the method which Hicks calls 'the static method in dynamic theory'.[15] The process of economic progress is divided into periods, the general equilibrium method being applied to each of

---

[14] See Walras, *Elements*, pp. 423–6.
[15] John Hicks, *Capital and Growth*, Oxford University Press, 1965, pp. 30–1.

them in order to obtain a picture of temporary equilibrium. Linking these snapshots together in an appropriate manner, a motion picture of economic progress and capital formation is obtained. Although the idea of a general equilibrium system and that of the static method for dynamics are both implicit (but literally discernible) in Ricardo, it was Walras who made them explicit and provided Ricardo's growth theory with a firm analytical formulation. Thus we may say, on the one hand, that Jaffé's view that there is no room for growth in Walras is a mere illusion, and on the other, that these two economists, Ricardo and Walras, complement, rather than compete with, each other. In addition, this view also leads me to reject the position of A. K. Dasgupta who insists that, whereas Ricardo was concerned with growth, Walras' interest was in a stationary economy.[16]

3 There is a popular and conventional view that marginalism emerged in opposition to classical economics. This view, however, is entirely wrong because Ricardian economics, in which the classical school is considered to have culminated, is indeed an economics based on marginalism. This has been stated above and will be shown in Chapters 1 and 2 below in considerable detail. Of course it is true that, with no idea of marginal utilities, both Ricardo and Marx used the labour theory of value.[17] It is also true that analysis was mainly made, in their economics, in terms of prices, wages and profits, rather than labour values. They both believed that prices are not equal (or proportional) to values, unless a stringent condition – that the composition of capital, that is the ratio of the capital to support labour to the capital invested in tools, machinery and the buildings, is the same throughout all processes of production – is fulfilled. Marx clearly stated: 'average prices do not directly coincide with the values of commodities, as Adam Smith, Ricardo, and others believe.'[18] It is interesting to notice in this quotation that even Marx was affected by the popular view and considered that Ricardo accepted the proposition of proportionality between prices and values; it will be seen later that Chapter 1 of Ricardo's *Principles* gives clear evidence that he believed the opposite, that is, that there was a disproportionality.

[16] A. K. Dasgupta, *Epochs of Economic Theory*, Basil Blackwell, 1985, p. 9.
[17] Though there is a passage in *Capital* which could be explained more intelligibly by introducing the concept of marginal utility. See my *Marx's Economics*, pp. 41–2.
[18] Marx, *Capital*, Vol. I, p. 166.

Still, it is true that the two economists analysed the economy in terms of value too. Their economics makes dual-standard valuations in terms of values and prices, respectively, while Walras, who totally rejected the labour value theory, adopted an approach of mono-standard valuation (in terms of prices, of course).

Marginalism was introduced into economics in relation to the rent theory. Because the marginal production coefficients of agriculture depend on the rate of cultivation m, they are regarded as constant where m remains unchanged. These, together with the production coefficients of industry, which are assumed to be constant, enable us to deduce the wage–profit frontier, or the Sraffa distribution line, for any given m, so that we obtain a family of the frontiers with m being a parameter. These are the results obtained from Ricardo's price–cost equations, and they are valid in Marxian economics too. It will be shown, in Chapter 3 below, that the frontier shifts downwards as m increases. Thus economic progress is accompanied by a downwards shift of the wage–profit frontier which finally ceases when a stationary equilibrium is reached. Also, as will be seen later, these shifting frontiers refute the incompatibility of falling profit and falling real wage insisted by Samuelson.[19]

In spite of having these results and knowing that values are generally disproportional to prices, Ricardo and Marx nevertheless continued to stick to the labour theory of value. Their reasons for this persistence are different. In the case of Marx, as has been seen in my *Marx's Economics*, value accounting is used to reveal exploitation concealed under the surface of price accounting, in order to show that exploitation is necessary and sufficient for positive profits. Ricardo, on the other hand, was not concerned with the problem of unmasking the essence of profits; he would have given the labour value theory up, if he had been able. In his theory of economic growth, the hard core of his economics, however, he required certain comparative statics laws, concerning the movement of prices and real wages, which play a most important role in the theory. For Ricardo, not being equipped with a mathematical ability to solve the complicated price–cost equations, it was absolutely impossible to deduce exact comparative statics laws of prices, using verbal deductive reasoning only. For him, therefore, it was necessary

[19] P. A. Samuelson, 'Wages and Interest: A Modern Dissection of Marxian Economic Models', in *The Collected Scientific Papers of Paul A. Samuelson*, Vol. I, MIT Press, 1966.

to simplify price–cost equations and obtain approximate solutions to the true equations, by regarding the simplified versions as if they were true. Naturally he took the value equations as simplified versions of the price–cost equations and labour values as approximations to prices.[20]

In my opinion, this is the main reason why Ricardo was concerned with comparative statics laws of labour values. If he could have derived laws of prices directly from price–cost equations, he would have agreed to discard the labour theory of value. I would imagine that Marx would also have agreed to dispense with it as far as this aspect of the use of the theory is concerned. The opinions of Ricardo, Marx and Walras would have concurred with regard to the labour theory of value in as far as it is used only as a rule of thumb for calculating prices and costs.

On the other hand neither Ricardo nor Walras were ever interested in identifying the essence (or source) of profits. If they had been, they would have encountered the problem of exploitation, because it can be shown, as will be done in a later chapter of this volume, for any economic model, that is, regardless of whether it is Marx's model, or Ricardo's, or Walras', or even Arrow–Debreu's, that exploitation is necessary and sufficient for positive profits; therefore, they would have accepted the labour theory of value as a tool for proving this proposition. Moreover, Marx discussed in *Capital* (Vol. I, pp. 85–7), how the use value of commodity i is related to the non-use value which commodity i provides to its owner as a depository of exchange value; I have shown that the two equations obtained by him together imply Walras' (and Marshall's) subjective equilibrium conditions for the consumer.[21] We may thus conclude that Walras, as well as Ricardo, would not have objected to the labour theory of value, so far as it appears in the proof of the essence of profits, while Marx would not have strongly opposed the utility theory, as long as it was used for explaining consumers' behaviour. Thus the three great economists would not have been antagonistic towards each other with respect to the theory of value.

4 Versions of what I have previously referred to as the three

[20] Even Marx, who could have mathematically formulated the price–cost equations in the 'transformation' problem, still felt difficulty in finding how prices behave, so that he too used the value equations to obtain a rule of thumb of price movements.

[21] See footnote 17 above.

Ricardo-like laws of the working of a progressive economy are to be found in various places in the works of Ricardo, Marx and Walras, whilst they do not appear in Hicks, *Value and Capital* or Keynes, *General Theory*. In the latter in particular Keynes did not follow in Ricardo's footsteps and apparently rebelled against him; he dispensed with Say's law which Ricardo regarded as a 'very important principle' and, since then, this position has been accepted and respected by most of his followers. According to Keynes, it is one of the three postulates made by the classical economists, and because 'these three assumptions', he maintains, 'all amount to the same thing in the sense that they all stand and fall together',[22] it is indeed *the* classical postulate. As he stated, under the postulate, if the economy is provided with enough capital – this condition is always satisfied where capital/labour ratio is perfectly flexible – there is no involuntary unemployment; the full employment of labour is always realized.

As Ricardo assumed Say's law throughout the *Principles*, unemployment is not discussed in the book at all, except in the final chapter, 'On Machinery'. This chapter first appeared in the third edition and deals with the problem of unemployment. Marx praised Ricardo on this point, because the latter who was originally of the opinion that 'all machinery that displaces workmen, simultaneously and necessarily sets free an amount of capital adequate to employ the same identical workmen', expressly disclaimed this point in the newly added chapter of the third edition, 'with the scientific impartiality and love of truth characteristic of him', as quoted previously. The more recent appraisals of the chapter are also favourable, and more or less similar to Marx's. However, if Say's law is understood to hold in the new chapter too, as it actually does, Marx was wrong in praising Ricardo's scientific impartiality; as I shall explain later, Ricardo should have stuck to his original view, because unemployment is impossible under Say's law. On the other hand, if the law were to be removed from Ricardo, due to Marx's criticism of it, then the conclusion of the machinery chapter would be acceptable, but all other chapters based on Say's law would have to be reexamined and revised on the new assumption that Say's law does not prevail. If so, Marx should have criticized Ricardo because of the lack of scientific consistency.

[22] J. M. Keynes, *The General Theory of Employment, Interest and Money*, Macmillan, 1936, p. 22.

Another basic assumption of Ricardo's economics is the wage fund theory. Where it prevailed, an expansion of the investment–goods sector gave rise to a reduction in the consumption–goods sector, because of the lack of wage funds. This is the complete opposite to the contemporary intersectoral multiplier theory which implies a positive repercussion from the investment sector to the consumption sector. At the time of Ricardo, agriculture was the dominant sector, and the production lag significant. Corn produced in one year was retained and used as wage funds the following year. The idea of wage funds due to the agricultural production lag was certainly appreciated by Ricardo and inherited by Marx as variable capital. It, however, completely disappeared in Walras. In this respect, among the trio, Walras was distinct from Ricardo and Marx and was nearer to contemporary economists who pay negligible attention to time lags. In this sense Walras was neoclassical, while Ricardo and Marx were classical. When choosing between production lags and simultaneous repercussions, the economists' emphasis has shifted towards the latter.

5 In Part I of this volume I shall deal with Ricardo's theory of value and discuss the Ricardo–Marx theorem which shows that prices and values are not proportional unless constant capital and variable capital, to use Marx's terminology, are proportional throughout all processes of production. Such economists as Pasinetti, Caravale and Tosato, Costa, and Casarosa assume that the agricultural output is an increasing function of its employment of labour, with diminishing returns.[23] However, there is no such simple production function in Ricardo. He assumed that agriculture is subject to constant returns to scale as long as the rate of cultivation m remains unchanged, while diminishing returns prevail where m increases. Hence it was vitally important for Ricardo to determine the value of m, and his marginalism was formulated in reference to the movement of m. Whereas the above mentioned writers assume full employment of land, Ricardo's conclusions included the proposition that rent is zero for the marginal land, provided that there is unemployed land of the same quality. All these will be discussed in Part I.

[23] L. L. Pasinetti, *Growth and Income Distribution*, Cambridge University Press, 1974; G. A. Caravale and D. A. Tosato, *Ricardo and the Theory of Value, Distribution and Growth*, Routledge and Kegan Paul, London, 1980. Also see, for Costa, and Casarosa, G. A. Caravale, *The Legacy of Ricardo*, Basil Blackwell, Oxford, 1985.

Part II sees various chapters of the *Principles* in a general equilibrium framework and derives a family of wage–profit frontiers, with the rate of cultivation as a parameter. It differs from Sraffa's single frontier interpretation.[24] It also shows that the fundamental Marxian theorem to the effect that profits are positive if and only if there is positive exploitation, holds true in the Ricardian system too. I explicitly introduce land into the theorem and confirm that the existence of land does not affect the theorem; it holds not only for Ricardo's economy, as well as Marx's, but also for the neoclassical models such as Hicks', Arrow–Debreu's, etc.

Part III formulates the Ricardian growth theory coupled with his theory of international trade. I interpret, as I have already stated, his dynamic analysis as a sequential analysis of short-run general equilibria, using the comparative statics method. Ricardo was concerned with an economy where capitalists invest in wage funds, as well as in capital goods. This obviously differs from recent macroeconomic formulations by Casarosa and Samuelson in terms of differential equations. They assume, among other things, that, if the rate of profit is higher than the minimum subsistence rate, capitalist's propensity to save (that is equal to their propensity to invest by virtue of Say's law) – hence the rate of capital accumulation – is positive. Casarosa, however, rules out capital goods proper (machines etc.), while Samuelson neglects the wage funds. They both are un-Ricardian in the sense that they do not deal with microeconomic problems in which Ricardo was interested, particularly the problem of allocating aggregate savings among two or more capital items, one being the wage funds and the other one or many capital goods. Being seen as a mathematical formulation of Ricardo's economics I would much prefer Walras' general equilibrium theory to the Casarosa–Samuelson macroeconomic model. In Chapter 5 below I critically review their interpretations.

In fact the Ricardo–Walras theory, together with Marx's one to be constructed on the bases of the theory of production prices and the reproduction schemes, could clearly be distinguished as the old general equilibrium theory from the contemporary one due to Hicks, Arrow, Debreu, Hahn and others. In the old theory, the price–cost equations are explicit and outputs as well as prices are regarded as independent variables. Outputs are regulated by excess profits from

[24] P. Sraffa, *Production of Commodities by Means of Commodities*, Cambridge University Press, 1960.

the respective outputs and prices by excess demands for the respective commodities. In the new theory, however, outputs are regarded, not as independent variables, but as functions of prices, and all prices are regulated by excess demands. Thus, in the old theory, the price–cost equations play an essential role, so that the general equilibrium theory of exchange where these equations are absent is completely different from that of production, where outputs and prices adjust themselves according to the dual adjustment rules stated above. In the new theory, on the other hand, the general equilibrium theories of exchange and production are homogenous; there is no role for the price–cost equations at all within them. Part III gives a formulation of Ricardo's economics from the viewpoint of the old theory of general equilibrium.

Part IV mainly deals with Say's law. As has been maintained by Keynes, Say's law is synonymous with the lack of an independent investment function; thus it is only true in an early stage of the capitalist economy, where each entrepreneur has only one source of capital, his own savings. Where he may use other persons' savings by borrowing directly from them or through a bank, the law will not hold true. An independent investment function will then have its place in the economy, and in this world of anti-Say's law there will be no guarantee of full employment. Thus investment decided independently (from savers) and full employment are generally incompatible under the anti-Say's law. This theory of over-determinacy, which has already been discussed in my *Walras' Economics*[25] is reexamined in Part IV; the thesis is revised in its proposition and a different proof is given. This part also carefully investigates Ricardo's chapter on machinery and shows that the introduction of machinery does not create unemployment, provided that the premise of Say's law is maintained.

Finally, Part V compares Ricardo's, Walras' and Keynes' economics. They are structurally similar but differ according to whether they satisfy Say's law or not and whether they assume the wage fund theory or not. These differences are shown to create vast disagreements about the workability of the economy between the three economists, especially between Ricardo and Walras on the one hand, and Keynes on the other. The final chapter discusses the historical character of economic theory and tries to specify the epoch of Ricardo's economics.

[25] Morishima, *Walras' Economics*, pp. 121–2.

Part I

PRICES AND RENT

1 Prices and the Ricardian marginalism

1 There are two kinds of commodities; one is scarce and the other can be increased in quantity by production. Concentrating on the latter, Ricardo considered that the ratio between supply and demand may, for a time, affect the market price of a commodity but this effect will be only of temporary duration, where production is made under competitive conditions. Abstracting from momentary or everyday fluctuations of price, its normal level (or what Ricardo called the natural price) is ultimately regulated by the cost of production. In a primitive society where goods are mainly produced by labour, without much use of machinery or tools, commodities are exchanged in inverse proportion to the quantities of labour necessary for producing them. As he quoted from Adam Smith, 'If among a nation of hunters, for example, it usually cost twice the labour to kill a beaver which it does to kill a deer, one beaver should naturally exchange for, or be worth two deer' (p. 13). This primitive labour theory of value, however, does not hold true in a more developed industrial society, where tools and machines are employed in producing various commodities. Ricardo clearly recognized this limit to the labour theory of value and, therefore, developed an extended theory of prices which has a dual structure, one section dealing with price determination and the other with the labour theory of value.

In this respect Ricardo was very similar to Marx who also knew the limit of the primitive value theory and therefore constructed a theory based on dual accounting principles in terms of prices and labour values, respectively. Why did they retain the obsolete, generally untrue labour theory of value? If they knew, as they did, that the theory is unsatisfactory as the theory of prices, they should have rubbed out or discarded it as Samuelson has suggested. The reason for the conservation of the old theory was different for each

of them. Marx reexamined various accounts in terms of prices from
the view point of labour value accounting and pointed out the fact
that an exchange between two commodities which is equal in terms
of prices may often turn out to be unequal in terms of labour values.
He then focussed upon the imbalance between the workers' supply
of labour and the capitalists' wage payment, that is 'exploitation'
in his sense of the word. The central theorem of his exploitation
theory is termed the fundamental Marxian theorem.

Ricardo was very different. Although he was not interested in the
problem of exploitation, he was concerned with how distribution of
the national product would be affected when the economy grew and
expanded. For this purpose he needed dynamic or comparative static
laws concerning price fluctuations. Moreover, as will be seen later,
this dynamic analysis was carried out within a framework
constructed with the spirit of general equilibrium analysis. Although
he did not explicitly state the equations of general equilibrium, it is
not very difficult to reconstruct his general equilibrium system by
excavating its parts from his *Principles* and putting them together
properly, as will be seen in later chapters. To solve these simultaneous
equations, Ricardo needed a powerful algorithm. Because, unlike
Walras who invented that tâtonnement algorithm, Ricardo had no
such procedure, he had nothing else to do but to simplify his general
equilibrium system so as to be able to use it. By using the value
equations rather than the price equations and assuming an
approximate or exact proportionality between prices and values, he
was able to obtain a simplified picture from his general equilibrium
system. And, regarding this as a first approximation to the reality,
he then examined deviations of prices from values, in order to obtain
a second approximation.

From a comparison of this use of the labour theory of value by
Ricardo with the one by Marx we must, of course, conclude that
the latter is more substantial than the former, though some or many
of us do not like Marx's subject – the revelation of the phenomena
of exploitation which are hidden underneath the free wage contract.
We must, however, recognize the fact that Ricardo's use of the value
theory is sensible, especially in view of the stage of development
which economics had reached when Ricardo was working. As a
matter of fact, it is much easier to derive comparative statics laws
from the value equations than from the price equations. If Ricardo
had discarded the value equations as suggested by Samuelson, a

disaster would have happened in Ricardo's study due to a lack of comparative statics laws of prices, and the progress of economics would have been hindered considerably.

2 Ricardo began by showing that prices obtained as solutions to the price equations are, in general, not proportional to 'labour values'; only in special cases where the composition of capital is equal through all industries, are prices proportional to values. This is a rigorous mathematical result, known to both Ricardo and Marx and, therefore, among Ricardians and Marxists. We shall refer to it as the Ricardo–Marx theorem and will prove it later.

In the formulation of the price determination and value determination theories, however, land as a second factor of production is ignored on purpose; commodities are regarded as if they are produced by a sole factor of production, labour. Nevertheless, this may be considered as the base, or the prototype, for explaining prices in more general circumstances where both labour and land are factors of production; to obtain this we only need to reinterpret the prototype price and value equations as the equations which hold at the margin of production. The price theory and the labour theory of value thus interpreted may be termed the marginal price theory and the marginal labour theory of value, respectively, and explain the reward of land in production as a part of the surplus. It is very important to reinterpret the price and value theories of the original, conventional forms as the marginal theories; by doing so, as will be seen later, we free these theories from the criticism that land is entirely ignored.

Another related topic is the derivation of the factor-price or the wage–profit frontier from the price equations. This problem is particularly important for contemporary Ricardians because it is closely related with the now famous Sraffa diagram depicting the linear relation between wages, as a proportion of 'the standard net product', and the rate of profit.[1] Sraffa's derivation is not the only one; we have Ricardo's original, Hicks' derivation and many others.[2]

[1] P. Sraffa, *Production of Commodities by Means of Commodities*, Cambridge University Press, 1960, p. 22.
[2] John Hicks, 'Sraffa and Ricardo: A Critical View', in G. A. Caravale (ed.), *The Legacy of Ricardo*, 1985, pp. 305–19. P. A. Samuelson, 'Parable and Realism in Capital Theory: The Surrogate Production Function', *The Review of Economic Studies*, XXIX, June 1962, pp. 193–206. M. Morishima, 'Prices, Interest and Profit in a Dynamic Leontief System', *Econometrica*, XXV, July 1958, pp. 358–80.

We are only briefly concerned with this problem in this chapter and postpone a more detailed comparison of the various forms of derivation to a later chapter; in this chapter we shall confine ourselves mainly to examining, first, the establishment of the Ricardo–Marx theorem and, secondly, the transformation of the price theory and the corresponding labour theory of value into their marginal version.

3 How are then the price and value determination systems formulated?

Let p be the (row) vector of prices; w the wage rate per unit of labour; and r the rate of profit. Let L be the (row) vector of labour-input coefficients and K the matrix of capital coefficients. The ith component of L, L_i, represents the amount of labour which is directly needed to produce commodity i, and the (j, i) element of K, K_{ji}, the jth capital good needed to produce one unit of i. Finally, K_i be the ith column of K and δ the diagonal matrix with the ith diagonal element δ_i being the rate of depreciation of capital good i.

Each producer must be provided with two kinds of capital, one being the capital that is to support labour and the other the capital that is invested in tools, machinery and buildings. Respectively, these are called, circulating and fixed capital by Ricardo, variable and constant capital by Marx. Thus in the case of Ricardo, like Marx, the total capital required for production of one unit of output i is given by $wL_i + pK_i$, while where production is instantaneous, it is pK_i. From this one may construe that Ricardo assumed a certain production lag for any industry, but he actually assumed the production period to be 1 for agriculture and 0 for manufacturing industries. This obvious contradiction will be ignored throughout the book until the last section, which deals with Wicksell's and von Neumann's new wage fund theory. The excess of price p_i over the cost, $wL_i + p(\delta K)_i$ (wages *plus* the user cost of capital goods),[3] gives profits; by dividing it by the total capital, $wL_i + pK_i$, the rate of profit for the production process i, r_i, is obtained. In the state of equilibrium where all r_i, $i = 1, 2, \ldots, n$, are equal to each other, we obtain the equal-rate-of-profit equation,

$$p - (wL + p\delta K) = r(wL + pK),$$

---

[3] $(\delta K)_i$ denotes the ith column of δK.

which is written in the following form and is referred to as the price, or price–cost, equation:

$$p = wL + p\delta K + r(wL + pK), \tag{1}$$

where r signifies the uniform rate of profit.

This equation is valid either (a) where prices are determined according to a kind of full cost principle with a given rate of mark-up r, or (b) where capital is transferred between production sectors with different rates of profit, from one at a lower rate to another at a higher one, so as to establish a uniform rate of profit throughout the economy. Ricardo considered that the intersectoral movement of capital was smooth and quick. This assumption will hold in an economy where production does not require a large initial fixed capital input as was generally so at the time of Ricardo.

In speaking of the laws which regulate the relative prices determined by (1), Ricardo introduced the concept of 'labour value' that is defined as the sum of 'the labour applied immediately to commodities' (direct labour) and 'the labour which is bestowed on the implements, tools, and buildings, with which such labour is assisted' (indirect labour). Let Λ be the (row) vector of labour values. Let us write $A = \delta K$, and let the ith columns of A and δK be A_i and $(\delta K)_i$, respectively; of course, $A_i = (\delta K)_i$. The total quantity of labour bestowed on A_i amounts to ΛA_i. This indirect labour is added to the direct labour L_i to give Λ_i, by the definition of the labour value. We have:

$$\Lambda = \Lambda A + L \qquad \text{(where } A = \delta K\text{)}. \tag{2}$$

Ricardo claimed that the relative price p_i/p_j, of commodity i, 'or the quantity of any other commodity [j] for which it will exchange, depends on the relative quantity of labour [Λ_i/Λ_j] which is necessary for its production' (p. 11). However, the dependence asserted by this does not necessarily imply equality between p_i/p_j and Λ_i/Λ_j. They are generally different from each other unless some stringent conditions, discussed below, are satisfied. Thus the problem of explaining prices of commodities in terms of the quantity of labour bestowed on their production is reduced to a comparison of the solutions to (1) with those to (2), that is, the problem which Marx called the problem of transformation of values into prices.

The price equation (1), the vector form of n individual price equations, contains $n + 2$ unknowns; n prices, the wage rate and the rate of profit. It looks, *prima facie*, as though it has two degrees of freedom. But the wage rate is equated with the living cost of the worker; we have, therefore, $w = pB$, where B is the (column) vector of the quantities of commodities consumed by a worker to support himself for a single period. The cost of living pB is compared with the basic cost pb with b the consumption vector at some basic level, so that we have

$$w = pb\omega, \qquad (3)$$

where ω is the ratio of pB to pb and is referred to as the real wage rate. By substituting this, (1) is reduced to a set of equations which are all homogenous of degree one in prices. They may, therefore, be normalized in terms of some measure of value (Walras' numeraire). Thus the price equation, after substitution and normalization, contains only $n - 1$ relative prices, besides the rate of profit and the real wage rate ω. Taking ω as a parameter, relative prices and the rate of profit are simultaneously determined as functions of ω. In particular, $r = r(\omega)$ thus obtained is called the wage–profit frontier (or the factor–price frontier) and will later be examined in full detail.

Similarly, the real wage rate ω may be defined by taking an arbitrary bundle b as the base; b is, of course, not necessarily a consumption bundle. For example, if we measure prices p and the money wages w in terms of a particular bundle which contains nothing other than one unit of gold, we find $\omega = w$ because $pb = 1$ in $\omega = w/(pb)$. In this case ω is a particular kind of the real wages, that is the wages in terms of gold. This may be referred to as the money wages under the gold standard. The money wage–profit frontier is derived in the same way as the wage–profit frontier based on the consumption bundle. This last is called the real wage–profit frontier, which Ricardo distinguished from the money wage–profit frontier but used both of them, as will be seen in Chapters 3 and 4 below, in his analysis of capital accumulation.

First, a most important theorem of the labour theory of value was found by Ricardo and Marx. It says that the quantity of labour bestowed on the production of commodities (i.e. the labour value of the commodities) regulates their relative prices if 'the proportions . . . , in which the capital that is to support labour, and the capital that is invested in tools, machinery and the buildings, may be variously combined' (p. 30) are the same through all production processes. This proposition is referred to as the Ricardo–Marx theorem. Ricardo and Marx discussed the theorem by using numerical examples, but it can be established mathematically as we shall see in the following.

As B expresses the vector of the quantities of commodities which are needed to support a unit of labour for one period, pBL_i represents the capital necessary to support L_i, and pK_i the capital that is invested in tools, machinery etc., to be used by L_i. Assuming that the ratios between these two types of capital are the same through all production processes i; this means

$$(pK_i)/L_i = k \qquad \text{for all } i \text{ and some } k \qquad (4)$$

then the theorem asserts that prices are proportional to values, that is

$$p = h\Lambda \qquad \text{for some positive number } h. \qquad (5)$$

To show this, let us write

$$\beta = (1+r)pB + rk.$$

Multiplying this equation by L, we have, in view of (4),

$$\beta L = (1+r)wL + rpK,$$

where $w = pB$, that is, the wages are paid at the rate which is just enough for a worker to live for one period. Adding $pA = p\delta K$ to both sides of the above equation, we obtain

$$pA + \beta L = (1+r)wL + rpK + p\delta K.$$

Obviously, the right-hand side of this equation is p by virtue of the price equation (1). Hence we have

$$pA + \beta L = p.$$

In view of the value equation (2) we now have $p = \beta\Lambda$, that is, prices are proportional to the labour value.

Let us next show that the converse of this result is also true as long as $r > 0$. Namely, provided $r > 0$, the proportionality of prices and values (5) implies the equality of the capital ratios (4). To establish this as valid, we first substitute (5) into the price equation and consider $w = pB$. Then we have

$$\Lambda = (1+r)\Lambda BL + r\Lambda K + \Lambda\delta K.$$

This, together with the value equation, enables us to write

$$L = (1 + r)\Lambda BL + r\Lambda K,$$

because $A = \delta K$. Hence,

$$[1 - (1 + r)\Lambda B]L = r\Lambda K,$$

which means $1 - (1 + r)\Lambda B > 0$ if $r > 0$. Writing

$$\alpha = [1 - (1 + r)\Lambda B]/r > 0$$

we have $\alpha L = \Lambda K$; multiplying both sides of this equation by h and putting $k = h\alpha$, we finally obtain, bearing (5) in mind, $kL = pK$; hence we have (4), the equality of the capital ratios.

Thus the condition (4) is necessary and sufficient for (5), provided $r > 0$. Also, we can establish the equivalence between (4) in terms of prices and its dual condition in terms of values,

$$\Lambda K_i/L_i = k' \qquad \text{for all } i. \tag{4'}$$

Calling the ratio, $\Lambda K_i/L_i$, the value composition of capital of process i, Marx showed that where the value composition of capital is the same through all processes, i.e. equation (4') holds, production prices are proportional to values and also that this proportionality is obtained only in this special case. This is Marx's version of the Ricardo–Marx theorem. Where $r = 0$, (4) is no longer necessary for (5). In this case, prices are proportional to values without any additional conditions.

4 Secondly, Ricardo claimed that 'it appears, too, that in proportion to the durability of capital employed in any kind of production, the relative prices of those commodities on which such durable capital is employed, will vary inversely as wages; they will fall as wages rise, and rise as wages fall' (p. 43). Also a passage to the same effect is stated by him as: 'I hope I have succeeded in showing ... that only those commodities would rise which had less fixed capital employed upon them than the medium in which price was estimated, and ... all those which had more, would positively fall in price when wages rose' (p. 46). However, as will be seen below, this law of price changes, which Ricardo obtained by analysing a numerical example, will be violated by a counter-example. As he knew that numerical analysis is not powerful enough to establish a general law and may be easily refuted by another example, Ricardo was not confident of

the validity of the law. In fact, such concessive expressions as 'it appears' or 'I hope I have succeeded ...' in the passages above indicate his intention that he was prepared to leave 'the law' as a conjecture for rigorous examination by future generations.

It can be shown, in fact, that his conjecture is not entirely valid. First, taking (3) into account, we can write (1) in the form

$$p = pb\omega L + pA + rp(b\omega L + K). \qquad (1')$$

As p is normalized such that p_i is unity for the numeraire, an increase in the real wage rate ω gives rise to a change in the rate of profit r. In fact, as will be seen later, the wage–profit frontier shows that where ω is sufficiently high to be, say, ω^0, r declines to the level 0, so that $(1')$ is reduced to

$$p = pb\omega^0 L + pA, \qquad (1'')$$

which can further be rewritten as

$$p = w^0 L + pA$$

by putting $w^0 = pb\omega^0$. From this and (2), we obtain $p = \omega^0 \Lambda$, that is, at the extreme point of the wage–profit frontier where $\omega = \omega^0$, the relative prices are equal to the relative values (see Figure 1).

Secondly, let commodity i be the numeraire, in terms of which prices are estimated, and j be the commodity upon which a smaller amount of fixed capital is employed than the numeraire. Suppose the relative price, p_j/p_i, determined by $(1')$, where $\omega < \omega^0$, is higher than the relative value, Λ_j/Λ_i; then when ω approaches ω^0, p_j/p_i should eventually approach Λ_j/Λ_i. This means that, for some values of ω, p_j/p_i must diminish when ω increases. Thus Ricardo's conjecture that it would rise is disproved for these values of ω.

Therefore, the third step of our argument is to show that p_j/p_i can be greater than Λ_j/Λ_i for some $\omega > \omega^*$, for a commodity j which has less fixed capital employed than the numeraire. For this purpose, we postmultiply $(1')$ by $(I - A)^{-1}$ and obtain

$$p^* = w^* L(I - A)^{-1} + r^*(w^* L + p^* K)(I - A)^{-1},$$

where p^*, r^* are solutions to $(1')$ which are in association with ω^*. Defining the capital ratio k_m as $p^* K_m/L_m$ and writing the diagonal matrix with $w^* + k_m$, $m = 1, \ldots, n$, on the diagonal as M, we obtain

$$p^* = w^* \Lambda + r^* L M (I - A)^{-1}, \qquad (1^*)$$

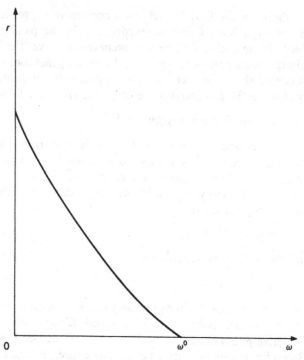

Figure 1

because $\Lambda = L(I-A)^{-1}$. Of course we have $k_j < k_i$ for the commodity j and the numeraire i.

To show the case $p_j/p_i > \Lambda_j/\Lambda_i$ being possible, let $k_h > k_i$ for an h having a negligible (h, i) element of $(I-A)^{-1}$, while $k_m = k_i$ for all other m's except j. Where k_j, which is less than k_i, is very close to it, the ith component of $LM(I-A)^{-1}$ is also very close to $(w^* + k_i)\Lambda_i$, because the (h, i) element of $(I-A)^{-1}$ is negligible, while $k_h > k_i$. On the other hand, the jth element of $LM(1-A)^{-1}$ is greater than $(w^* + k_i)\Lambda_j$ unless the (h, j) element of $(I-A)^{-1}$ is negligible, because $k_h > k_i$. Hence we obtain from (1*)

$$p_j^*/p_i^* > \Lambda_j/\Lambda_i.$$

This shows that at some ω, between ω^* and ω^0, the relative price p_j/p_i must diminish (rather than rise as Ricardo claimed) towards Λ_j/Λ_i. This completes the argument.

5 Thirdly, let us derive the wage–profit frontier which is stated in Ricardo's words as:

> There can be no rise in the value of labour without a fall of profits. If the corn is to be divided between the farmer and the labourer, the larger the proportion that is given to the latter, the less will remain for the former. So if cloth or cotton goods be divided between the workman and his employer, the larger the proportion given to the former, the less remain for the latter. [Thus] . . . owing to a rise of wages, profits fall . . . (p. 35)

Interpreting this trade-off between wages and profits as a relationship between the real wage rate ω and the rate of profit r, we can provide the following rigorous proof to the conjecture that an increase in ω creates a decline of r. Let ω^0 and ω^1 be any two ω's such that $\omega^0 < \omega^1$, and let p^0, r^0 be prices and the rate of profit associated with ω^0; similarly p^1, r^1 with ω^1. Let us define

$$\hat{A} = \omega bL + A, \qquad \hat{K} = \omega bL + K$$

and call them the augmented input-coefficient matrix and the augmented capital-coefficient matrix, respectively, because the former includes the labour-feeding inputs ωbL as well as the physical current inputs, while the latter includes the capital to support labour ωbL as well as the proper capital goods in the form of machines, tools, factory building, etc. They both depend on the real wage rate ω. The price equation (1′) may simply be put, by use of them, in the form,

$$p = p\hat{A} + rp\hat{K}. \tag{1'}$$

As we know from Leontief's input–output analysis

$$(I - \hat{A})^{-1} > 0$$

provided that ω does not exceed a certain limit, $\hat{K}(I - \hat{A})^{-1}$ is found to be a positive matrix. Therefore, by virtue of the Frobenius theorem on non-negative matrices,[4] it has one and only one positive eigenvalue λ, which is associated with a positive (row) eigenvector v and a positive (column) eigenvector X. Thus

$$\lambda v = v\hat{K}(I - \hat{A})^{-1}, \qquad \lambda X = \hat{K}(I - \hat{A})^{-1}X,$$

---

[4] G. Frobenius, 'Über Matrizen aus nicht negativen Elementen', *Sitzungsberichte der königlich preussischen Akademie der Wissenschaften*, 1912, pp. 456–77.

from which we obtain

$$v = v\hat{A} + \frac{1}{\lambda} v\hat{K}.$$

In view of $\hat{A}$ and $\hat{K}$ depending upon ω, we observe that $1/\lambda$, v equal r^0, p^0, respectively, for the ω set at ω^0, while r^1, p^1 for the ω at ω^1. Thus we have

$$p^0 = p^0 \hat{A}^0 + r^0 p^0 \hat{K}^0, \tag{6.0}$$

$$p^1 = p^1 \hat{A}^1 + r^1 p^1 \hat{K}^1, \tag{6.1}$$

where $\hat{A}^0$ and $\hat{A}^1$ are the augmented input-coefficient matrices with ω set at ω^0 and ω^1, respectively; and, similarly, for $\hat{K}^0$ and $\hat{K}^1$. For ω^1 we also have

$$X^1 = r^1 \hat{K}^1 (I - \hat{A}^1)^{-1} X^1. \tag{7}$$

On the other hand, since $\omega^0 < \omega^1$, we have $\hat{A}^0 < \hat{A}^1$ and $\hat{K}^0 < \hat{K}^1$. Therefore

$$p^0 < r^0 p^0 \hat{K}^1 (I - \hat{A}^1)^{-1}$$

from (6.0). Postmultiply this by X^1 and premultiply (7) by p^0 and compare. We then at once find $r^1 < r^0$.

Besides this way of deriving the wage–profit frontier, there are many others – Ricardo's, Sraffa's, Hicks' and so on, as I have already mentioned. Because this frontier plays a most crucial role in the Ricardian economics, I shall carefully examine the various methods of deriving the frontier and discuss their merits and demerits in a later chapter.

6   We have so far made no reference to land and rent. It has implicitly been assumed that land is homogenous in quality and abundant in quantity, so that land is free and no rent is paid. Some economists have criticized the labour theory of value in this respect. Samuelson, for instance, is concerned with the case where labour is reproducible without limit. Then homogenous labour would not become scarce; production of commodities and labour would be restricted by the availability of land. In his words, 'Land, being the only primary (i.e. non-reproducible) item in the simplest model, has imputed to it – either as a residual or as a marginal product – all the net product

of the system.'[5] Thus 'scarce land ... destroys the possibility of a labour theory of value. Instead, under the special Ricardian long-run assumptions, a single grade of land would itself provide a simple "land theory of value", based upon all prices equal to mathematically definable "embodied land".'[6] Schumpeter, prior to Samuelson, has also emphasized the importance of land as an independent source of value and advocates a two-factor (labour and land) theory of value against the conventional single-factor (labour) theory.[7] He conclusively says: 'Böhm-Bawerk was indeed the first who expressly said that the whole value of the product must in principle be divided between labour and land.'[8] These views, however, do not represent Ricardo's value and rent theory in a fair manner.

Both Samuelson and Schumpeter do not accurately take into account the fact that, in the case of land being scarce, Ricardo modified (or generalized) his original labour theory of value which assumed that land is free, into what I call the marginal labour theory of value so as to allow for the productivity of land. This theory will be expounded below, under the assumption of one homogenous grade of land, postponing the examination of the more general case with several grades of land to the next chapter. It will be shown that Ricardo's marginal labour theory of value is in fact the two factor theory of value which Schumpeter and Samuelson seek.

As soon as land becomes scarce, capital and land are employed more intensively. Let us assume, for the sake of simplicity, that (1) there is no mining industry, while (2) no land is used by the manufacturing industry where (3) constant returns to scale prevail. In agriculture (or sector 0) labour-feeding input of the amount $\omega b L_0$ and employment of fixed capital of amount K_0, which depreciates at the rate A_0, are made in order to cultivate one acre of land. When the same area of land is cultivated more intensively, more labour and capital are employed per acre; we assume in the following that labour and capital are inputted proportionately. Therefore, inputs

[5] P. A. Samuelson, 'A Modern Treatment of the Ricardian Economy: I. The Pricing of Goods and Labour and Land Services', in *The Collected Scientific Papers of Paul A. Samuelson*, Vol. 1, MIT Press, 1966, p. 392.

[6] *Ibid.*

[7] J. Schumpeter, *Theorie der wirtschaftlichen Entwicklung*, Duncker und Humblot, Berlin, 1964 (unveranderter Nachdruck der 1934 erschienen vierten Auflage), SS. 19–23.

[8] *Ibid.*, p. 41; J. Schumpeter, *The Theory of Economic Development*, Harvard University Press, 1951, p. 32.

at the intensity level m are $m\omega b L_0$ and mK_0 with depreciation mA_0, where $m \geq 1$. In the following b includes consumption of corn.

Let x_0 be the output of agriculture, say, of corn, from one acre; then the production function may be written as $x_0 = f(m\omega b L_0, mA_0, mK_0, 1)$ (or more simply $x_0 = f(m, 1)$), where the last element 1 refers to the area of land cultivated that is one acre. Ricardo assumed that the productivity of agriculture with respect to the intensity level, dx_0/dm, declines if the intensity level is further increased, i.e. $d^2x_0/dm^2 < 0$, while keeping m constant, if inputs of labour, capital goods and land are increased proportionately, output will also increase proportionately.[9] If normal profit is included, the marginal cost in terms of money amounts to

$$[p(\omega b L_0 + A_0) + rp(\omega b L_0 + K_0)] \frac{dm}{dx_0}. \qquad (8)$$

Suppose now the land is cultivated at the intensity m^0. Since dx_0/dm depends on m^0, its reciprocal dm/dx_0 is also dependent on m^0. Let us put, for simplicity,

$$L_0(m^0) = L_0 \frac{dm}{dx_0}; \text{ similarly for } A_0(m^0) \text{ and } K_0(m^0). \qquad (9)$$

If the marginal cost (8) evaluated at the margin m^0 exceeds the price of corn p_0, the intensity of m^0 must be decreased until they become equal to each other. In equilibrium, therefore, we obtain

$$p_0 = p(\omega b L_0(m^0) + A_0(m^0)) + rp(\omega b L_0(m^0) + K_0(m^0)). \qquad (10)$$

In Ricardo's words this price equation is expounded as: 'that corn which is produced by the greatest quantity of labour [i.e. the corn produced at the margin m^0] is the regulator of the price of corn; rent does not and cannot enter in the least degree as a component part of its price' (p. 77). 'The exchangeable value of all commodities ... is always regulated ... by the greater quantity of labour necessarily bestowed on their production ... by those who continue to produce them under the most unfavourable circumstances' (p. 73). At the margin m^0, therefore, where the circumstances are worst,

[9] Let $\bar{x}_0$ be produced at $m = 1$; that is, $\bar{x}_0$ is the output which is obtained by employing $\omega b L_0, A_0, K_0$ on one acre of land. As the productivity $f(m, 1)/m$ diminishes with respect to m, we have

$$\bar{x}_0 > f(m, 1)/m > f' = dx_0/dm > 0 \qquad \text{for all } m > 1.$$

the marginal cost in terms of labour value, that is $L_0(m^0) + \Lambda A_0(m^0)$, is equated with the labour value of the marginal output of corn, Λ_0. Thus,

$$\Lambda_0 = L_0(m^0) + \Lambda A_0(m^0). \tag{11}$$

In this way Ricardo obtained, in the circumstances where land is no longer free, the marginal pricing equation (10) and the marginal labour value equation (11), whose importance Ricardo stressed in a footnote to a passage describing the principle of marginal pricing. He stated, 'Clearly understanding this principle is, I am persuaded, of the utmost importance to the science of political economy' (p. 77n). This has been missed by Samuelson and Schumpeter.

Let commodities $1, \ldots, n$ be products of manufacturing industries. Their augmented input-coefficient matrix and augmented capital-coefficient matrix are constant because their use of land is neglected and constant returns to scale prevail. Let us denote these augmented matrices by

$$(\hat{A}_1, \ldots, \hat{A}_n) \quad \text{and} \quad (\hat{K}_1, \ldots, \hat{K}_n).$$

These together with those for the agriculture, $\hat{A}_0(m^0) = \omega b L_0(m^0) + A_0(m^0)$ and $\hat{K}_0(m^0) = \omega b L_0(m^0) + K_0(m^0)$, constitute the whole augmented input-coefficient and capital-coefficient matrices of the economy:

$$\hat{A}(m^0) = [\hat{A}_0(m^0), \hat{A}_1, \ldots, \hat{A}_n],$$
$$\hat{K}(m^0) = [\hat{K}_0(m^0), \hat{K}_1, \ldots, \hat{K}_n].$$

The marginal version of the price determination equations and that of the value equations are written as

$$p = p\hat{A}(m^0) + rp\hat{K}(m^0), \tag{12}$$

$$\Lambda = L(m^0) + \Lambda A(m^0), \tag{13}$$

where $L(m^0) = [L_0(m^0), L_1, \ldots, L_n]$; similarly for $A(m^0)$.

7 With prices and labour values thus determined outputs and inputs are evaluated; in particular, where cultivation is made at the intensity m^0 an acre of land yields $p_0 x_0^0$ or $\Lambda_0 x_0^0$ worth of output (where $x_0^0 = f(m^0, 1)$) by spending the cost (including the normal profits) of $p\hat{A}_0 m^0 + rp\hat{K}_0 m^0$, or $L_0 m^0 + \Lambda A_0 m^0$. In view of the price and labour value determination equations for corn, (10) and (11), $p_0 x_0^0$

and $\Lambda_0 x_0^0$ are equal to

$$p\hat{A}_0(m^0)x_0^0 + rp\hat{K}_0(m^0)x_0^0, \qquad L_0(m^0)x_0^0 + A_0(m^0)x_0^0$$

respectively. Bearing the definition (9) in mind, we obtain

$$A_0(m^0)x_0^0 = A_0 \frac{dm}{dx_0} x_0^0,$$

which is greater than $A_0 m^0$ because $dx_0/dm < x_0^0/m^0$, which follows from the diminishing returns with respect to m. Similarly, $L_0(m^0)x_0^0 > L_0 m^0$ and $K_0(m^0)x_0^0 > K_0 m^0$. These inequalities show that similar inequalities hold for agriculture's augmented inputs (current and capital) too. All these imply

$$p_0 x_0^0 > p\hat{A}_0 m^0 + rp\hat{K}_0 m^0, \qquad \Lambda_0 x_0^0 > L_0 m^0 + \Lambda A_0 m^0.$$

The differences between the left-hand and right-hand sides of these expressions gives the rents per acre of land, in terms of money and labour values, respectively. Let these rents be R and V. Then we have from the above inequalities

$$p_0 = p\hat{A}_0 \frac{m^0}{x_0^0} + rp\hat{K}_0 \frac{m^0}{x_0^0} + \frac{R}{x_0^0}, \tag{14}$$

$$\Lambda_0 = \Lambda A_0 \frac{m^0}{x_0^0} + L_0 \frac{m^0}{x_0^0} + \frac{V}{x_0^0}, \tag{15}$$

where R/x_0^0 and V/x_0^0 are rents per unit of output.

These equations explain how output is distributed among factors of production, labour, capital and land. Land is used more intensively because it has a productive power which enables the farmer to employ labour and capital of the amounts, $L_0 m^0$ and $K_0 m^0$, profitably. Paying them, as well as the commodities consumed $A_0 m^0$ during the process of production, at the wage rate, $w = \omega pb$, and the prices, p, determined by the marginal price determination equation (12), the value of output still exceeds the cost (including the normal profit) evaluated in this way, and this excess is attributed to the productive power of land. Thus, the equation (14) derived from the marginal pricing equation (12) recognizes the productive power of land as well as those of labour and capital. The equation (15), similarly derived from the marginal labour-value-theory equation (13), may be taken as an equation of 'the two-factor theory

of value' which is advocated by both Samuelson and Schumpeter.
It is indeed important to realize that the *marginal labour theory* of
value is *not* a theory which imputes the value of output entirely and
exclusively to labour and concealed labour, but a theory attributing
it to both labour and land.[10]

It must be noted, however, that we have to be provided with the
value of m^0, to solve (12) or (13). Otherwise, we cannot determine
the values of p and Λ. Therefore, in (14) and (15), rents R and V
are left indeterminate. We need one equation to obtain m^0 and
another one to solve that equation if it contains, besides m^0, at least
one new variable, and so forth. Thus the marginal pricing equation
and the marginal value-theory equation are merely components of
some greater self-contained system – the Ricardian general
equilibrium system. This is a point clearly indicated by Walras in
Lesson 39 of his *Elements*.[11] Unlike the original price and value
determination equations under the constant returns to scale, which
form a closed decomposable subset in the whole Ricardian system,
their marginal version (12) and (13) can only provide us with p and
Λ as functions of m^0. It is especially important to observe that labour
values are not constants determined solely by technology; they
fluctuate economically according to whether the circumstances of
the market require the intensity of cultivation to change.

8 Let us finally examine Marx's theory of absolute rent which asserts
that, where the private ownership of land imposes some amount of
rent as a fee for the use of land for a given period of time upon the
farmer (or the tenant), even the land of the lowest quality brings
forth rent as long as it is cultivated. Rent of this type is the door
fee which capital must pay when it enters a lot of land. 'Landed
property itself has created rent.'[12] This is true for the marginal land
too, and Marx observed that the existence of absolute rent gives rise

[10] It may be unfair to criticize Samuelson in this manner, because a paragraph of p.
381 of his paper and a footnote attached to it evidently show that his interpretation
of Ricardo does not conflict with my view as expressed in the text. If so, then, he
should withdraw or at least soften his critical comment to the effect that 'the
existence of scarce land has destroyed the simple labour theory of value'.
(Samuelson, 'A Modern Treatment', p. 279) If it is replaced by the marginal labour
theory of value as Ricardo did, productive powers of labour and land are both
taken account of.

[11] Leon Walras, *The Elements of Pure Economics*, pp. 404–18.

[12] Marx's italics. Karl Marx, *Capital III*, Progress Publishers, Moscow, 1966, p. 755.

to an increase in the price of agricultural produce. Furthermore he stated that 'the rent from soil A would not be simply a consequence of the rise in grain prices, but, conversely, the fact that the worst soil must yield rent in order to make its cultivation at all possible, would be the cause for a rise in the grain price to the point where this condition may be fulfilled.'[13]

Thus, for absolute ground rent, Marx concluded, 'the increase in the price of the product is not the cause of rent, but rather that rent is the cause of the increase in the price of the product.'[14] In this respect, the absolute rent is completely different from differential rent which cannot be considered as the cause of an increase in the price of the product but is the result of the latter that itself, in turn, is a result of diminishing returns in agriculture. Marx, accordingly, stated that the absolute rent 'forms a portion of the value, or, more specifically, surplus-value, of commodities, and instead of falling into the lap of the capitalists, who have extracted it from their labourers, it falls to the share of the landlords, who extract it from the capitalists.'[15]

This kind of analysis assumes that the imposition of absolute rent does not affect the intensity of cultivation m^0 of marginal land. When it changes, as it should do, a completely different story is obtained. It is true that Marx payed some attention in his analysis to intensive cultivation of land when he referred to 'the surplus-profits arising from the last investments of capital in a particular soil type.'[16] But this does not apply to the worst quality land which he implicitly assumed is never cultivated intensively. In order to examine the new scenario let us retain, for the sake of simplicity, our assumption that all land is homogenous in quality. Let us now suppose that the absolute rent of the amount R^* is imposed per acre. There is no necessity that this R^* should equal the R of equation (14) which is the Ricardian rent obtained per acre when land is cultivated at the intensity m^0. If R^* is greater than R, then the degree of intensity m^0 is increased such that a greater amount of surplus product, R, is produced per acre; and it finally becomes equal to R^*. Because this increase brings forth an increase in the amount of grain produced per acre, the scale of cultivation has to be adjusted to the demand for grain, so that a number of fields would cease to be cultivated.

[13] *Ibid.*, p. 755.
[14] *Ibid.*, p. 763.
[15] *Ibid.*, p. 771.
[16] Especially, see Marx, *ibid.*, pp. 764–5.

As Marx pointed out, the legal ownership of land gives the landowner 'the power to withdraw his land from exploitation until economic conditions permit him to utilize it in such a manner as to yield him a surplus.'[17] $R*$ is the minimum surplus insisted by the owner of land. Then the owners of uncultivated land will not agree to a cut of the absolute rent below $R*$. In this way, 'in all civilised countries a comparatively appreciable portion of land always remains uncultivated.'[18] This means that the imposed absolute rent $R*$ equals Ricardian rate R after the adjustment, that is the integral of the surplus products obtained from successive investment of capital on the same land form $m = 0$ to m^1, where m^1 is the intensity of cultivation after the adjustment. At the margin m^1 the marginal surplus product vanishes, and the absolute rent is thus transmuted into the Ricardian rent. In this case it is noted, however, that there may exist uncultivated land, side by side with the cultivated one earning rent $R*$ per acre.

On the other hand, if $R*$ is less than R of the equation (14), there is no need to change m^0, because the farmer's reserve for the rent payment R is large enough to pay the door fee $R*$. The absolute rent is then absorbed as a part of Ricardian rent and is in fact paid out of it, without any adjustment in the intensity of cultivation. The monopolistic position of the landowner and competition among farmers enable the former to capture all the surplus product after paying profits to capitalists at the normal rate, as rent either in the form of absolute rent $R*$ or in the form of excess rent, $R - R*$, the sum of these two being equal to Ricardo's rent R.[19]

Finally it is noted that in the opposite case of $R < R*$, m^0 has to be revised, and of course it takes time for this adjustment. The transformation of absolute rent to Ricardian rent is completed only in the long run. It is nevertheless true that as far as the long-run equilibrium is concerned, no independent position can be found for Marx's absolute rent within Ricardian economics.

---

[17] *Ibid.*, p. 757.

[18] *Ibid.*, p. 757. One may consider that it is irrational for an individual landowner to keep a portion of his land unemployed. But to explain the existence of uncultivated land (of the same quality as the marginal land) in most of actual economies we must accept that there is some minimum $R*$ to the absolute rent. In this way, positive rent may appear for the marginal land before it is fully employed. This negation of the rule of free goods for land by Marx may be considered as a predecessor of Keynes' one for labour.

[19] $R - R*$ is captured by the landowner in exactly the same way as R is captured by him in the absence of absolute rent. As for this process of transformation of surplus profit into ground rent, see Marx, *ibid.*, pp. 637–9.

2   Differential rent

1 We have seen how immediately and smoothly Ricardo's price theory is connected to his theory of differential rent. In this chapter we elaborate the latter by abandoning the simplifying assumption we have adopted in the last chapter that all land is homogenous in quality. We shall here instead assume, as Ricardo himself did, that land is differentiated in quality into several or infinitely many classes: the first class of the highest quality, the second best class, and so on. In the following, as we have done in the previous chapter, we use the device of the production function to describe the productivity of land.

In the days of Ricardo, no economist had a clear idea of the production function. But Ricardo was far in advance of his contemporaries and had almost got it. He stated: 'Thus suppose land – No. 1, 2, 3 – to yield, with an equal employment of capital and labour, a net produce of 100, 90, and 80 quarters of corn' (p. 70). This means that the production function of corn per acre of land shifts downwards when the quality of land utilized is lower. He also stated:

> It often, and, indeed, commonly happens, that before No. 2, 3, 4, or 5, or the inferior lands are cultivated, capital can be employed more productively on those lands which are already in cultivation. It may perhaps be found, that by doubling the original capital employed on No. 1, though the produce will not be doubled, will not be increased by 100 quarters, it may be increased by eighty-five quarters. (p. 71)

This implies that the marginal productivity of land No. 1 will diminish when more capital is invested on the same land; similarly, for other lands, No. 2, 3, and so on. It is noted that Ricardo's capital includes the funds which are to employ labour and therefore labour employed always increases or diminishes with the increase or diminution of capital. In the following we assume, for simplicity, that labour and investment on capital goods change proportionately.

Thus capital (consisting of the seed corn and other capital goods) and labour are employed in a fixed set for the production of corn, and we denote the number of the sets invested on an acre of land of the quality of No. i, by m_i. Then the output of corn produced from the same land, designated by Φ_i, is a function of m_i; that is, $\Phi_i = F_i(m_i, 1)$, where the second argument of the function, that is fixed at 1, signifies that one acre of land is used. We assume that at least one set of capital and labour is required to cultivate the land, so that where $m_i < 1$, only m_i acre of the land is cultivated, the rest, i.e. $1 - m_i$ acre, being left uncultivated. This means that, on each land No. i, $i = 1, 2, 3, \ldots$, constant returns to scale prevails as far as the intensity of cultivation m_i is confined between 0 and 1. For $m_i > 1$, Φ_i is doubled when labour, capital and land employed are all doubled, keeping m_i constant.

The first passage quoted above from Ricardo implies that

$$F_1(m_1, 1) > F_2(m_2, 1) > F_3(m_3, 1) > \cdots, \tag{1}$$

where $m_1 = m_2 = m_3 = \cdots$. The second passage above means that as long as the acreage of land cultivated is fixed at, say, 1, the law of diminishing returns prevails. With every subsequent portion of labour and capital a less productive return is obtained; in other words, for all i

$$F_i'(m_i, 1) > 0 \quad \text{and} \quad F_i''(m_i, 1) < 0, \quad \text{where } m_i > 1,$$

and F_i' and F_i'' are the first and second derivatives of the production function F_i with respect to m_i. In addition to these we may safely assume that the marginal productivity of land of grade i is higher than that of land of grade $i + 1$, if both lands are cultivated alike, in other words,

$$F_i'(m_i, 1) > F_{i+1}'(m_{i+1}, 1) \quad \text{if } m_i = m_{i+1}. \tag{2}$$

The production functions of these properties are depicted in Figure 2. This specification of Ricardo's production functions is similar to the interpretation of Ricardo by Walras who defined, for

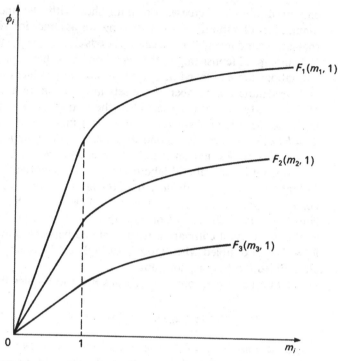

Figure 2

each kind of land, the production function *per hectare*.[1] It is, however, different from the aggregate agricultural production function used by Pasinetti and Negishi to give Ricardo's rent theory a mathematical formulation. They neither classify lands according to their quality nor take, in the production function, the area of land employed into account explicitly.[2] The output of corn is thus a function of labour and capital only, while the role of land in production is implicit. By their models, therefore, it is impossible to decide whether land is scarce or abundant. With their production function it is impossible to discuss, for example, the following

[1] Walras, *Elements*, pp. 409–10.
[2] L. Pasinetti, *Growth and Income Distribution*, Cambridge University Press, 1974, p. 7. T. Negishi, *Economic Theories in a Non-Walrasian Tradition*, Cambridge University Press, 1985, p. 136.

propositions claimed by Ricardo:

> When in the progress of society, land of the second degree of
> fertility is taken into cultivation, rent immediately commences on
> that of the first quality, and the amount of that rent will depend
> on the difference in the quality of these two portions of land. (p. 70)
> It may perhaps be found ... that this quantity [the produce
> obtained by doubling the original capital employed on No. 1]
> exceeds what could be obtained by employing the same capital on
> land No. 3. In such case, capital will be preferably employed on
> the old land, and will equally create a rent; for rent is always the
> difference between the produce obtained by the employment of
> two equal quantities of capital and labour. (p. 71)

Their models are also unsuitable for examining, as we have done in
the last part of Chapter 1, Marx's assertion that because a high
absolute rent is insisted an appreciable portion of land is intensively
cultivated, while the remaining land of the same quality is kept virgin.

2 Let (λ, κ) be the set of labour and capital employed where land i
is cultivated at the unitary level of intensity, $m_i = 1$. As several kinds
of capital goods may be used, κ is a column vector, while λ, standing
for the labour input coefficient of the agriculture, is a single number
because of our assumption that all labour is homogenous. We
assume, for the sake of simplicity, the depreciation rate is identical
for all capital goods. We then write

$$c = (1 + r)w\lambda + (\delta + r)p\kappa, \tag{3}$$

which represents the cost of production at $m_i = 1$, including the
interest of the circulating and fixed capitals as well as the depreciation
cost; p is a row price vector of capital goods. Let π be the price of
the agricultural produce. As surplus of the amount,

$$P_i = \pi F_i(m_i, 1) - m_i c$$

accrues from the cultivation of land i of one acre, at the intensity m_i,
the condition

$$\pi \frac{dF_i}{dm_i} \leqq c \tag{4}$$

is satisfied at m_i^0 where the surplus P_i is maximized. This m_i^0 takes on
a non-negative value if strict equality holds for the above condition,
while it is zero if strict inequality '$<$' holds.

Let us suppose that for some (π, c), $m_u^0 = 1$ for some u. Then (2) and (4) together imply that the strict inequality

$$\pi \frac{dF_j}{dm_j} < c$$

does hold for $j = u + 1, u + 2, \ldots$, and therefore $m_{u+1}^0, m_{u+2}^0, \ldots$ are all zero. Thus if $m_u^0 = 1$, land u is the marginal land and all the lands of lower quality will not be used.

On the other hand, for i which is less than u, the condition (3) must hold with $m_i^0 > m_u^0 = 1$ because of (2). We can, furthermore, show that

$$1 = m_u^0 < m_{u-1}^0 < m_{u-2}^0 < \cdots < m_1^0.$$

That is to say, the lands of better quality will be cultivated more intensively.

As has been stated above, the equilibrium equation,

$$\pi F_i'(m_i^0, 1) = c, \tag{5}$$

holds at a positive intensity m_i^0, while for $m_i < m_i^0$, the inequality

$$\pi F_i'(m_i, 1) > c,$$

is obtained because of the assumption of the diminishing marginal productivity with respect to investment of circulating (wages) and fixed capital (i.e. $F''(m_i, 1) < 0$). Let us write the marginal surplus output as $r_i(m_i)$; then

$$\pi F_i'(m_i, 1) = c + r_i(m_i).$$

Therefore,

$$\pi \int_0^{m_i^0} F_i' dm_i = \int_0^{m_i^0} c \, dm_i + \int_0^{m_i^0} r_i(m_i) dm_i.$$

Hence,

$$\pi F_i(m_i^0, 1) = c m_i^0 + R_i(m_i^0).$$

This final equation implies that, where one acre of land of grade i is cultivated at the intensity m_i^0, an amount of the surplus output, $R_i(m_i^0)$, remains after having paid for labour and capital. This payment includes not only wages and the price of capital goods the farmer uses, but also the interest on circulating and fixed capitals.

Since the workers and the capitalists have thus been paid, the remaining surplus products are attributed to the relative superiority of the land employed, so that they are remitted to the landowners, in the form of rent.

It is obvious that $r_i = dR_i/dm_i$, and (5) implies that this marginal surplus product vanishes at the margin m_i^0. This means that the intensity of cultivation is decided such that the rent is maximized at m_i^0. That is to say, we have

$$R_i(m_i^0) \geqq R_i(m_i) \qquad \text{for all } m_i, \tag{6}$$

where

$$\pi F_i(m_i, 1) = m_i c + R_i(m_i). \tag{7}$$

This maximum rent may now be compared with the maximum rent of the land of a lower grade, say, $i+1$ per acre, that is, $R_{i+1}(m_{i+1}^0)$ such that

$$\pi F_{i+1}(m_{i+1}^0, 1) = m_{i+1}^0 c + R_{i+1}(m_{i+1}^0). \tag{8}$$

We can show $R_i(m_i^0) \geqq R_{i+1}(m_{i+1}^0)$. This is because (6) and (7) hold for $m_i = m_{i+1}^0$:

$$R_i(m_i^0) \geqq R_i(m_{i+1}^0), \tag{6'}$$

$$\pi F_i(m_{i+1}^0, 1) = m_{i+1}^0 c + R_i(m_{i+1}^0). \tag{7'}$$

As land i is superior to land $i+1$, we have from (1) that $F_i(m_{i+1}^0, 1) > F_{i+1}(m_{i+1}^0, 1)$. Therefore, (7') and (8) imply $R_i(m_{i+1}^0) > R_{i+1}(m_{i+1}^0)$, and this together with (6') yields

$$R_i(m_i^0) > R_{i+1}(m_{i+1}^0).$$

In this way rent per acre diminishes as the grade of the land used declines, and it finally vanishes for the marginal land u if its intensity of cultivation m_u^0 is less than or equal to 1.

3 Let Φ_i^* be the output of land i per acre when the level of cultivation intensity is equal to one and let m_i^* be the particular level of cultivation where the marginal productivity of land i, $F_i'(m_i^*, 1)$, equals the initial productivity $\Phi_{i+1}^*/1$ of land of the next grade $i+1$. If the actual intensity m_i^0 reaches m_i^*, then farming is expanded to the new land of grade $i+1$. The farmed area of the land of this grade will expand as the demand for agricultural produce increases;

when it is exhausted, it will start to be used more intensively. Then m_{i+1}^0 will be more than 1. Where it becomes equal to m_{i+1}^* which is similarly defined as m_i^*, the land of grade $i+2$ is brought into cultivation.

It is clear that, where the intensity of cultivation of land i is m_i^0, λm_i^0 workers are employed per acre. The total agricultural employment will then amount to

$$\lambda[m_1^0 T_1^0 + m_2^0 T_2^0 + \cdots + m_{u-1}^0 T_{u-1}^0 + m_u^0 T_k], \tag{9}$$

where T_i^0 stands for the total acreage of land i available in the economy. For the marginal land u, the acreage of the farmed area T_u does not exceed T_u^0. As long as $T_u < T_u^0$, m_u^0 equals 1, whereas it may be more than 1 if T_u reaches T_u^0.

Where m_u^0 is given, c/π is obtained as $\dfrac{dF_u}{dm_u}(m_u^0) = c/\pi$. Once c/π is given, $m_i^0, i = 1, \ldots, u-1$, are determined by (4). Thus, agricultural employment (9) may be written:

$$\lambda[G(m_u^0) + m_u^0 T_u] \begin{cases} m_u^0 = 1, & \text{if } T_u < T_u^0, \\ m_u^0 \geq 1, & \text{if } T_u = T_u^0, \end{cases} \tag{9'}$$

where

$$G(m_u^0) = m_1^0 T_1^0 + \cdots + m_{u-1}^0 T_{u-1}^0.$$

In (9) or (9') the part in the square brackets shall be simply designated as η.

Thus we obtain an equation,

$$w\lambda[G(m_u) + m_u T_u] = w\lambda\eta, \tag{10}$$

which is equivalent to Walras' equation (4)[3], a constituent of the equation system formulated by Walras as an interpretation of Ricardo's rent theory. In equation (10), the right-hand side represents the total amount of circulating capital employed by the agricultural sector, while the left-hand side shows how this total amount is distributed among land of various grades. If η is given, (10) includes two variables, m_u and T_u. Where T_u, satisfying (10) with $m_u = 1$, does not exceed T_u^0, these m_u and T_u are solutions to (10), while, when such a T_u is greater than T_u^0, m_u is increased and becomes larger than 1. With an m_u which is less than m_u^* but larger than 1, the T_u

[3] Walras, *Elements*, p. 410.

fulfilling (10) equals T_u^0; these m_u and T_u are the solutions we are seeking. If $T_u > T_u^0$, the land of the next grade, $u + 1$, becomes the marginal land. In this way equation (10) eventually determines the equilibrium intensity of cultivation of the marginal land, m_u^0, and its cultivated area, T_u. Once m_u^0 is decided, the intensities, $m_1^0, m_2^0, \ldots, m_{u-1}^0$, are correspondingly decided for all sorts of land which are superior to the land of grade u.

Walras, nevertheless, stated: 'According to Ricardo, it seems that in every economy there is a certain amount of capital ... At any given moment, the amount of capital is determinate. Let us call such a determinate amount X.'[4] X is written as $w\lambda\eta$ in our notation. Where it is determinate, the degrees of cultivation, $m_1^0, \ldots, m_u^0$ are decided, as has just been seen; hence the total amount of rent is found out to be

$$R_1(m_1^0)T_1^0 + \cdots + R_{u-1}(m_{u-1}^0)T_{u-1}^0 + R_u(m_u^0)T_u,$$

where $R_u(m_u^0) = 0$ if $m_u^0 = 1$ and $T_u = T_u^0$ if $m_u^0 > 1$. Walras continued: 'Thus in final analysis rent depends on the capital of a country, and is determined without regard to wages, interest or the prices of products. This is the essence of the English theory of rent.'[5]

Walras criticized Ricardo for regarding his X (our $w\lambda\eta$) as given and not determining it simultaneously with wages, prices and other variables in a well-formulated and self-contained system of general equilibrium. The same sort of criticism is repeated by him when he discussed the English theories of wages and interest.[6] It seems at least for me, however, that this criticism is not applicable to Ricardo. It is of course true that Ricardo never used mathematics (except a number of numerical examples), so that there is no set of equations which describes general equilibrium. But it is also true that Ricardo's economics is perfectly logically constructed, so that it is not very difficult to rewrite his theory with mathematics. Ricardo's economics is, in fact, a general equilibrium theory, which determines $\lambda\eta$ (hence, intensities, m_i, and rents, R_i, $i = 1, \ldots, u$) together with w, p, r and agricultural output of land i, Φ_i, and industrial output x.

4 Let us now reveal the whole equations which constitute Ricardian general equilibrium. The economy consists of agriculture which uses

[4] *Ibid.*, p. 410.
[5] *Ibid.*, p. 411.
[6] *Ibid.*, pp. 419–28.

various grades of land, and n industries, which use no land. Agriculture produces output (corn) with the production lag of one year, while the industrial production is assumed to be instantaneous. A part of the industrial production is consumed by workers and landowners, and the rest is used for production in the future, either as material or as capital goods (see equation (9) of Chapter 5). Material is, in fact, a kind of capital goods which is usable only once, so that its rate of depreciation is 1 and cannot be assumed to be equal to the rates of depreciation of the other durable capital goods. In spite of this, material is included in the vector of the fixed capital goods, M, throughout this volume, because, as is easily shown, the argument *mutatis mutandis* holds true for the general case of the rate of depreciation being different from one capital goods to another.

Then, first, from (3) and (4) we obtain

$$\pi F_i'(m_i, 1) = (1 + r)w\lambda + (\delta + r)p\kappa,$$

$$i = 1, \ldots, u, \text{ where } m_i \geqq 1, i = 1, \ldots, u. \quad (11.1)$$

As for the marginal land u, however, we need a proviso, that is, m_u may be zero, and if so, the above equation holds for u with inequality '$<$' rather than equality '$=$'. The price equations for the n manufacturing industries may be written in terms of a vector equation, as

$$p = (1 + r)wl + (\delta + r)pk, \quad (11.2)$$

where p is a 1 by n vector of prices, l a 1 by n vector of labour input coefficients, and k an n by n matrix of capital coefficients. In the following we sometimes simplify our system by assuming that there is only one manufacturing industry; in such a case, p, l and k may be reduced to a single number, rather than a vector or a matrix. As far as this chapter is concerned, however, we assume that there are n industries. Also, in the following, we take the agricultural product as a numeraire, so that its price π always takes on the value of 1.[7]

Secondly, ξ_i is the total agricultural output produced by the land of quality i. When $i < u$, the land is fully utilized; so we must have

$$\xi_i = F_i(m_i, 1)T_i^0, \qquad i = 1, \ldots, u - 1, \quad (12)$$

[7] In other chapters, however, we take gold, one of the n goods, as numeraire and set $p_G = 1$.

while for u, land is not necessarily in full employment. Therefore we only have

$$\xi_u = F_u(m_u, 1).T_u, \tag{12'}$$

where $T_u \leqq T_u^0$.

The third component of the system is the wage fund theory. Let ξ be the total output from the agricultural activity in the previous period which is available in the market in the present period. We make, for the sake of simplicity of argument, the 'classical' assumption of consumption and saving behaviour – workers do not save, and capitalists do not consume. As for the landowners, we assume that they consume, in the current period, a constant percentage of their total rent income in the previous period. Then, subtracting the landowners' consumption, $c(\bar{R})$, where $\bar{R}$ is the total amount of rent in the previous period, from the total output ξ of the same period, we obtain $\xi - c(\bar{R})$, which constitutes the wage fund for the present period. Since the total demand for the wage fund by agriculture is $w\lambda\eta$, while the one by the manufacturing industries is wlx, where x is the industrial output vector, the total demand for the wage fund is equalized to its supply, where the following equation is established

$$\xi = w(\lambda\eta + lx) + c(\bar{R}). \tag{13}$$

Similarly, the available fixed capital goods are fully utilized if equation

$$\kappa\eta + kx = M \tag{14}$$

holds; in this expression M is an n by 1 vector which has the stock of capital good i at the commencement of the current period as its ith element. Equation (14), together with equation (13), assures that the fixed and circulating capitals are all entirely employed in the state of equilibrium.

Equation (15) below describes the full employment of labour. Let N be the total number of workers available in the present period. On the other hand, their employment by agriculture is $\lambda\eta$, while the one by industry is lx. It is clear that full employment is established where we have the following equation,

$$\lambda\eta + lx = N. \tag{15}$$

In addition to these we have the rent equation (7), which may be rewritten, in view of $\pi = 1$ and the definition of c, in the form

$$F_i(m_i, 1) = m_i[(1 + r)w\lambda + (\delta + r)p\kappa] + R_i(m_i),$$

$$i = 1, 2, \ldots, u, \quad (16)$$

with the qualification that $R_u = 0$ if $T_u < T_u^0$, while $R_u \geqq 0$ if $T_u = T_u^0$. Finally, we have (10), that is equivalent to

$$m_1 T_1^0 + m_2 T_2^0 + \cdots + m_{u-1} T_{u-1}^0 + m_u T_u = \eta \quad (17)$$

on which Walras' attention is focussed.

5 The system of equations, (11)–(17), which might be called the Ricardian system of general equilibrium, can be solved in the following way. First, equations (14) and (15) determine the full employment levels of activity, η^0 and x^0, of the agricultural and industrial sectors. As the number of equations contained in (14) and (15) is equal to the number of their variables η, x, so, in general, (14) and (15) have solutions η^0 and x^0. These, however, are economically meaningless unless they are non-negative. Ricardo as an economic theorist of the first generation was not concerned with this problem of some of η^0 and x^0 being possibly negative and simply took their positiveness for granted.

Now in view of (14) we may put (13) in the form

$$\frac{\xi}{N} = w + c\frac{\bar{R}}{\xi}\frac{\xi}{N}. \quad (13')$$

Solving with respect to w,

$$w^0 = (1 - c\theta)\frac{\xi}{N}, \quad (13'')$$

where θ represents the share of rent in the agricultural product in the previous period, $\bar{R}/\xi$. As $c, \theta, \xi/N$ are all given at the beginning of the present period, the full employment wage rate w^0 is determined by the wage fund equation $(13'')$. We then obtain from (11.2) prices p as a function of r. Therefore, in (11.1) the right-hand side is a function of r only, so that it gives m_i as a function of r.[8]

---

[8] Remember that π is normalized such that $\pi = 1$.

Then equation (17) may be written as

$$m_1(r)T_1^0 + \cdots + m_{u-1}(r)T_{u-1}^0 + m_u(r)T_u = \eta^0, \qquad (17')$$

by means of which r and T_u are determined at, say, r^0 and T_u^*, respectively; $T_u^* \leqq T_u^0$. Then $m_1, \ldots, m_u$ are accordingly determined, and we obtain rents per acre, $R_1, \ldots, R_u$ from (16).

This is an outline of a proper algorithm to get Ricardo's general equilibrium. In this procedure the most delicate part is a step to establish the final equation (17) or (17'), which is worth a more detailed explanation. Aiming for (17'), we begin with (13''), which determines the real wage rate w^0. With this w given, we have from (11.2)

$$p = (1+r)w^0 l[I - (\delta + r)k]^{-1}. \qquad (18)$$

As k is a non-negative square matrix, we can show that p is an increasing function of r. Substituting (18) into (11.1) we have, with $\pi = 1$, equation

$$F_i'(m_i, 1) = (1+r)w^0\{\lambda + l[I - (\delta + r)k]^{-1}(\delta + r)\kappa\}, \qquad (19)$$

whose right-hand side is apparently an increasing function of r. Bearing in mind the assumption that F_i' is a decreasing function of m_i, we find from (19) that m_i decreases when r increases.

We now solve (17') in the following way. Suppose r takes on a positive value, say, r^0. Select u such that $m_i \geqq 1$ for all $i \leqq u$, while $m_j = 0$ for all $j > u$. Then solve (17') with respect to T_u. If $0 < T_u \leqq T_u^0$, r^0 and T_u are taken as solutions to (17'). If T_u thus determined is either zero or negative, we have the following possibilities. First, $T_u = 0$ and $m_u(r^0) = 1$; then this r^0 and the T_u being 0 are solutions to (17'). If not, r^0 is changed and a higher value r^1 is assigned to r. After the change we may still obtain $m_i(r^1) \geqq 1$, $i = 1, \ldots, u$, and $m_i(r^1) = 0$, $i = u+1, u+2, \ldots$; T_u will increase. If $0 < T_u < T_u^0$, then this r^1 is the solution. On the other hand, if the T_u obtained when r is fixed at r^0 exceeds T_u^0, r^0 has to be revised to a lower value r^1. All m_i's, $i = 1, \ldots, u$, increase and T_u decreases. If the new T_u is less than or equal to T_u^0 and all m_i, $i = u+1, u+2, \ldots$ remain at zero, the new r^1 and T_u are solutions to (17'). However, we must remember that, when we revise the preassigned value of r, the marginal land u may change. In this case we must search for the new marginal land u' and afterwards proceed the *tâtonnement* on u'.

6 The procedure to get solutions to (17') may be conveniently shown graphically. If the preassigned value of r is very high, no m_i, $i = 1, 2, \ldots$, can be positive, so that the left-hand side of (17') is nil. At some $r^1 > 0$, m_1 becomes equal to 1, all other m_i's being zero; therefore, the left-hand side of (17') may take on any value between 0 and T_1^0. Where r decreases further $m_1(r)$ increases, keeping all other m_i, $i = 2, 3, \ldots$, at zero. At some $r^2 < r^1$, we have $m_2(r^2) = 1$. Then the left-hand side of (17') may take on any value between $m_1(r^2)T_1^0$ and $m_1(r^2)T_1^0 + T_2^0$. Similarly we have a staircase-like curve AA' with steps at r^3, r^4 and so on. Finally, r reaches zero, and (19) may be reduced to equations

$$F_i'(m_i, 1) = w^0[\lambda + l(I - \delta k)^{-1}\delta \kappa], \qquad i = 1, 2, \ldots, \qquad (19')$$

which have solutions $m_i^0 \geqq 1$ for $i = 1, 2, \ldots, j$ and no solutions for $i > j$. The curve AA' may reach its highest level when

$$m_1^0 T_1^0 + \cdots + m_j^0 T_j^0, \qquad \text{if } m_j^0 > 1,$$

or

$$m_1^0 T_1^0 + \cdots + m_{j-1}^0 T_{j-1}^0 + T_j, \qquad \text{if } m_j^0 = 1,$$

where $T_j \leqq T_j^0$. Equation (17') implies that the rate of profit r and the cultivated area of the marginal land T_u are determined at the intersection of curve AA' with the horizontal line BB' of the height η^0 (see Figure 3).

It is easy to confirm that at $r = 0$, Ricardo's labour values, which I call the marginal labour values, prevail. They are defined by the following set of equations:

$$\Lambda_0 F_i'(m_i, 1) = \lambda + \Lambda_1 \delta \kappa, \qquad (20.1)$$

$$\Lambda_1 = l + \Lambda_1 \delta k, \qquad (20.2)$$

where Λ_0 is the value of the agricultural product, corn, and Λ_1 the n-dimensional vector of labour values of the industrial products. Equation (15) of Chapter 1 corresponds to (20.1); $L_0(m^0)$ there stands for $\lambda/F_i'(m_i, 1)$ here, whilst $A_0(m^0)$ there is $\delta \kappa/F_i'(m_i, 1)$ here. Solving (20.2) and substituting, we obtain

$$\Lambda_0 F_i'(m_i, 1) = \lambda + l(I - \delta k)^{-1}\delta \kappa. \qquad (21)$$

Comparing this with (19'), we find $\Lambda_0 = 1/w^0$. In other words, the

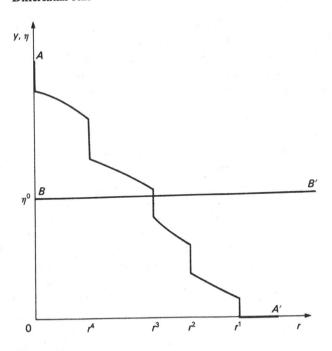

Figure 3*
*y stands for the left-hand side of (17')

marginal labour value of corn is the reciprocal of the real wage rate w^0 in terms of corn.

Figure 3 shows that the two curves AA' and BB' do not necessarily intersect at $r = 0$. This means that the marginal labour values do not necessarily (and usually) prevail in the market. This is consistent with Ricardo's own finding, as has been seen in Chapter 1, that prices are *not* generally proportional to values. In fact, there are always discrepancies between relative prices and labour values except in the most unrealistic case where the ratio of circulating capital (i.e. variable capital in Marxian terminology) to fixed capital (i.e. his constant capital) is equal throughout all production sectors of the economy. Ricardo nevertheless used the labour theory of value, as a useful first approximation to the theory of production prices (11.1) and (11.2), because we can derive, from the former more easily than the latter, a comparative statics law concerning production prices.

In order to find out how prices in terms of corn will change where land is cultivated more intensively, we have to solve (11.1) and (11.2) simultaneously. Assuming w is given at w^0 by (13″), equation (19), obtained by substituting (11.2) into (11.1), gives the rate of profit r as a decreasing function of m_i. Substituting the r function thus obtained into (18), that is equivalent to (11.2), then p is given as an increasing function of r, and hence, a *decreasing* function of the intensity of cultivation m_i. To reach this conclusion, we have to know that $[I - (\delta + r)k]^{-1}$ increases when r does so. This knowledge became common among economists around 1950. Therefore, it was almost impossible for Ricardo to say how prices would behave when m_i was increased. He had to be satisfied with making a conjecture about price movements.

For this purpose, Ricardo used his marginal labour theory of value. Thus we first find from (20.2) that the values of industrial products, Λ_1, are constant. This enables us to say from (20.1) that the value of corn Λ_0 increases when m_i does so, because the right-hand side of (20.1) is constant. Consequently the relative value, Λ_1/Λ_0, declines where land is used more intensively. We can then say, as a first approximation to the true law of prices, that the prices of industrial products in terms of corn, p, will also decline, provided we consider, as Ricardo did, that a change in prices is regulated by a change in values. In fact, whilst he rejected the proportionality between prices and values, he assumed, without giving any convincing rationale, that p was a positive function of Λ_1/Λ_0. Throughout his analysis of the accumulation process (which is discussed in a later chapter), the marginal labour theory of value plays the most important role in conjecturing the direction of price movements which will occur when the economy progresses and capital is accumulated.

7 The above general equilibrium system may be compared with the one proposed by Pasinetti as an interpretation of Ricardo.[9] As has already been mentioned, Pasinetti does not classify various sorts of land according to their quality. He instead has only one aggregate production function for agriculture as a whole, with the logical consequence that he is unable to explain the rent of a land as the surplus which it yields – i.e. an excess of output of a land over the

[9] See L. Pasinetti, *Growth and Income Distribution*, pp. 6–10.

amount that the least productive land in cultivation can produce. His theory of rent, accordingly, can hardly be a theory of differential rent, though it may be called a marginal productivity theory of rent.

Secondly, in his two-sector Ricardian model consisting of the wage-good industry (i.e. the corn production sector) and the luxury-good industry (i.e. the gold industry), no fixed capital is used. Consequently, there is no room in his model for what I name the Ricardo–Marx theorem in Chapter 1; it means that prices always equal labour values. This is entirely opposite to the view of Ricardo who insisted that prices generally deviate from values, and who considered them to coincide with each other only in a highly exceptional case.

To this Pasinetti model the following comment by Walras directed at J. S. Mill would perfectly apply. 'The capital he (Mill) has in mind does not include fixed capital; it does not even include all the circulating capital, but only that part of it which is expanded on the payment of wages, i.e. *the amount of working capital used for hiring labourers.*'[10] But this does not apply to Ricardo. In his system there are both (1) fixed capital and (2) circulating capital, in addition to (3) the fund paid to workers as wages. Our ξ above, that is Pasinetti's K, stands for this last category (3); and, while capitals (1) and (2) are absent in Pasinetti, they are shown by M in our model. If the rate of depreciation δ is less than 100 per cent, the corresponding element of vector M is capital of category (1), i.e. durable fixed capital, while a capital good with $\delta = 100$ per cent is circulating capital (materials etc.) which is consumed during the production process or embodied in the product. As it is an aim of the general equilibrium analysis to show how all kinds of capital which are used in production will be reproduced, it is important to construct a model which explicitly contains M and ξ representing all three sorts of capital.

Finally, a comment should be made on which variables should be regarded as exogenous. In the previous sections, I have considered ξ, M and N as given, because the first two represent the existing amounts of wage goods and capital goods, respectively, while the last the number of workers in the economy. Pasinetti, however, takes his K and x (my ξ and w, respectively) as given. This means that his equilibrium, like von Neumann's, is feasible only in an 'open'

---

[10] Walras, *Elements*, p. 421, his italics.

economy where workers freely emigrate or immigrate so as to keep
the real wage at a given level w^0.[11] Pasinetti, in particular, fixes it at the
natural level which is defined as that wage rate which keeps population constant.[12]

This model, however, is very different from that of Ricardo who
was concerned in his *Principles* with an economy that is *closed* with
respect to the population of workers. Although he discussed
international trade in one of the chapters, he assumed even in that
chapter that no worker can immigrate or emigrate. Then the real
wage rate has to be flexibly adjusted to ξ/N which is taken as constant
in the short-run analysis, since both ξ and N are given at any moment
in time.

In the long-run analysis Pasinetti defines the long-run equilibrium
as a state where the real wage rate is set at the natural rate and the
profits are zero.[13] There is no doubt that Ricardo also has the same
definition. But there is a big difference between the models of the
two authors. Ricardo's economy is a closed economy, whilst
Pasinetti's fixed wage model requires that it an open economy. If he
had clearly paid attention to this fact and had seen that workers can
freely immigrate or emigrate, he would have seen that the long-run
equilibrium real-wages need not be at the natural level, because the
wage rate at which the population remains stationary has no relevance
in such an 'open' economy. The wage rate can be kept at an arbitrary
level even in the long run.

8 There is one more difference between Pasinetti's interpretation of
Ricardo and the model in this chapter. It concerns the consumption
and savings of the landowners. According to Pasinetti, the
landowners do not consume corn at all; they instead spend their
entire income on buying luxuries, gold in his case. In the present
model, on the other hand, the landowners spend a part of their
income on buying corn, the rest being saved; there are no luxuries
for them to buy. Also for workers no consumption good, other than
corn, is available.

[11] J. von Neumann, 'A Model of General Economic Equilibrium', *Review of
Economic Studies*, 1945–6, pp. 1–9.
[12] Pasinetti, *Growth and Income Distribution*, p. 10. Hicks too once considered
Ricardo in a similar way. See his *Capital and Time*, Oxford, 1973, p. 49 and J.
Hicks and S. Hollander, 'Ricardo and the Moderns', in his *Classics and Moderns*,
Basil Blackwell, 1983, pp. 41–2.
[13] *Ibid.*, p. 14.

It is clear that either of these two views deviates from Ricardo. He himself refers to 'food and other necessaries, on which the wages of labour are expended' (p. 15). These other necessaries, such as 'the shoes and clothing of the labourer' as he pointed out, are produced by the manufacturing industries. This means that Ricardo's industry produces at least one wage good in addition to luxury goods. In a later chapter we shall generalize our present model by introducing wage-good and luxury producing industries.

As for saving by landowners, Pasinetti's assumption that they do not save, though valid through most parts of Ricardo's *Principles*, conflicts with the latter's description of the landowners as 'the monied men'. 'These men are engaged in no trade, but live on the interest of their money, which is employed in discounting bills, or in loans to the industrious part of the community' (p. 89). He also stated: 'The whole produce of the land and labour of every country is divided into three portions: of these, one portion is devoted to wages, another to profits and the other to rent. It is from the *two last portions* only, that any deductions can be made for taxes, or for *savings*' (p. 348, my emphasis). It is thus clear that Ricardo considered both capitalists and landowners as savers, though, as Hollander has pointed out, the latter's propensity to save is likely to be lower than the former's.[14]

Let us now establish a position for the savings-investment equation in the previous model. First, concerning savings, it is assumed that capitalists do not consume, so that their savings are equal to their income, which is

$$r[w(\lambda\eta + lx) + p(\kappa\eta + kx)].$$

On the other hand, landowners' savings are written as

$$R - c(\bar{R}),$$

where R is the aggregate rent income in the current period, while $\bar{R}$ is that from the previous period. R is the sum of the rents paid to all sorts of lands of various qualities:

$$R = R_1(m_1)T_1^0 + \cdots + R_{u-1}(m_{u-1})T_{u-1}^0 + R_u(m_u)T_u,$$

where $R_u(m_u) = 0$ if $T_u < T_u^0$; otherwise, $T_u = T_u^0$. Total savings,

---

[14] S. Hollander, *The Economics of David Ricardo*, Heinemann Education Books, 1979, p. 324.

therefore, are written

$$S = r[w(\lambda\eta + lx) + p(\kappa\eta + kx)] + R - c(\bar{R}). \qquad (22)$$

Next, as assumed tacitly so far, we now explicitly assume Say's law. This law which is called the law of market (debouche) is open to interpretation and has been given diverse meanings throughout its history. It is clear that Ricardo welcomed and accepted it.[15] In what follows, we define the law in the same way that Keynes did. That is, there is no independent investment function, so that the amount of capital goods produced is flexibly adjusted such that full employment of labour and capital is established. It is then clear that by virtue of the full employment equations (14) and (15) the two parts in the parentheses on the right-hand side of (22) equal N and M respectively. Thus S is seen to be the full employment level of savings. Since we have the equation,

Total output = wages + depreciation + profits + rent,

and wages equal workers' consumption, which is ξ, we may rewrite the above equation in the form,

Total output − depreciation − ξ = profit + rent.

In view of the expression that total output = $\xi + px$ and equation (22) we finally obtain

$$\xi - c(\bar{R}) - \xi + px - \text{depreciation} = S.$$

The left-hand side obviously stands for net investment, that is the sum of net investment in the form of the wage fund and the net investment on capital goods. The equation shows that total net investment equals total savings at the full employment level.

Thus under Say's law investment is always equal to full employment savings. That is to say, as Keynes claimed, there is no obstacle to realizing the full employment of all resources (i.e. labour and capital). There is no unemployment problem in Ricardo, because it is assumed that lack of effective demand would never happen. Behind this, there is perhaps a tacit assumption that the marginal efficiency of capital, in Keynes' sense, does not diminish. Ricardo's outlook on investment was then inherited by Walras, who also assumed flexible investment and proved mathematically that there exists a full employment equilibrium to the general equilibrium

[15] Ricardo, *Principles*, pp. 6–7.

system of capital formation and credit.[16] Even Marx assumed, as will be discussed in a later chapter, that his extended reproduction scheme fulfilled Say's law in Keynes' sense that the animal spirit of capitalists is strong enough to exhaust full employment savings.

After Keynes, even now many economists, especially those who are influenced by Walras, still believe that equilibrium solutions to any model of general equilibrium do exist. One of the equilibrium conditions states that supply equals demand for labour; hence the equilibrium is a full employment equilibrium. Of course, this is true for a certain class of economic models. But in the case of those which include investment as one of their variables we meet the problem of Say's law in Keynes' sense. If the marginal efficiency of capital does not diminish and, accordingly, investment is perfectly flexible, then effective demand can never be insufficient and full employment will be realized. On the other hand, where the marginal efficiency diminishes, investment is limited. Where it sharply diminishes, investment is so low that full employment equilibrium is impossible. The former is the world with which Ricardo and Walras were concerned – the classical and neoclassical regime – while the latter is, of course, the Keynesian world. We shall later examine the process of transition from the Ricardo–Walras paradigm, based on Say's law, to Keynes' paradigm of anti-Say's law. Here we see an evolution of economic theory, or a shift in its interest, from one which assumes no unemployment to another whose prime concern is unemployment.

16 Walras, *Elements*, pp. 267–95. Also see Morishima, *Walras' Economics*, Cambridge University Press, 1977, pp. 100–22 and 185–94.

Part II

WAGES AND PROFITS

3 Wages, profits and general equilibrium

1 A careful reader of the previous chapters will have found that, in the capital coefficient matrix of the economy, the industrial sectors are decomposable from the agricultural sector. This assumes that agricultural products are not used as materials in the production of commodities; that is, the capital coefficient matrix (regarding material as a 'capital good' which can be used only once for production) is of the following form:

$$K = \begin{bmatrix} 0 & 0 \\ \kappa(m_u) & k \end{bmatrix},$$

where $\kappa(m_u)$ is a n by 1 vector and k a n by n matrix. The ith element of $\kappa(m_u)$ represents the marginal quantity of capital good i required for an increase in the agricultural output on the marginal land, i.e.

$$\kappa_i(m_u) = \kappa_i \frac{dm_u}{dF_u} \qquad \text{or} \qquad \kappa_i/F_u'(m_u, 1).$$

Industry is decomposable from agriculture because of the 0 at the top of the second column of K, which shows that industry does not use corn as a material. (It seems that a direct and explicit textual support for this decomposability is hardly found in Ricardo's *Principles*. Nevertheless we may take the italicized part of the quotation below as evidence that Ricardo's derivation of the wage–profit frontier is based on the decomposability.)

Ricardo took advantage of this assumption in deriving the wage–profit frontier (i.e. the factor–price frontier as Samuelson calls it), one of the most important 'parts' of Ricardian economics. Because of this, the labour theory of value is simplified and, therefore, it can be used to prove the reciprocal relationship between wages and profits. Thus Ricardo's approach may be characterized as applying the labour theory of value to an economy whose industry is decomposable from its agriculture. In addition to this, his method of establishing the reciprocal relationship may be characterized as semi-dynamic (or, more properly, shifting); in fact, he saw the relationship as being in a process of economic expansion. This dynamic, labour-value theoretic and decompositional character of Ricardo's approach to the wage–profit frontier, is precisely shown, in a condensed form, in the following passage:

> Supposing corn and manufactured goods always to sell at the same price, profits would be high or low in proportion as wages were low or high. *But suppose corn to rise in price because more labour is necessary to produce it; that cause will not raise the price of manufactured goods in the production of which no additional quantity of labour is required.* If, then, wages continued the same, the profits of manufacturers would remain the same; but if, as is absolutely certain, wages should rise with the rise of corn, then their profits would necessarily fall. (pp. 110–11; my italics)

As more inferior land is put into cultivation as the economy progresses, corn will be produced under more unfavourable conditions and its labour value will be increased. However, this will not affect the labour values of manufactured goods because of the assumed decomposability of manufacturing industries from agriculture. (In fact, if at least one industry uses corn as a material, a rise in the labour value of corn will give rise to an increase in the labour value of the output of that industry, and hence a further increase in the labour values will be created in other industries where the products which are made of corn are further used as materials or means of production.) From this Ricardo conjectured that the price of corn would rise, and the production prices of manufacturing industries would remain constant. Where the price of corn rises, the workers' cost of living will also rise, and therefore wages should rise. This obviously means a decrease in the manufacturers' profits because the prices of manufactured goods are all unchanged.

2 Later economists, especially after Sraffa,[1] were concerned with establishing the wage–profit frontier without appealing to the labour theory of value and without assuming decomposability. In reviewing these works I shall begin with my article which was published before

---

[1] P. Sraffa, *Production of Commodities by Means of Commodities*, Cambridge University Press, 1960.

Sraffa's book.[2] Although this article may establish a base from which Ricardo's result is derived, it itself is not a quasi-dynamic analysis but only a comparative static one. It deals with two possible equilibria in comparison, one at a higher wage rate and the other at a lower rate, both carrying out cultivation at the same level of intensity m_u.

In this sort of analysis, we must clearly define, as Ricardo did, what is taken as the standard of measure of prices and wages. This is Sraffa's problem of standard commodity or the problem of numeraire, which is dealt with significantly differently by Ricardo, Sraffa and myself. Ricardo assumed that there is a peculiar commodity called 'money' which is 'invariable in value, and therefore every variation of price to be referable to an alteration in the value of the commodity' (p. 110n), while I do not assume existence of such a commodity because I do not take the labour-value theoretic approach. Instead, like Walras, I consider that any commodity, or any bundle of commodities, could serve as numeraire. Although I defined, in the above mentioned article, the real wage rate and prices of commodities in terms of the bundle of consumption goods, $b = (b_0, b_1, \ldots, b_n)$, where b_i is the quantity of the ith good which is necessary for subsistence for a man for one period, it could be any bundle.[3]

Alternatively, it may be the current consumption bundle of the workers, or anything else which includes Sraffa's standard commodity. Sraffa and his followers stick to his peculiar standard commodity but there is no need to be faithful to any particular sort of bundle.

Throughout the following, we fix m_u at some constant level m, and, assuming that the economy is not necessarily decomposable, we write the capital coefficient matrix as

$$K = \begin{bmatrix} \theta(m) & h \\ \kappa(m) & k \end{bmatrix},$$

where $\theta(m) = \theta \dfrac{dm_u}{dF_u}(m) = \theta/F_u'(m, 1)$ which is the quantity of corn

---

[2] M. Morishima, 'Prices, Interest and Profits in a Dynamic Leontief System', *Econometrica*, XXVI, 1958, pp. 358–80; it is also contained in my *Equilibrium, Stability and Growth*, Oxford University Press, 1964.

[3] If $b_0 = 1$ and all other b_i's are zero, then corn is the standard, while, where $b_G = 1$, G standing for gold, with $b_i = 0$ otherwise, gold is the standard commodity.

used as seed in the production of one unit for corn and h, a 1 by n vector, represents corn used as material in n manufacturing industries, $1, \ldots, n$. It is noted that K is a constant matrix. We denote the labour input coefficient vector $(\lambda(m), l_1, \ldots, l_n)$ by L, where $\lambda(m) = \lambda \dfrac{dm_u}{dF_u}(m) = \lambda/F_u'(m, 1)$, and the price vector $(\pi, p_1, \ldots, p_n)$ by p. In this section and Section 7, the agricultural product is referred to as commodity 0, and p_0 stands for its price π. It is also noted that L is a constant vector. Now we may put the price equations in the matrix form:

$$p = (1+r)wL + (\delta + r)pK. \tag{1}$$

The real wage rate ω and the prices in terms of the composite commodity b are defined as

$$\omega = w/pb \qquad \text{and} \qquad q = p/pb,$$

respectively. Then equation (1) may be written as

$$q = (1+r)\omega L + (\delta + r)qK. \tag{1'}$$

Of course $qb = 1$. By virtue of (1') we can now establish that an increase in ω gives rise to a decrease in r, and vice versa.

Suppose $\omega^0 < \omega^1$. Let (ω^0, r^0, q^0) and (ω^1, r^1, q^1) be solutions to (1'). If we suppose the contrary, i.e. r does not decrease (that is, $r^0 \leq r^1$) where ω is increased ($\omega^0 < \omega^1$) and, in this case, if q remained unchanged ($q^0 = q^1$), we would clearly have

$$q^0 = (1+r^0)\omega^0 L + (\delta + r^0)q^0 K < (1+r^1)\omega^1 L + (\delta + r^1)q^0 K = q^0,$$

which is an obvious contradiction. Hence $r^0 > r^1$.

Next, examine the remaining case where $q^0 \neq q^1$. As $qb = 1$, at least one price q_i must decrease. Let $q_j^1 = \alpha_j q_j^0$ and let α_i be the smallest among $\alpha_0, \ldots, \alpha_n$. Then we have

$$q_i^0 > q_i^1, \tag{2}$$

and

$$\frac{q_j^0}{q_i^0} \leq \frac{\alpha_j}{\alpha_i} \frac{q_j^0}{q_i^0} = \frac{q_j^1}{q_i^1} \qquad \text{for all } j. \tag{2'}$$

Where $r^0 \leqq r^1$ and $\omega^0 < \omega^1$, we have from (1'), in view of (2) and (2'),

$$1 = (1 + r^0) \frac{\omega^0}{q_i^0} l_i + (\delta + r^0) \sum_j \frac{q_j^0}{q_i^0} k_{ji}$$

$$< (1 + r^1) \frac{\omega^1}{q_i^1} l_i + (\delta + r^1) \sum_j \frac{q_j^1}{q_i^1} k_{ji} = 1,$$

because we assume $l_i > 0$; of course k_{ji} is an element of K. Obviously, this is a contradiction, which means that $r^0 \leqq r^1$ is not compatible with $\omega^0 < \omega^1$. Therefore we may now conclude that the rate of profit r is a decreasing function of the real wage rate ω.[4]

3 Sraffa takes a different approach. First, he assumes that wages are paid at the end of the production period, whereas Ricardo himself assumed that wages were advanced to the workers at the beginning of the period (p. 41). Although this simplifies the argument, it is not a crucial assumption, under which the price equation (1) is reduced to

$$p = wL + pA + rpK, \tag{1''}$$

where $A = \delta K$.

Next, let us consider a hypothetical situation where no wage payment is made to the workers. Then there would be neither labour-feeding inputs, nor workers' demand for consumption goods. In this situation we would have a dynamic input–output system:

$$X = AX + K\Delta X. \tag{3}$$

In the state of balanced growth, where $X = X^*$ and $\Delta X = gX^*$, (3) is written as

$$X^* = AX^* + gKX^*. \tag{3'}$$

We can further show that the rate of balanced growth g is equal to the particular rate of profit r^* which is obtained in the hypothetical situation where $\omega = 0$, and, therefore, the price equation

$$p^* = p^*A + r^*p^*K \tag{4}$$

holds.[5] So, in (3'), g may be replaced by r^*, and the equation thus

---

[4] See Morishima's above-mentioned *Econometrica* paper, p. 373, and his *Equilibrium, Stability and Growth*, pp. 81–3. Note that k_{ij} are elements of the indecomposable K; in particular, $k_{00} = \theta(m)$, $k_{j0} = \kappa_j(m)$ and $k_{0i} = h_i$. Also $l_0 = \lambda(m)$.

[5] Premultiply (3') by p^* and postmultiply (4) by X^*, and compare. We then at once have $g = r^*$.

obtained may be premultiplied by p. This, together with (1″) postmultiplied by X^*, yields

$$wLX^* + pAX^* + rpKX^* = pAX^* + r^*pKX^*,$$

from which we get

$$r = r^*\left(1 - \frac{wLX^*}{r^*pKX^*}\right). \tag{5}$$

Since $r^*pKX^* = p(I - A)X^*$ from (3′), the second term of the part within the parentheses of the above formula stands for 'the share of wages' in 'the net output'. Sraffa denotes it by W and derives the formula

$$r = r^*(1 - W). \tag{6}$$

If he, like Ricardo, assumed that wages are advanced to the workers, he would obtain, by a similar method, instead of (6), the formula,

$$r = r^*(1 - W)\frac{1/r^*}{W + 1/r^*}. \tag{6'}$$

In any case, in view of the fact that r^* is constant, we find from (6) or (6′) that an increase in 'the wage share' W gives rise to a decrease in the rate of profit r.

Sraffa interprets (6) in the following manner. He calls the system (3′) 'the standard system' and the eigenvector X^* 'the composition of the standard composite commodity'. It is noted that the demands for commodities by the workers are all neglected (or nil because no wage payment is made) in the system (3′). Remembering $g = r^*$ in (3′) we observe that the standard net products $(I - A)X^*$ equal r^*KX, where r^* is called by Sraffa 'the standard ratio' which is the ratio of the net products, $(I - A)X^*$, to the means of production, KX^*, in the standard system.[6] Of course in this system too, labour is needed for producing commodities, even though no wage payment is made. (I ignore, at the present stage of the argument, this paradoxical character of the standard system and do not ask whether workers will work without reward. Even slaves would not really work if they were not rewarded, in the form of food at least.) 'Standard' employment, LX^*, and 'standard' net output, r^*KX^*, are both evaluated at the equilibrium price p of the actual system.

[6] Sraffa, pp. 20–1.

Sraffa's W, that is 'the proportion of the net product that goes to wages', is the ratio of the total wages that the standard employment, LX^*, would earn if it were paid at the actual rate w, to the standard net output, r^*KX^*, evaluated at the current equilibrium prices p.

Alternatively, if $(I - A)X^* = \sigma$, Sraffa's system is a system in terms of the composite-commodity numeraire σ. Defining $\omega = w/p\sigma$, and $q = p/p\sigma$, we get from (1")

$$q = \omega L + qA + rqK. \tag{1'''}$$

Using the method adopted in the previous section, we can obtain the downwards sloping wage–profit frontier directly from (1''') without using (3'). Also, taking into account the equation, $r^*pKX^* = p\sigma$, we can immediately see that (5) is written as

$$r = r^*(1 - \omega LX^*). \tag{6''}$$

This establishes a linear, declining relationship between r and ω.

Whatever terminology and rhetoric are used, the hypothetical character of the standard system is clear. It is doubly hypothetical. First, it neglects the workers' demand for commodities as well as the wage payment. Secondly, it assumes that commodities are produced in the fixed proportions necessary for the standard economy to grow at a uniform rate. Such an imaginary state is extremely remote from the actual observed economy, and Sraffa's share W, as a proportion of 'the standard net product', has nothing to do with the workers' share in the actual economy. In addition to this, Sraffa's formula (6) has a defect in that this real wage rate in terms of the standard commodity σ does not accurately reflect the consumers' true 'real wage rate' in terms of their consumption bundle b, although there is some parallelism between them.

Let us write

$$\omega = w/p\sigma \quad \text{and} \quad \omega^* = w/pb.$$

Then $\omega = \omega^*pb/p\sigma$. Taking this into account we find from (6") that Sraffa's W or ω depends on both ω^* and p. Where the true real wage rate ω^* changes, it influences p, so that the relationship between ω and ω^* may be non-linear. That is to say, we obtain the Sraffa conclusion that the rate of profit is a linear function of the wage share W, only in the case of the peculiar standard commodity σ being taken as numeraire. Otherwise, a change in ω^* has two effects upon W, one directly and the other indirectly via p.

Finally, it is noted that, where the Ricardo–Marx condition of the ratios of the two capitals (circulating and fixed) being equal is fulfilled throughout all production processes, the wage–profit frontier which I derived and Sraffa's formula become identical with each other. This can be shown in the following way. As the Ricardo–Marx theorem holds true, we have $p = h\Lambda$, so that the capital–labour ratios in terms of values are equal to each other. Thus

$$\Lambda K_i / L_i = k_0, \qquad i = 1, \ldots, n.$$

Then, taking the composite commodity σ as numeraire, the price equation (1) may be put in the form

$$h\Lambda = \omega h\Lambda \sigma L + h\Lambda A + r\omega h\Lambda \sigma L + rhk_0 L$$

because $w = \omega p\sigma$. Hence

$$\Lambda = (\omega \Lambda \sigma + r\omega \Lambda \sigma + rk_0)L + \Lambda A,$$

which is compared with the value equation, $\Lambda = L + \Lambda A$. We then have

$$1 = \omega \Lambda \sigma + r\omega \Lambda \sigma + rk_0,$$

from which we have

$$r = \frac{1}{k_0}(1 - \omega \Lambda \sigma)\frac{k_0}{\omega \Lambda \sigma + k_0}. \tag{7}$$

As $\Lambda \sigma$ and k_0 are independent of both ω and r, r decreases where ω increases. We can show that, where all production processes have an identical capital composition, the Sraffa formula (6′) is also reduced to (7), because, under the assumption of equal composition of capital, we have $r^* = 1/k_0$ from (4) and $W = \omega \Lambda \sigma$ from the definition of W. Where the wages are not advanced, the formula (7) is reduced to

$$r = \frac{1}{k_0}(1 - \omega \Lambda \sigma),$$

which is exactly the same as the original one, (6), that Sraffa obtained; in particular, r is linear with respect to ω.

It is not surprising at all to see that the wage–profit frontier and Sraffa's distribution formula coincide with each other, where all production processes have the same capital composition; in fact, in this case prices are proportional to values, so that there is no (relative) price effect upon W and r in the Sraffa formula. The sole relationship we can derive from it is the one between r and ω, that is the wage–profit frontier in our sense. We may now conclude that this is the only case in which Sraffa's formula [(6) or (6')] is meaningful; otherwise it deviates from the wage–profit frontier, because of the relative price effects, and is nothing else but a law concerning the *imaginary* 'standard' system.

4 Although Sraffa, like Ricardo, is concerned with an economy where prices may deviate from values, Tosato, like Pasinetti, discusses the case where prices are proportional to values.[7] He assumes, first of all, that the rate of depreciation δ is one in the price equation (1). We have, therefore,

$$p = [wL + pK](1 + r). \tag{8}$$

He also makes the following assumptions which play crucial roles in his argument.[8] First,

$$[p_G - (pK)_G]/L_G = 1; \tag{9}$$

and then

$$[p_G - (pK)_G]/L_G = [p(I - K)X]/N, \tag{10}$$

where G stands for gold, which is taken as numeraire, so that p_G is the price of gold, L_G the labour input, and $(pK)_G$ the capital input, per unit of gold output, whilst X is the actual output vector and N the total employment of labour. Obviously,

$$LX = N. \tag{11}$$

(9) and (10) mean that the total value added equals total labour.

Notwithstanding Tosato's claim that he has given an interpretation of the Ricardo–Sraffa theory of profit, he departs from Sraffa in two important respects. First, while Tosato's X is the actual output vector, Sraffa's X^* represents the imaginary 'standard' output structure. Secondly, relating to this difference, Sraffa need not make any additional assumption like (10), whereas Tosato's restriction of his analysis to the case of (10) evidently implies, because the actual

---

[7] D. Tosato, 'A Reconsideration of Sraffa's Interpretation of Ricardo on Value and Distribution', in G. A. Caravale (ed.), *The Legacy of Ricardo*, Basil Blackwell, 1985.
[8] Tosato, *ibid.*, p. 198 and p. 200.

output X may vary so that (10) must hold for *any* given X, that he is concerned with the case of equations

$$\frac{p_G - (pK)_G}{L_G} = \frac{p_i - (pK)_i}{L_i}, \qquad i = 1, \ldots, n, \tag{12}$$

being fulfilled. In view of (8), we have

$$\frac{p_i}{L_i} = w(1 + r) + \frac{(pK)_i}{L_i}(1 + r). \tag{13}$$

Substituting from this, it is at once clear from (12) that this holds true if and only if the composition of capital is the same for all industries; that is, we have

$$\frac{(pK)_G}{L_G} = \frac{(pK)_i}{L_i}, \qquad i = 1, \ldots, n. \tag{14}$$

Thus, in Tosato's model, the premise of the Ricardo–Marx theorem is satisfied and hence, unlike Sraffa and Ricardo, he implicitly assumes that prices are proportional to values.

It seems, however, that Tosato does not realize this proportionality. This may mean that instead of assuming (10) for any value of X, he might alternatively assume, as he seems to have done, that (10) is true only for a given vector X of actual outputs. In this case, (14) does not automatically follow from (10) and we have instead, from (8), (9) and (10)

$$r = \frac{N - wN}{wN + pKX} = R(1 - w), \tag{15}$$

where R is the reciprocal of $w + pKX/N$. Since p is affected by a change in w, pKX/N does not remain unchanged when w changes. Thus Tosato's distribution formula is entirely different from Sraffa's (6') because his r^* is constant with respect to W. This is true, even though we assume, like Sraffa, that wages are paid after work, because, in this case, R reduces to $1/(pKX/N)$, which varies whenever w changes, while Sraffa's r^* is constant. In fact, his linearity disappears as soon as the aggregation is made in terms of actual outputs X rather than in terms of 'standard' outputs X^*, though it is of course true, as will be seen below, that the linearity might be preserved if we could additionally impose some other stringent conditions such as (14).

On the other hand, if (14) were held true, we would obtain

$$r = \frac{1 - w/h}{w/h + \Lambda K X/N} = \frac{1 - w/h}{w/h + k_0} = \frac{w/h}{w/h + k_0} \frac{1 - w/h}{w/h} \qquad (16)$$

from (8), (10) and the value equation

$$\Lambda = L + \Lambda K.$$

In equation (16), h represents the proportionality factor between p and Λ (i.e. $p = h\Lambda$), so that w/h is the 'real' wage rate in terms of labour value, while $\Lambda K X/N$ is equal to the uniform value composition of capital k_0, because (14) implies that each $(\Lambda K)_i/L_i$ is equal to some constant value k_0. The distribution formula (16) is essentially the same as the previous one (6'), though it is based on different assumptions. Evidently we can see that, under the assumption of wage payment after work, (16) is demoted to a simpler form

$$r = \frac{1}{k_0}(1 - w/h),$$

which corresponds to the original Sraffa formula (6).

It will now be seen that the second term on the extreme right-hand side of (16) is nothing else than the rate of exploitation à la Marx. Let b be the basic consumption bundle and ω the number of the bundles bought by a worker. Then his budget equation is written as

$$w = pB,$$

where $B(= \omega b)$ represents the amounts of consumption goods bought by the worker. Where p is proportional to Λ, the above equation may be put in the form $w = h\Lambda B$; hence $w/h = \Lambda B$. Thus real wages in terms of labour value, w/h, equal the total value of consumption goods which a worker buys. On the other hand, each worker supplies one unit of labour; accordingly, where the wages in terms of labour, w/h, are lower than the supply of labour, 1, the worker is exploited (or unpaid) by the amount, $1 - w/h$, and the rate of exploitation e is defined as $(1 - w/h)/(w/h)$. In view of this Marxian definition of the rate of exploitation, we can put (16) in the following simple form:

$$r = Ue, \qquad (16')$$

where U stands for $\Lambda B/(\Lambda B + k_0)$ and is obviously positive. Equation (16′) implies that the rate of profit r is positive if and only if the rate of exploitation is positive.

This shows that Tosato's Sraffa-like formula of the rate of profit is very closely related to the theorem which I call the fundamental Marxian theorem,[9] claiming that exploitation is necessary and sufficient for positive profits. It is noted, however, that such a result is acquired, in the case of Tosato, by assuming (14) or (10) which imply proportionality between prices and values. In the general case of the Ricardo–Marx theorem being inapplicable, so that prices may relatively deviate from values, we have only (15), instead of (16). It is of course true that, even in the case of (15), r is positive if and only if w is less than 1. But it is entirely unclear what is meant by the condition $1 > w$. In other words, under what conditions does w become less than 1? And how are prices and wages normalized in this general case? It is evident that the use of (9) and (10) is essential for deriving (15). Although (9) is a formal extension of Tosato's original assumption, $p_G/L_G = 1$, we need, in order to rationalize it, something more than the numeraire condition, because the latter only requires $p_G = 1$. Moreover, (10) together with (9) implies an equation, $p(I - K)X = N$, which is hardly provided with an economic justification, because the left-hand side of the equation gives an amount in terms of the numeraire, while the right-hand side the number of workers in the economy. Thus, the way in which w is normalized is unintelligible, and, as a consequence, the condition $1 > w$ is not economically meaningful. This means that Tosato is unable to explain under what economic conditions the rate of profit becomes positive. We shall leave the problem of exploring the conditions for positive profits to the next chapter; here we shall only point out that Sraffa's problem of the distribution of income between workers and capitalists is closely associated with my fundamental Marxian theorem.

5 The semi-dynamic (or shifting) character of Ricardo's original reasoning has been restored by Hicks.[10] He grasps the wage–profit correspondences in an economy by examining them in a phase of

[9] For this theorem, see my *Marx's Economics*, pp. 63–8, Cambridge University Press, 1973.

[10] John Hicks, 'Sraffa and Ricardo: A Critical View', in G. A. Caravale (ed.), *The Legacy of Ricardo*, Basil Blackwell, 1985.

transition towards the long-run equilibrium by use of the two vertically integrated production functions. There are two sectors, food production and non-food production, which I call agriculture and industry respectively. The product of the latter is taken as numeraire, with its price being fixed at 1. Let a_n be the labour, and t_n the average time required to produce a unit of non-food goods; w is the wages in terms of the numeraire and r the rate of profit. Hicks writes the price equation of the industry in the form:

$$1 = wa_n(1 + r)^{t_n}. \tag{17}$$

Similarly, the price equation of agriculture is given in a vertically integrated form:

$$p_f = wa_f(1 + t)^{t_f}, \tag{18}$$

where p_f is the price of food, a_f the labour required to produce a marginal unit of food, and t_f the average production period.

Hicks accepts the same assumptions as Ricardo. Constant returns to scale prevails in industry, so that a_n is constant, while diminishing returns are generally seen in agriculture; that is, a_f increases where agriculture expands its scale. He also assumes, as he says Ricardo clearly supposed, that both t_n and t_f are technologically fixed.

Once these two equations are given, we can easily derive two wage–profit frontiers. One is the industrial wage–profit frontier,

$$w = \frac{1}{a_n(1 + r)^{t_n}}, \tag{17'}$$

obtained from (17). In view of a_n and t_n being constant, it clearly shows that an increase in w gives rise to a decrease in r, and vice versa. The other frontier is the agricultural one,

$$\frac{w}{p_f} = \frac{1}{a_f(1 + r)^{t_f}} \tag{18'}$$

resulting from (18), which shows the wages in terms of food as a function of r. As long as a_f remains unchanged, the wages in terms of food, w/p_f, are a diminishing function of the rate of profit r, whilst, where a_f increases as the expansion of agriculture proceeds, the w/p_f as the function of r shifts downwards. The agricultural wage–profit frontier (18') expresses these two effects in combination, while the other, usual and familiar frontier of industry, (17'), lacks

the second shift effect because of the assumed constant returns to
scale in industry. As will be seen below, it is 'the agricultural
wage–profit frontier' which plays a most important role in Ricardo's
economics. It is Hicks' short article which infused a fresh idea into
the frontier argument.

Samuelson's comment on Marx is related with this point. In one
of his earlier articles on Marxian economics,[11] he derives the
wage–profit frontier, and assuming the constancy of production
coefficients, he concludes that real wages and the rate of profit change
in opposite directions. He says:[12]

> We should note a contradiction in Marx's thinking that analysts
> have pointed out. Along with the 'law of the falling rate of profit',
> Marxian economists often speak of the 'law of the falling (or
> constant) real wage of labour'. . . . But he [Marx] perhaps didn't
> fully realize the inconsistency of his two inevitable laws. As Joan
> Robinson points out: 'Marx can only demonstrate a falling
> tendency in profits by abandoning his argument that real wages
> tend to be constant.' Our model is well-designed to show this.

This criticism is meant to be cast on Marx, bearing in mind that
these two laws both evidently came from Ricardo, it would not be
altogether meaningless to point out that, strictly speaking, it does
not apply to Ricardo. In fact, in deriving these tendencies, Ricardo
did not assume the constancy of production coefficients. On the
contrary, the diminishing returns of land are the ultimate cause of
his two tendencies. In his words,

> As population increases, these necessaries [the products of
> agriculture – M.M.] will be constantly rising in price, because
> more labour will be necessary to produce them. . . . [Then the
> wages paid to the labourer] would rise. . . . [T]his increase in his
> wages would necessarily diminish the profits of the manufacturer;
> for his goods [non-food products – M.M.] would sell at no higher
> price, and yet the expense of producing them would be increased.
> . . . [The labourer] receive[s] more money wages, it is true, but
> his corn wages [w/p_f] will be reduced. . . . While the price of corn
> rises to 10 per cent., wages will always rise less than 10 per cent.
> The condition of the labourer will generally decline . . .
> (pp. 101–3)

[11] P. A. Samuelson, 'Wages and Interest: A Modern Dissection of Marxian Economic
Models', in *The Collected Scientific Papers of Paul A. Samuelson*, Vol. I, MIT
Press, 1966.
[12] *Ibid.*, p. 349.

This passage from Ricardo's *Principles* clearly shows that he was concerned with a situation where more and more labour is required for a unit production of food, so that a_f is increasing in the wage–profit frontier of agriculture (18'). It is clear that Hicks' formulation fits better with Ricardo's than Samuelson's. More precisely, we may modify Hicks' model slightly in order to interpret the above passage more exactly. Consider a system consisting of four equations,

$$p_n = wa_n(1 + r)^{t_n}, \qquad p_f = wa_f(1 + r)^{t_f},$$

$$p_n = 1, \qquad\qquad w = (p_f b_f + p_n b_n)\omega,$$

the last being the budget equation of the worker. With given ω, the unknowns w, r, p_f, p_n are determined by the four equations. Where a_f increases, p_f rises. The budget equation shows that this (say, a rise of 10 per cent) creates an increase in w at a rate less than 10 per cent, because p_n is fixed at 1, which, in turn, produces a reduction of r, by virtue of the first equation. The wage–profit frontier, that is the curve r as the function of the real wage rate ω, thus shifts downwards. Hence, a decrease in r, though it gives rise to an increase in the 'money wages' w (that is, the wages in terms of the non-food product, gold), reduces the corn wages (w/p_f) because of the diminishing returns of land. Samuelson's conclusion that falling profits and falling wages are incompatible is perfectly right as a proposition concerning the relationship between r and the 'money wages' w, but his allegation against Marx is wrong if it is applied to Ricardo, because the last asserts that both r and the corn wages w/p_f, rather than the money wages, will fall together.

6 After this, Samuelson examines the effects of technological change under perfect competition.[13] These effects may also be examined by the use of Hicksian frontiers (17') and (18'). As will be seen in the next section, the total amounts of labour, a_f and a_n, necessary to produce one unit of food and non-food, respectively, are complexes consisting of labour- and capital-input coefficients of the two sectors. Therefore, generally speaking, a technological improvement occurring in either sector, say for example, the farm-tools making industry, will affect not only a_n but also a_f. Similarly, an increase or a decrease in the productivity of the agricultural sector will give

[13] *Ibid.*, pp. 350–2.

rise to a change in *both* a_n and a_f. Hicks, however, has supposed in deriving frontiers that diminishing productivity in agriculture has no effect upon a_n. That is to say, Hicks, unlike Sraffa, but like Ricardo, is concerned with an economy where agriculture and industry are technologically decomposable from each other. This is not an 'indecomposable' economy where agriculture and industry are coupled interdependently with each other as is usually observed in the actual world.

Intersectoral dependency is obscured in the vertically integrated model. In this respect, the Sraffa–Leontief type approach is preferable. Tosato, in the previously examined article, tries to connect Hicks and Sraffa, on the assumption that $\delta = 1$. Solving the price equation (8) with respect to p, Tosato has

$$p = wL(1 + r)[I - K(1 + r)]^{-1}. \tag{19}$$

Since

$$[I - K(1 + r)]^{-1} = I + K(1 + r) + [K(1 + r)]^2 + \cdots,$$

(19) can be written in the form

$$p = wL^{(0)}(1 + r) + wL^{(1)}(1 + r)^2 + wL^{(2)}(1 + r)^3 + \cdots, \tag{20}$$

where $L^{(0)} = L$, $L^{(1)} = LK$, $L^{(2)} = LK^2, \ldots$ Obviously, $L^{(0)}$ is the quantity of direct labour required for the production of one unit of goods, $L^{(1)}$ the quantity of direct labour contained in the means of production K, which we call the quantity of indirect labour of order 1; $L^{(2)}$ the quantity of indirect labour of order 1 contained in K, i.e. the indirect labour of order 2. The total amount of indirect labour contained in K is given by

$$L^{(1)} + L^{(2)} + \cdots,$$

which is added to direct labour $L^{(0)}$ to make the value of commodities Λ.[14] Let us write: $a_i^{(0)} = L_i/\Lambda_i$, $a_i^{(1)} = L_i^{(1)}/\Lambda_i$, $a_i^{(2)} = L_i^{(2)}/\Lambda_i$, and so on. Then it follows from (20) that

$$p_i = w\Lambda_i[a_i^{(0)}(1 + r) + a_i^{(1)}(1 + r)^2 + a_i^{(2)}(1 + r)^3 + \cdots].$$

[14] It is evident that

$$L^{(0)} + L^{(1)} + L^{(2)} + \cdots = L[I + K + K^2 + \cdots]$$
$$= L[I - K]^{-1} = \Lambda,$$

because $\delta = 1$. See Tosato, 'A Reconstruction of Sraffa's Interpretation'.

By determining t_i such that $(1 + r)^{t_i}$ approximates the part in the square brackets, we finally get[15]

$$p_i = w\Lambda_i(1 + r)^{t_i}. \tag{21}$$

This is the equation which connects Sraffa to Hicks. If we interpret Hicks' price equations (17) and (18) as having been derived in this way, we should regard t_f and t_n as variables which increase as r increases, whereas Hicks gets similar equations with constant t_f and t_n.

Let us now consider a two-sector economy with

$$L = (\lambda(m), l) \quad \text{and} \quad K = \begin{bmatrix} \theta(m) & h \\ \kappa(m) & k \end{bmatrix},$$

where Greek letters are coefficients for the food sector and Roman letters those for the non-food sector. Then the indirect labour of order 1 is given as

$$LK = [\lambda(m)\theta(m) + l\kappa(m), \lambda(m)h + lk].$$

Therefore, unless $h = 0$, the quantity of indirect labour of order 1 of the non-food sector depends on the labour input coefficient of the food-producing sector. Similarly, in order for the non-food sector's indirect labour of higher orders all to be independent of the input coefficients of the food sector, we must have $h = 0$. As Λ is the sum of $L, LK, LK^2, \ldots$, the same result does hold for Λ. Hence, except in the case of $h = 0$, the decline of productivity in agriculture will influence not only the wage–profit frontier of agriculture but also that of industry. Hicks supposes that the latter remains undisturbed, so that $h = 0$ is implicitly assumed. In other words, in Hicks' economy, industry is 'decomposable' from agriculture.[16] It is now clear that the simplicity and clearcut nature of Hicks' analysis are

---

[15] Although Tosato seems to consider that t_i is a constant, it depends, strictly speaking, on the value of r at which t_i is determined. Where r is large, t_i would be large, and vice versa. Moreover, t_i is different from one commodity to another; all t_i's are equal to each other, only in the case where the premise of the Ricardo–Marx theorem is satisfied.

[16] With a general n by n matrix K, the second group of industries said to be 'decomposable' from the first if K can be partitioned, after some identical permutations of rows and columns, as

$$\begin{bmatrix} K_I & 0 \\ H & K_{II} \end{bmatrix}$$

with square sub-matrices K_I and K_{II}, whilst H is, in general, rectangular.

obtained not by his vertical aggregation but by the decomposability he tacitly assumes.

7 In establishing the existence of a downwards sloping wage–profit frontier the proportionality between prices and values is often assumed. Also concepts referring to some imaginary state of affairs, such as Sraffa's 'standard commodity' X^*, are sometimes used. Furthermore, it is occasionally assumed that there are no durable capital goods, $\delta = 1$. These concepts are all restrictive and may be dispensed with. Among the various approaches reviewed above, my 1958 proof is the only one which avoids all these assumptions. It makes only the general assumptions that the economy forms an indecomposable system, that the composition of capital may be different from one sector to another, so that prices may deviate from Λ, and that the durability may differ from one capital good to another. It also employs no metaphysical concept such as X^*.

My 1958 proof, however, is static. It does not see the frontier in the phase of transition from a less intensive use of land to a more intensive one. It assumes that the degree of land utilization is constant. In order to make it a useful tool for examining Ricardo's economics, it must be 'semi-dynamized'; that is to say, we must show how the frontier will move when the economy progresses and land is used more intensively.

Consider now two states of affairs with different intensities of cultivation, m^0 and m^1. Suppose $m^1 > m^0$, so that the agricultural production coefficients are greater at m^1 than m^0. With the same real wages ω, the equilibrium rate of profits and the equilibrium prices in terms of the basic consumption bundle b are r^0 and q^0 at m^0, while r^1 and q^1 at m^1. Of course, $q_0^i = \pi^i/p^i b$ and $q_j^i = p_j^i/p^i b$, $i = 0, 1; j = 1, \ldots, n$. We shall show that $r^0 > r^1$. This means with ω given the static wage–profit frontier $r(\omega)$ shifts downwards wherever land is used more intensively.

To show that, we shall use the method we applied to derive the static frontier in Section 2 above. Suppose the contrary, that is, $r^0 \leqq r^1$. First we examine the case, $q^0 = q^1$. As

$$\lambda(m^0) < \lambda(m^1), \qquad \theta(m^0) < \theta(m^1), \qquad \kappa(m^0) < \kappa(m^1), \quad (22)$$

we have

$$q^0 = (1 + r^0)\omega L(m^0) + (\delta + r^0)q^0 K(m^0)$$

$$< (1 + r^1)\omega L(m^1) + (\delta + r^1)q^0 K(m^1) = q^0,$$

where $L(m^0)$ and $L(m^1)$ are vector L with $\lambda(m^0)$ and $\lambda(m^1)$ as their first components, respectively. Similarly, matrices $K(m^0)$ and $K(m^1)$ are *mutatis mutandis* defined. The inequality $r^0 \leqq r^1$ obviously produces a contradiction. Hence $r^0 > r^1$.

Next we turn to the case of $q^0 \neq q^1$. As q is normalized such that $qb = 1$, at least one price must decrease. Let q_i show the greatest decrease. Then we of course have

$$q_i^0 > q_i^1, \tag{23}$$

$$\frac{q_j^0}{q_i^0} \leqq \frac{q_j^1}{q_i^1} \quad \text{for all } j. \tag{24}$$

Also we have supposed that

$$r^0 \leqq r^1. \tag{25}$$

Then, from equilibrium conditions

$$q^0 = (1 + r^0)\omega L(m^0) + (\delta + r^0)q^0 K(m^0)$$

and

$$q^1 = (1 + r^1)\omega L(m^1) + (\delta + r^1)q^1 K(m^1),$$

we get, if $i = 0$,

$$1 = (1 + r^0)\frac{\omega}{q_0^0}\lambda(m^0) + (\delta + r^0)\left[\theta(m^0) + \sum_1^n \frac{q_j^0}{q_0^0}\kappa_j(m^0)\right]$$

$$< (1 + r^1)\frac{\omega}{q_0^1}\lambda(m^1) + (\delta + r^1)\left[\theta(m^1) + \sum_1^n \frac{q_j^1}{q_0^1}\kappa_j(m^1)\right] = 1$$

or, if $i \geqq 1$,

$$1 = (1 + r^0)\frac{\omega}{q_i^0}l_i + (\delta + r^0)\left[\frac{q_1^0}{q_i^0}h_i + \sum_1^n \frac{q_j^0}{q_i^0}\kappa_{ji}\right]$$

$$< (1 + r^1)\frac{\omega}{q_i^1}l_i + (\delta + r^1)\left[\frac{q_1^1}{q_i^1}h_i + \sum_1^n \frac{q_j^1}{q_i^1}k_{ji}\right] = 1$$

because (22), (23), (24) and (25) hold. Either of these two inequalities implies a contradictory statement, $1 < 1$. Hence, in this case too, we must have $r^0 > r^1$, and the downwards shift of the frontier is confirmed.

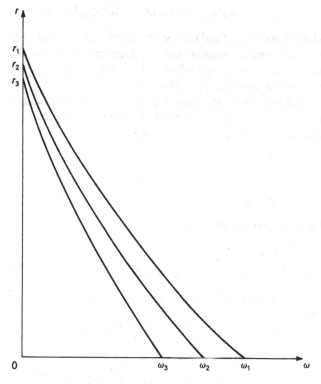

Figure 4

There is an additional point to be noted. Where $\omega = 0$, the price equation is reduced to

$$q(I - A) = rqK,$$

where $A = \delta K$. It is seen that the effect upon r of a decline in the agricultural productivity through L disappears because $\omega = 0$. Only an increase in $\theta(m)$ and $\kappa(m)$ affects A and K, and r is reduced. (It will be unchanged if $\theta(m) = h = 0$, so that K is of the form I have mentioned at the beginning of this chapter.) The decrement of r is smaller than the one that will be obtained when ω is positive. The higher the level of the real wage rate ω, the larger the effects of $\lambda(m)$ upon the augmented current and capital input matrices, $(\omega bL + A)$ and $(\omega bL + K)$, will be. Therefore, as the real wage rate becomes higher, the shift of the wage–profit frontier increases as Figure 4 illustrates.

We have so far measured the real wages ω in terms of the basic consumption bundle b. But we may alternatively take b as a vector with the component for gold being 1 and other components being all zero. Take gold as numeraire, i.e. $p_G = 1$. Then $pb = 1$, so that $w = \omega$; thus the 'money wages' are a particular kind of real wages that are measured in terms of gold. In any case, the proof establishing the static wage–profit frontier (ω, r) in Section 2 above and the proof of the downwards shift of the frontier in this section *mutatis mutandis* hold for the money–wage frontier (w, r).[17] That is to say, money wages decrease wherever the rate of profit increases; and, provided that K is *indecomposable*, the frontier shifts downwards wherever land is used more intensively.

In the case of industry being *decomposable* from agriculture in K, the price equations of industries are independent of the price of corn. It can easily be observed that the frontier (w, r) is determined by the price equations of industries alone and any change in the level of cultivation m has no effect upon it. Even in this case, real wages in terms of the basic consumption bundle b, ω, trace out a family

---

[17] Suppose $w^0 < w^1$. If $p^0 = p^1$, then $r^0 > r^1$. Otherwise we would have

$$p^0 = (1 + r^0)w^0 L + (\delta + r^0)p^0 K < (1 + r^1)w^1 L + (\delta + r^1)p^0 K = p^0,$$

a contradiction. (Note that p has the price of corn as its first component; L and K too include input coefficients of agriculture.) Next, where $p^0 \neq p^1$, suppose first $p_i^0 < p_i^1$ for all i's other than $i = G$. Then we have for G

$$1 = (1 + r^0)w^0 l_G + (\delta + r^0) \sum p_j^0 k_{jG} < (1 + r^1)w^1 l_G + (\delta + r^1) \sum p_j^1 k_{jG} = 1$$

if $r^0 \leqq r^1$. This is a contradiction, so that $r^0 > r^1$. Secondly, if there is a price which diminishes, then for good i whose price is decreased most, we must have

$$p_i^0 > p_i^1,$$

$$\frac{p_j^0}{p_i^0} \leqq \frac{p_j^1}{p_i^1} \qquad \text{for all } j.$$

Then, if $r^0 \leqq r^1$, we should have

$$1 = (1 + r^0)\frac{w^0}{p_i^0} l_i + (\delta + r^0) \sum_j \frac{p_j^0}{p_i^0} k_{ji}$$

$$< (1 + r^1)\frac{w^1}{p_i^1} l_i + (\delta + r^1) \sum_j \frac{p_j^1}{p_i^1} k_{ji} = 1,$$

which is a contradiction again; hence $r^0 > r^1$.

The downwards shift of the money wage–profit frontier may be proved in a similar way.

of real wage–profit frontiers which shift downwards, because the price equations of industries are linked with that of agriculture through the workers' demand for corn. This is the case where, while K is decomposable, the *augmented* current and capital input matrices are indecomposable. Ricardo accepted this assumption and was, therefore, provided with a single, static, money wage–profit frontier and a semi-dynamic map of multiple real wage–profit frontiers.

4 The equal rate of profit and exploitation

1 It has been seen that Ricardo's economics consists of various parts – the price–cost equations, the demand–supply equations for factors (capital services and labour), the marginal productivity equations for land, etc. – which together form a system of general equilibrium. Moreover, these parts cannot stand independently but are interrelated. For example, it is only in exceptional cases that we can derive the wage–profit frontier from the price–cost equations alone; our derivation of the frontier in the previous chapters, to say nothing of Sraffa's own derivation, is misleading because it is confined to the realm of exceptional cases assuming no joint output etc. In this chapter I shall show that parts of the Ricardian model are interlinked by certain rules, such as that of dual cross adjustment, and in doing so I shall elaborate my argument of Section 6 of the last chapter. I also shall take this opportunity to correct the misunderstanding which Roemer and Petri have with regard to my Generalized Fundamental Marxian Theorem,[1] its validity being warranted where the dual cross adjustment mechanism of the Ricardo–Marx–Walras type works. I shall furthermore be concerned with the assertion of Schumpeter, Samuelson and many other economists, that the labour theory of value should be extended to a multi-factor (say, land and labour) theory of value, which is also due to their misunderstanding of Ricardo and Marx. This has partly been discussed in the previous chapter and will be reexamined below to complete the argument.

2 A passage from Ricardo's *Principles* has already been quoted to the effect that more (or less) funds will be employed in an industry and, therefore, its output will be increased (or decreased) if the profit

---

[1] See M. Morishima, 'Marx in the Light of Modern Economic Theory', *Econometrica*, July 1974, pp. 611–32, and J. E. Roemer, 'A General Equilibrium Approach to Marxian Economics', *Econometrica*, March 1980, pp. 505–30.

rate is higher (or lower) in the industry than the average rate. This means that output of industry i, x_i, increases or decreases according to whether its supernormal profit, $p_i - (1 + r)wl_i - (\delta + r)pk_i$, is positive or negative, where r stands for the normal rate of profit and k_i is industry i's capital coefficient vector. The set of industries includes agriculture which is industry 0. Its output x_0 may be written as ξ, as before. Its input coefficients l_0 and k_0 are marginal coefficients, $\lambda(m)$ and $\kappa(m)$ which depend on the degree of cultivation of land in agriculture. We have then the following adjustment equations:

$$\frac{dx_i}{dt} = a[p_i - (1 + r)wl_i - (\delta + r)pk_i], \qquad i = 0, 1, \ldots, n,$$

where a is the adjustment coefficient which is positive. The speed of adjustment may be different from one industry to another – but we assume that it is the same for all industries and is signified by a to avoid unnecessary complication. In view of the budget equation of the worker,

$$w = p\omega b,$$

where b stands for the basic bundle of consumption goods, and ω is the real wage rate or the number of bundles which a worker buys, the above equation can be put in the form,

$$\frac{dx_i}{dt} = a[p_i - (1 + r)p\omega bl_i - (\delta + r)pk_i], \quad i = 0, 1, \ldots, n. \quad (1)$$

As for the adjustment of prices, Ricardo had the following view:

> It is the cost of production which must ultimately regulate the price of commodities, and not, as has been often said, the proportion between the supply and demand: the proportion between supply and demand may, indeed, for a time, affect the market value of a commodity, ... but this effect will be only of temporary duration. (p. 382)

He also says,

> The opinion that the price of commodities depends solely on the proportion of supply to demand ... has become almost an axiom in political economy, and has been the source of much error in that science. (p. 382)

He nevertheless accepted, on the other hand, that the market prices of a commodity obeys the law of 'the proportion of the supply to the demand'.[2] That is to say, he clearly recognized the view that the market price of a commodity is regulated by its excess demand or supply.[3] We can thus find apparently contradictory statements in Ricardo's *Principles*, but they do not produce any difficulty for us because he reconciled them in the following synthetic proposition: 'However much the market prices of [a commodity] may deviate from its natural [or equilibrium] price, it has ... a tendency to conform to it' (p. 94).

Ricardo's view of price adjustment may be formulated in the following way. It is evident that excess demand for commodity j is given by

$$\omega b_j Lx + c_j + \delta k^j x + h_j - s_j,$$

where L is a row vector of labour input coefficients $(l_0, l_1, \ldots, l_n)$, k^j is the jth row vector of the capital matrix K, which is $k^j = (k_{j0}, k_{j1}, \ldots, k_{jn})$,[4] and finally x is the output column vector $(x_0, x_1, \ldots, x_n)'$. Obviously, $\omega b_j Lx$ represents the workers' demand for good j, while c_j, $\delta k^j x$ and h_j are, respectively, capitalists' consumption, replacement and net investment for j and s_j is the supply of j. For agriculture s_0 equals $\bar{\xi}$, because of the production lag, but for all other industries s_j equals x_j as production is assumed instantaneous. We then have the following adjustment equations:

$$\frac{dp_j}{dt} = b[\omega b_j Lx + \delta k^j x + c_j + h_j - s_j]$$

$$\text{with } s_j = \begin{cases} \bar{\xi} & \text{for } j = 0 \\ x_j & \text{for } j > 0, \end{cases} \quad (2)$$

where the adjustment coefficient b is assumed to be the same for all j, for simplicity's sake.

[2] Ricardo, *Principles*, Chapters IV and V, particularly pp. 88–95.
[3] Following Hicks and Samuelson, it has become prevalent among economists to assume that prices are adjusted according to excess demand for respective commodities. However, it is evident that even though the amount of excess demand may be the same, say 100 units, the effect upon the price would be different if in one case demand was 200 and supply 100, while in another demand was 800 and supply 700. Ricardo's idea that price of commodities depends on the proportion of supply to demand would be more appropriate than Hicks' and Samuelson's excess demand hypothesis. In spite of this, in the following, we do not distinguish between the two and regard them as if they were equivalent.
[4] Note that k_i is the ith column vector of K.

The adjustment of quantities x and prices p generated by differential equations (1) and (2) is called *dual* adjustment because it involves both x and p. It is also called *cross* adjustment because an excess price over cost, for commodity i, gives rise to a change in its quantity and an excess quantity demanded over supply, for commodity j, produces a change in its price. Where this process of adjustment is completed, dx/dt and dp/dt vanish, so that we obtain equilibrium equations,

$$p = p[(1 + r)\omega bL + (\delta + r)K], \qquad (3)$$

$$s = [\omega bL + \delta K]x + c + h, \qquad (4)$$

from (1) and (2), respectively. In (4) s is the supply vector and h the net investment vector. Like later economists such as Walras who assumed that a general equilibrium is established by an imaginary *tâtonnement* process and Hicks who assumes 'an easy passage to temporary equilibrium',[5] Ricardo too tacitly assumed a perfectly organized economy where equilibrium is established quickly and smoothly within a given period, say, one year. During the year, agricultural output, $s_0 = \xi$, in the previous year is, of course, kept unchanged, while current outputs x, as well as prices p, fluctuate and approach their equilibrium values at the end of the year. In the following we assume that adjustment is completed by the end of January and production, exchange, consumption and investment are all accomplished during the rest of the year. Fluctuating outputs during the process of adjustment, like those in Walras' *tâtonnement* process, are never produced; after the establishment of equilibrium, production is carried out according to the equilibrium effective contracts finally made. Outputs produced, other than that of agriculture, are either consumed or invested at the end of the year. Agricultural output, $x_0 = \xi$, is carried over to the next year in order to sustain the workers for one year.

3 Let us now show that the Ricardian subsystem, (3) and (4), constitutes a very von Neumann-like general equilibrium system. For this purpose we shall alter our assumption slightly and assume, first, that not only agriculture but also all other industries take one period to produce their output. Then, in (2) and (4), we have $s = \bar{x}$, not only for $j = 0$ but also for all other j's, where $\bar{x}$ is the output

[5] J. R. Hicks, *Value and Capital*, Oxford University Press, 1939, p. 123.

vector in the previous period. Then the net investment on good j, h_j, is given by $k^j x - k^j \bar{x}$, so that $h = K(x - \bar{x})$. Once one period of production lag is introduced for capital goods industries, the term for replacement investment, $\delta k^j x$, of equation (2) and, hence, the same term for equation (4) should be altered to $\delta k^j \bar{x}$. The production in the previous period which began with capital stocks $K\bar{x}$ would end up with capital $K\bar{x} - \delta K\bar{x}$, so that replacement investment of the amount of $\delta K\bar{x}$ is required in order to keep capital stocks intact. As $K\bar{x} - \delta K\bar{x} +$ replacement $(\delta K\bar{x}) +$ net investment $(h) = Kx$, we have $h = K(x - \bar{x})$, as has been said. Thus, under the assumption of one period of production lag, we have, in place of (4),

$$\bar{x} = \omega bLx + \delta K\bar{x} + K(x - \bar{x}) + c.$$

Secondly we may, like von Neumann, assume without loss of generality that $\delta = 1$ for all capital goods. This is not a restrictive assumption at all but, in fact, more general than the usual *prima facie* less restrictive assumption that δ takes on some positive value not exceeding 1. This is because von Neumann distinguishes capital goods not only in kind but also by age and regards capital goods of the same kind but at different stages of wear and tear as qualitatively different goods. He considers that the capital goods available for production at the beginning of the period are transformed into one period older capital goods by the end of the period. He regards these last, left over to the next period for further production, as by-products of the respective production processes. Thus, according to von Neumann's procedure, inputs include capital goods inherited from the preceding period, while outputs include qualitatively different capital goods to be handed down to the next generation.[6] The von Neumann system has an output matrix which is no longer a diagonal matrix but a general non-negative matrix, denoted by B, that may have two or more positive elements in at least one column because of his way of treating capital goods. Taking $\delta = 1$ and introducing B to the left-hand side, the above equation may be written as

$$B\bar{x} = [\omega bL + K]x + c. \tag{4'}$$

It can easily be seen that (3) should correspondingly be rewritten as

$$pB = (1 + r)p[\omega bL + K] \tag{3'}$$

[6] M. Morishima, *Theory of Economic Growth*, Oxford University Press, 1969, p. 89.

Once we allow for joint production, the number of commodities n may not be equal to the number of production processes m; in the extreme case, a single process may produce every commodity. Also, where we regard capital goods at different states of wear and tear as different goods, we must allow for alternative processes to produce the same kind of main output; to produce cars, for example, we may use a brand-new robot, or alternatively an old robot. Therefore, we can no longer assume that $n = m$; n may be greater or smaller than m. If it is so, we cannot generally establish the m equations (3') by adjusting n-dimensional vector p, and the n equations (4') by m-dimensional x. They have to be replaced by inequalities.

Let us continue to follow von Neumann's footsteps further. As long as (3') holds with strict inequality '>' for some process i, the corresponding x_i is increased limitlessly by the adjustment rule (1), while, if '<' holds, x_i decreases. This downwards movement of x_i will be stopped when x_i reaches 0, even though the inequality '<' still holds for process i in (3'). Thus, where

$$pB \leqq (1 + r)p[\omega bL + K] \qquad (3^*)$$

holds, the production activity x remains stationary if x_i's are zero for those processes i for which (3*) holds with strict inequality '<'. This means that throughout the production processes in operation (i.e. the processes with $x_i > 0$) there prevails a uniform rate of profit r, while those processes whose rates of profits are not as high as r are not employed so that their x_i's are zero. We call this rule of production operation the rule of profitability which prevails at the point where x_i is stationary.[7]

Secondly, as long as (4') holds with inequality '<' for some j, the corresponding p_j is increased without limit by the rule (2); while where it holds with '>' for commodity j its price moves downwards until it is impossible for p_j to decrease further because it has reached the boundary, $p_j = 0$. We thus find that p is stationary where

$$B\bar{x} \geqq [\omega bL + K]x + c, \qquad (4^*)$$

provided p_j's are zero for those j for which (4*) holds with strict inequality '>'. This implies that the following rule of pricing holds true at the point of stationary prices; those commodities which are

---

[7] *Ibid.*, p. 101.

supplied abundantly (i.e. much more than the level of demand) are free, so that their prices are set at 0. We call this rule the rule of free goods.[8]

In this way, the subsectors (3) and (4) of the Ricardian general equilibrium system can naturally be modified into the form (3*) and (4*). The cross adjustment rule works behind these dual inequalities; that is, the above inequality (3*) concerning p, which is rewritten as

$$pB \leqq (1 + r)p[\omega bL + K], \tag{5a}$$

is supplemented by the rule of profitability concerning x, while the other inequality (4*) concerning x is supplemented by the rule of free goods concerning p. Thus we may perhaps be allowed to say that von Neumann's work is an elaboration of a subsector of Ricardo's economics. In fact, where there is a proportional growth of x, we have $x = (1 + g)\bar{x}$, so that, neglecting capitalists' consumption c,[9] we may put (4*) in the form,

$$Bx \geqq (1 + g)[\omega bL + K]x. \tag{5b}$$

This constitutes the von Neumann growth equilibrium, together with the condition (5a), the rule of profitability implying

$$pBx = (1 + r)p[\omega bL + K]x, \tag{5c}$$

the rule of free goods implying

$$pBx = (1 + g)p[\omega bL + K]x \tag{5d}$$

and the condition that the total value of output should be positive. This last equation is, of course, written in the form,

$$pBx > 0. \tag{5e}$$

4 Implications of von Neumann's dual cross adjustment (3*) and (4*) have been discussed. Among the results obtained, most significant is a theorem which I have referred to as the generalized fundamental Marxian (GFMT).[10] Between this and the original fundamental Marxian theorem (FMT),[11] there are two important

---

[8] *Ibid.*, p. 103.

[9] For a more general case where the capitalists' consumption c is not neglected, see my *Equilibrium, Stability and Growth*, Oxford University Press, 1964, pp. 131–53.

[10] M. Morishima, 'Marx in the Light of Modern Economic Theory', *Econometrica*, 1974, pp. 611–32.

[11] M. Morishima, *Marx's Economics*, Cambridge University Press, 1973, pp. 53–71.

88   Ricardo's economics

differences. First, the original one is confined to the case of there being no joint production and no alternative production process, while in the generalized one, input and output matrices K and B are usually rectangular and B has, moreover, positive off-diagonal elements. Secondly, the original theorem is concerned with equations (3) and (4), whereas the generalized theorem relates to the inequality system (3*) and (4*). Due to these differences, the original concept of the rate of exploitation, defined as the ratio of the surplus labour to the necessary labour, is redefined in the GFMT as the ratio of the *maximum* surplus labour to the corresponding *minimum* necessary labour, as is given by formula (9) below. These maximum surplus and minimum necessary labour are obtained by solving the linear programming problem to minimize Lx subject to (7′) below. The theorems state:

Fundamental Marxian theorem   The rate of profits is positive if and
   only if the rate of exploitation is positive.
Generalized fundamental Marxian theorem   The warranted rate of
   profits and the capacity rate of growth are both positive if and
   only if the rate of exploitation is positive.

In the GFMT the warranted rate of profits is defined as the minimum value of r satisfying (3*) with non-negative, non-zero p, which is the profit rate that is guaranteed by the given technology (K, L, B), provided that the real wage rate is fixed at a given level ω. It is possible that the actual rate of profits may be higher than the warranted rate. Therefore, it is possible that, although the actual rate of profits is positive, the rate of exploitation and the warranted rate of profits may be non-positive. An example of this possibility has been presented by Petri,[12] erroneously as a counter-example to my GFMT. In order to avoid this perversity, Roemer restricts the technology to the case where production is 'independent',[13] and finds that the independence of production is a necessary and sufficient condition on technology for the validity of the equivalence of positive

[12] F. Petri, 'Positive Profits Without Exploitation: A Note on the Generalized Fundamental Marxian Theorem', *Econometrica*, 1980, pp. 531–3.
[13] Let a bundle of net outputs a be produced with some labour. The technology is said to be 'independent' if any bundle b such that $b < a$ and $b \neq a$, can be produced with strictly less labour. See J. Roemer, *Analytical Foundations of Marxian Economic Theory*, Cambridge University Press, 1981, p. 47.

profits and positive exploitation.[14] This result is referred to as Roemer's fundamental Marxian theorem (RFMT). As the von Neumann technology (K, L, B) is not necessarily 'independent' in Roemer's sense, the RFMT does not hold true for general technologies, but is only valid for their 'independent' subset. Consequently, where a von Neumann technology is given, no one – not even Marx – can say whether positive exploitation always exists behind positive profits. Thus the RFMT is a theorem which contradicts the spirit of Marxism, so that it cannot provide a foundation for Marxian economic theory.

Although the original version of the relevant part of Roemer's book and Petri's article were published in the same issue of *Econometrica*, I had no chance to read the former before its publication, while I was given an opportunity to read, and reply to, the latter.[15] I would have made the same comment on the RFMT if I had been provided with the opportunity. Petri's and Roemer's 'counterexample' to my GFMT are, in fact, avoided if we assume the capitalists' propensity to consume to be less than one; their perverse cases are obtained only in such an un-Marxian situation of all capitalists consuming their whole profits.

This result may be referred to as the strong general fundamental Marxian theorem (SGFMT) and is spelt out in the following way:

SGFMT In any state of balanced growth equilibrium, where capitalists' savings are positive, positive profits are obtained where, and only where, workers are positively exploited.

This theorem, like my original GFMT but unlike Roemer's RFMT, is valid for all von Neumann technologies, 'independent' or 'non-independent'. However, as is evident in my reply to Petri, I have so far confined myself to the case of balanced growth equilibrium. Assuming the 'generalized von Neumann system' which is a system like (5a)–(5e) but further includes capitalists' consumption, and using the equilibrium equation $g = sr$, where s is the capitalists' propensity to save, I have shown that the theorem is true if $0 < s < 1$. In the following I remove the condition of balanced growth and show that it still holds unless the aggregate rate of growth exceeds the capacity rate defined below.

[14] *Ibid.*, p. 50.
[15] M. Morishima, 'Positive Profit Without Exploitation: A Note on the Generalized Fundamental Marxian Theorem', *Econometrica*, 1980, p. 535.

5 Proof: In order to prove the GFMT, two lemmas have been used, the first of which does not assume a state of balanced growth.

Lemma 1 The fact that the rate of exploitation is positive implies that the warranted rate of profit is positive.

There is no need to reprove Lemma 1. The other lemma, however, has to be reproved by removing the concept of balanced growth from the original proof. We prove for any $\bar{x}$ satisfying $L\bar{x} > 0$:

Lemma 2 The fact that the capacity rate of growth is positive implies that the rate of exploitation is positive.

To show this we first define the capacity rate of growth g^c as the maximum of g such that

$$[\omega bL + K]x \geqq (1 + g)[\omega bL + K]\bar{x} \qquad (6)$$

$$B\bar{x} \geqq [\omega bL + K]x + c, \qquad x \geqq 0. \qquad (7)$$

Next, to define the rate of exploitation we minimize Lx subject to

$$Bx \geqq Kx + \omega b, \qquad x \geqq 0, \qquad\qquad (7')$$

where ωb is the amount of daily necessaries per worker. Let x^0 be a solution to this minimum problem so that $\min Lx = Lx^0$. We assume, throughout the following, that

$$Lx^0 > 0. \qquad (8)$$

If the minimum amount of labour is less than the labour offered by one worker (that is taken as 1), we may say that there is positive exploitation; that is to say, the rate of exploitation e is defined, as has already been stated, as the ratio of the maximum surplus labour, $1 - Lx^0$, to the minimum necessary labour, Lx^0. Thus we have

$$e = \frac{1 - Lx^0}{Lx^0}, \qquad (9)$$

where the right-hand side of this formula shows that e is equal to the ratio of surplus labour to necessary labour. It is well known that there is a dual maximization problem with this minimization problem. This fundamental duality theorem of linear programming is explicitly formulated in this case as maximizing $\Lambda\omega b$ subject to

$$\Lambda B \leqq \Lambda K + L, \qquad \Lambda \geqq 0. \qquad (10)$$

Let Λ^0 be a solution to this problem; then max $\Lambda\omega b = \Lambda^0\omega b$, and by the duality theorem we have

$$\Lambda^0\omega b = Lx^0. \tag{11}$$

We can now prove Lemma 2. Let $g = g^c$, $x = x^c$ and $c = c^c$ which satisfy conditions (6) and (7). Premultiply (7) by Λ^0 and postmultiply (10) by $\bar{x}$; we then have

$$\Lambda^0 B\bar{x} \geqq \Lambda^0[\omega bL + K]x^c + \Lambda^0 c^c, \tag{12}$$

and

$$\Lambda^0 B\bar{x} \leqq \Lambda^0 K\bar{x} + L\bar{x}. \tag{13}$$

In view of (6) premultiplied by Λ^0, (12) can be written as

$$\Lambda^0 B\bar{x} \geqq \Lambda^0[\omega bL + K]\bar{x} + g^c\Lambda^0[\omega bL + K]\bar{x} + \Lambda^0 c^c.$$

This together with (13), establishes

$$L\bar{x}[1 - \Lambda^0\omega b] \geqq g^c\Lambda^0[\omega bL + K]\bar{x} + \Lambda^0 c^c. \tag{14}$$

By virtue of (8) and (11), $\Lambda^0\omega b > 0$. As $L\bar{x}$ is assumed to be positive, we obtain $\Lambda^0[\omega bL + K]\bar{x} > 0$. On the other hand, $\Lambda^0 c^c \geqq 0$. Hence, where $g^c > 0$, (14) implies $1 > \Lambda^0\omega b$ so that $e > 0$ by (9) and (11). Therefore, Lemma 2 has been proved.

Next we establish, again avoiding the concept of balanced growth, the following equilibrium condition:

$$g = sr, \tag{15}$$

where s represents the capitalists' propensity to save and g the rate of growth of aggregate capital. To obtain (15) we first apply the rule of free goods to (4*); then,

$$pB\bar{x} = p[\omega bL + K]x + pc.$$

Therefore,

$$pB\bar{x} - pK\bar{x} = p\omega bL\bar{x} + pc + p[\omega bL + K]\Delta x, \tag{16}$$

where $\Delta x = x - \bar{x}$. The left-hand side of this equation stands for the net output, while on the right-hand side the first term represents the part of the net output consumed by workers, the second term the part consumed by capitalists and the last term the part invested in wage funds and stocks of capital goods. Thus (16) effectively states that savings equal investment. If we assume, therefore, that workers do not save, capitalists' savings must equal investment. As capitalists' savings equal their propensity to save, s, times total profits which is, in turn, the rate of profit times total capital, equation (16) implies

$$srp[\omega bL + K]\bar{x} = p[\omega bL + K]\Delta x.$$

Dividing both sides by $p[\omega bL + K]\bar{x}$, we finally obtain (15), as g is the rate of growth of total capital.

We can now easily establish the SGFMT. (i) First, by Lemma 1, the positive rate of exploitation ($e > 0$) implies that the warranted rate of profit is positive ($r^w > 0$). As the rate of profits of the level r^w is guaranteed, the actual rate of profits r is at least as high as r^w. Hence $r > 0$. (ii) Secondly, $r > 0$ implies $g > 0$ because $s > 0$ in (15). By assumption the actual equilibrium rate of growth g cannot exceed the capacity growth rate g^c. Therefore, $g^c > 0$, which implies $e > 0$ because of Lemma 2. Evidently (i) and (ii) establish the SGFMT.

Throughout the argument above we have not used Roemer's strange assumption that technology is 'independent'. Instead, in an essential way, we make use of the assumption that capitalists always save. Of these two assumptions it is clear that Roemer's is not essential for Marx's economic theory at all, while ours is emphasized everywhere in his work; we may conclude from this that the SGFMT is the theorem which is of crucial importance to Marx. It is, of course, true that, as Roemer tacitly implies, the technology Marx assumes may be more general than the one which I have assumed in my *Marx's Economics*. It is very easy to see, however, that my polygonal (or polyhedral) frontier approaches the smoothly curved frontier at the limit where the number of vertices of the polygonal (or polyhedral) frontier is infinitely large. Thus Roemer's extension of my von Neumann-like Marxian economics into his set-theoretic one is rather trivial and self-evident.

6 It has so far been taken for granted that no land is used for production. So it may be queried whether fundamental Marxian theorems are not applicable in an economy with agriculture as a significant sector of production. It is indeed a reasonable query, because both factors of production, land and labour, are able to produce and thus it would be natural to conjecture that either land or labour must be exploited in order to get positive profits. It then follows that the exploitation of labour is not a necessary condition for profits; thus it may be conjectured that the fundamental Marxian

theorem is negated as soon as land appears as a second factor of production.

In the following we shall show that the introduction of land does not affect the Marxian theorem in its strong form at all. I also want to show simultaneously that it is valid not only for the Marx or Marx–von Neumann economies but even for the ordinary neoclassical, or marginalist models. For this purpose, we shall examine a standard general equilibrium model with two factors, land and labour, to show that, in spite of the presence of land, the economy produces surplus output if and only if labour is positively exploited. In this case, however, profits are no longer equal to the total value of surplus output but only to a part of it. The remaining part of the surplus output is distributed to landowners as rent. Where there is an exploitation of labour but profits are zero, the entire surplus output is received by the landowners.

We assume an Arrow–Debreu economy of the simplest form. Let $\bar{x}_h$ be the vector of initial endowments of household h and x_h^* the vector of the stock of commodities which h wants to hold for consumption after transactions in the market. x_h^* is determined such that it maximizes utility, $U_h(x_h)$, subject to

$$p^* x_h \leqq p^* \bar{x}_h + \sum_f d_{hf}(p^* y_f^*), \qquad (17)$$

where p^* is the equilibrium price set and d_{hf} is household h's share of profits of the firm f. It is noted that, on the right-hand side of the budget inequality above, the first term represents the market value of h's initial endowments and the second term the total income from the holding of shares; $p^* y_f^*$ is, as will be seen at once, the profits of the firm f. On the other hand, the input–output vector of the firm f is denoted by y_f, where positive elements represent outputs and negative elements inputs. y_f must of course belong to the production possibility set Y_f; otherwise production of y_f would be infeasible. Thus $y_f \in Y_f$.

The equilibrium input–output vector y_f^* maximizes profits, $p^* y_f$, subject to $y_f \in Y_f$. As we assume throughout the following that it is always possible for the firm to engage in no production, $0 \in Y_f$, the maximum profits are non-negative:

$$p^* y_f^* \geqq 0.$$

Obviously, x_h^* and y_f^* are functions of prices. The market equilibrium is established at $p^* \geqq 0$ whenever there is no excess demand in any market; that is to say, whenever

$$\sum_h (x_h^* - \bar{x}_h) \leqq \sum y_f^*. \tag{18}$$

(As outputs appear in y_f^* as positive elements, it is clear that (18) claims that in equilibrium demand should not exceed supply. In the case of inputs, corresponding elements of y_f^* are negative, so that we have, from (18), $\sum_h (\bar{x}_h - x_h^*) \geqq -\sum_f y_f^*$, which means that inputs should not exceed the amounts of factors of production supplied by households.)

Let us begin with examining the conventional, simplest case of the fundamental Marxian theorem in this Arrow–Debreu framework. We assume that there is no land and that labour is homogenous. The single kind of labour which exists is labelled as $n+1$. There is only one firm in each industry $i = 1, \dots, n$, which produce output i, x_i. Signifying a transposition of vector by prime, we write:

$$y_i' = (-x_{1i}, \dots, -x_{i-1 i}, x_i, -x_{i+1 i}, \dots, -x_{ni}, -x_{n+1 i}).$$

Let the labour value vector be denoted by $\Lambda = (\lambda_1, \lambda_2, \dots, \lambda_n, 1)$. By definition,

$$\Lambda(y_1^*, y_2^*, \dots, y_n^*) = 0. \tag{19}$$

Furthermore, we assume that labour is not a free good and normalize prices p^* such that $p_{n+1}^* = 1$. Therefore, if no firm has positive profits, i.e. $p^*(y_1^*, \dots, y_n^*) = 0$, it follows from (19) that $p^* = \Lambda$ as p^* satisfies the normalization condition.

To discuss the case of $p^* y_i^* > 0$ for some i, it is assumed that (i) consumer goods industries form an 'indecomposable' subset within the whole production system,[16] and (ii) the output of any non-consumer goods industry is employed for production by at least one consumer goods industry. Then we can easily prove that if $p^* y_i^* > 0$ for some industry producing either consumer or non-consumer goods then $p_j > \lambda_j$ for all consumer goods j. We need no explanation for this; it is a familiar result derived from a well-known application of the standard input–output analysis.

We now define the rate of exploitation in the following manner.

---

[16] For the definition of indecomposability, see p. 75n above.

Let x_h^{**} be a bundle of commodities which maximizes $U_h(x_h)$ subject to $p^* x_h \leqq p^* \bar{x}_h$. It should be noted that the household's income from share holding is not included on the right-hand side of the budget equation, so that x_h^{**} is the bundle of commodities which the household would consume if wages were its sole income. Households as a whole offer commodities, $\sum_h \bar{x}_h$, in which labour of the amount, $\Lambda \sum_h \bar{x}_h$, is embodied. This is to be compared with the amount of labour, $\Lambda \sum_h x_h^{**}$, which is embodied in the commodities $\sum_h x_h^{**}$ that households receive in exchange for $\sum_h \bar{x}_h$. If $\Lambda \sum_h x_h^{**}$ is smaller than $\Lambda \sum_h \bar{x}_h$, households are said to be exploited, and the rate of exploitation is defined as:

$$e = \frac{\Lambda \sum_h \bar{x}_h - \Lambda \sum_h x_h^{**}}{\Lambda \sum_h x_h^{**}}.$$

Let us now specify $\bar{x}_h$ and x_h^{**} such that elements of them are all zero for non-consumer goods, while elements of $\sum_h (\bar{x}_h - x_h^{**})$ for consumer goods take on non-positive values, with at least some of them being negative; that is to say, we assume that households do not supply any consumer goods but demand some of them. We can now prove the Marxian theorem.

First we have seen that the premise $p^* y_f^* > 0$ for some f and $\geqq 0$ for all f implies that $p_i > \lambda_i$ for all consumption goods. This, together with the specifications we have just made concerning $\sum_h (\bar{x}_h - x_h^{**})$ – its ith element being 0 if i is a non-labour, non-consumer good, while it is non-positive for all consumer goods but negative for some of them – yields the inequality,

$$p^* \left(\sum_h \bar{x}_h - \sum_h x_h^{**} \right) < \Lambda \left(\sum_h \bar{x}_h - \sum_h x_h^{**} \right).$$

In view of the fact that the budget constraint $p^* x_h^{**} \leqq p^* \bar{x}_h$ is fulfilled, with equality for all h under the normal condition of there being no satiation point in the individual preference field, the left-hand side of the above inequality is 0 and, therefore, the right-hand side is positive. This means $e > 0$.

Secondly, the converse is also true. On the one hand,

$$\Lambda\left(\sum_h \bar{x}_h - \sum_h x_h^{**}\right) > 0 \qquad \text{where } e > 0.$$

On the other hand,

$$p^*\left(\sum_h \bar{x}_h - \sum_h x_h^{**}\right) = 0$$

as we have just seen. Hence $p^* \neq \Lambda$, which means $p^* y_f^* > 0$ for some f and ≥ 0 for all f, as we have already shown. Thus $e > 0$ implies $p^* \sum_f y_f^* > 0$. Q.E.D.

7 We have now finally reached the problem of extending the Marxian theorem to the case where land is also a factor of production. Labelling land as commodity $n + 2$, we write

$$y_i' = (-x_{1i}, \ldots, -x_{i-1i}, x_i, -x_{i+1i}, \ldots, -x_{n+1i}, -x_{n+2i}).$$

In spite of the existence of land, we define the labour value of commodities in exactly the same way as before; that is to say, we treat land as if it has no value, and write

$$\Lambda = (\lambda_1, \ldots, \lambda_n, 1, 0),$$

where $\lambda_1, \ldots, \lambda_n$ are determined such that

$$\Lambda(y_1^*, \ldots, y_n^*) = 0. \tag{20}$$

Of course $p_{n+2} \geq 0$, whereas $\lambda_{n+2} = 0$. In the following we continue to normalize p^* such that $p_{n+1}^* = 1$. That is to say,

$$p^* = (p_1^*, \ldots, p_n^*, 1, p_{n+2}^*).$$

This assumption of the labour theory of value, the entire neglect of the productive services of land – the 'free gift of Nature' – has been frequently criticized by many authors throughout its history. For example, as has already been mentioned, following Menger, Wieser, and Böhm-Bawerk, Schumpeter advocates an extension of a single-factor-of-production theory of value such as the labour theory of value into a two-factor (or land and labour) theory of value by aggregating the two factors in terms of their respective 'marginal productive use (Produktivitätsgrenznutzen)'.[17] Samuelson even insists on the possibility of the pure land theory of value killing the labour value theory.[18]

For Ricardo and Marx the significance of the value theory did not lie in the precise reproduction of actual prices but for the former it was the ability to make intuitive conjectures concerning price movements whereas for Marx it lay in the revelation of unobservable phenomena, such as exploitation by capitalists, which are hidden behind observed transactions of commodities in terms of prices. With the same intention as Marx, we have purposefully assigned the value 0 to land in our labour theory of value.

Taking employment of land into consideration we redefine z_i as

$$z_i' = (-x_{1i}, \ldots, -x_{i-1i}, x_i, -x_{i+1i}, \ldots,$$

$$-x_{ni}, -x_{n+1i} - p y_i, -x_{n+2i}).$$

Then it follows from the definition of y_i that we have

$$p^*(z_1^*, \ldots, z_n^*) = 0.$$

Using the same argument as in the previous section, we can show that $p^* = \Lambda$ if the sums of rent and profits, $p_{n+2}^* x_{n+2i}^* + p^* y_i^*$, are zero for all i, while $p_i^* > \lambda_i$ for all consumer goods if the sums are non-negative for all i and positive for some i.

We can now prove the extended fundamental Marxian theorem which states, either profits or rent or both are positive if and only if $e > 0$. To show this we first give attention to $p^* y_i^* \geqq 0$ and $p_{n+2}^* x_{n+2i}^* + p^* y_i^* \geqq 0$ for all i. If this last is strictly positive for some i, $p_i^* > \lambda_i^*$ for all consumer goods; we thus have

$$p^* \left(\sum_h \bar{x}_h - \sum_h x_h^{**} \right) < \Lambda \left(\sum_h \bar{x}_h - \sum_h x_h^{**} \right).$$

The left-hand side of this inequality vanishes as has already been seen. This means that the right-hand side is positive; hence $e > 0$. Conversely, if $e > 0$,

$$\Lambda \left(\sum_h \bar{x}_h - \sum_h x_h^{**} \right) > 0.$$

[17] J. A. Schumpeter, *The Theory of Economic Development*, Harvard University Press, 1934, p. 25.
[18] P. A. Samuelson, 'A Modern Treatment of the Ricardian Economy: The Pricing of Goods and of Labour and Land Services', in J. E. Stiglitz (ed.), *The Collected Scientific Papers of Paul A. Samuelson*, Vol. I, MIT Press, 1966, pp. 373–407.

On the other hand,

$$p^*\left(\sum_h \bar{x}_h - \sum_h x_h^{**}\right) = 0.$$

Therefore, $p^* \neq \Lambda$. Hence $p_{n+2}^* x_{n+2i}^* + p^* y_i^* > 0$ for at least one i. Q.E.D.

This extended Marxian theorem claims that the aggregate surplus output produced by exploitation is distributed between the capitalists and landowners as profit and rent, respectively. Applying it to the state of long-run stationary equilibrium, which would be established at the end of Ricardian growth, we may conclude that the persistent exploiter is the landowner, since the capitalist would eventually fade away as profits vanished in the final state. In this way we would have a capitalist economy without capitalists, or with demoralized capitalists, in the last years of the capitalist regime. Schumpeter has analytically and vividly developed a possible scenario of capitalism in its closing stages.[19] However, in any case, it would be fair to say that Ricardo's stationary state, Schumpeter's transition to socialism, and Marx's revolution are all analytical conjectures – or economic science fictions.

8 Finally a few remarks. We can show that, in the Arrow–Debreu economy with no land and no production lag, the rate of exploitation is positive or zero, according as returns to scale diminish or are constant, so that we may say that diminishing returns are the source of profits. This familiar view does not conflict with the Marxian theorem but is nothing else other than a special case which is valid only under the assumption of instantaneous production, whereas the Marxian theorem has a wider applicability and holds true for other types of economic models too. For its proof we may assume Ricardo's, Marx's, Walras' or the Marx–von Neumann model which I discussed in an earlier part of this chapter. In this sense it is a very basic and general theorem for the capitalist economy. Applying it to the problem of economic growth one can easily find that the rate of growth is positive if and only if the rate of exploitation is positive. In relation to this implication of the theorem we may ask whether the socialist economy can grow without exploitation. Then,

---

[19] J. A. Schumpeter, *Capitalism, Socialism and Democracy*, George Allen and Unwin, 1943, pp. 131–63.

irrespective of the answer to this question, we may further ask whether and how people can be exploited in the socialist economy. We cannot repeat the discussion of these problems here, as I have already dealt with them in the book which I wrote jointly with G. Catephores.[20]

Next it is pointed out that we have so far assumed a single kind of labour being available. In the actual world, there is an enormous variety of labour of different qualities. As Ricardo quoted from Smith's *Wealth of Nations*,

> It is often difficult to ascertain the proportion between two different quantities of labour. The time spent in two different sorts of work will not always alone determine this proportion. The different degrees of hardship endured, and of ingenuity exercised, must likewise be taken into account... But it is not easy to find any accurate measure, either of hardship or ingenuity. (p. 21n)

As far as the Marxian theorem is concerned, however, these different sorts of labour may safely be aggregated, in proportion to their relative wages, into a labour index. Let there be m kinds of labour and let their quantities employed by the firm i be $q_{1i}, q_{2i}, \ldots, q_{mi}$. These are aggregated in terms of their relative wages $v_1, v_2, \ldots, v_m$ as:

$$x_{n+1\,i} = v_1 q_{1i} + \cdots + v_m q_{mi},$$

where $x_{n+1\,i}$ is the labour index for the firm i. By replacing the $x_{n+1\,i}$ in the previous proof of the Marxian theorem by this labour index and making a similar alteration to the households' supply of labour we can show that the theorem still stands firm. This is easily confirmed by refollowing the proof.

The careful reader has probably noticed that the concept of value which we employ for the proof of the Marxian theorem is different from the concept of marginal value used by Ricardo. In our value equation (20), involving land and labour, y_i^* may be written as

$$y_i^{*\prime} = (-a_{1i}^*, \ldots, -a_{i-1\,i}^*, 1, -a_{i+1\,i}^*, \ldots, -a_{ni}^*, -a_{n+1\,i}^*, -a_{n+2\,i}^*)x_i^*$$
$$= (-a_i^*)x_i^*,$$

where $a_{ji}^* = x_{ji}^*/x_i^*$, $j = 1, \ldots, n+2$, which are the average production coefficients of industry i. Then the value equation (20)

[20] M. Morishima and G. Catephores, *Value, Exploitation and Growth*, McGraw-Hill, 1978, pp. 59–88.

is seen to be equivalent to its conventional form:

$$\Lambda_M(a_1^*, a_2^* \ldots a_n^*) = 0$$

by eliminating the minus sign and x_i^*'s. We may refer to the Λ_M thus determined as the Marxian value.

On the other hand, as we have seen in Chapters 1 and 2, Ricardo's value theory is developed as the theory of 'marginal labour value', where the production coefficients employed to determine values are not average but marginal production coefficients. In his economy, only agriculture uses land so that it is the industry where marginal and average coefficients differ from each other, while they are the same for all other industries where constant returns to scale prevail as they do not use land. Let industry 1 be agriculture and let b_{j1}^* be agriculture's marginal production coefficient of input j and define

$$(-b_1^*)' = (-b_{11}^*, \ldots, -b_{i-11}^*, 1, -b_{i+11}^*, \ldots, -b_{n+11}^*, -b_{n+21}^*)'.$$

Then we obtain Ricardian values by solving equation,

$$\Lambda_R(b_1^*, a_2^*, \ldots, a_n^*) = 0.$$

Obviously, $\Lambda_M \neq \Lambda_R$.

This difference in the definition of value between Marx and Ricardo reflects the difference in their intentions when using the value theory. Marx's value equation is perfectly fitted to the fundamental Marxian theorem, while the Ricardian value equation is constructed so as to simplify the marginal price-determination equation and still maintain the main features of the latter. It is from this construction of the Ricardian equation that we are able to conjecture a number of comparative-statics laws of price movement.

Part III

GROWTH

5   Ricardian growth

1 Ricardo's theory of capital accumulation has been put into mathematical formulations by various writers; notable examples include Pasinetti, Samuelson and Casarosa.[1] Their common policy has been to construct as simple a system as possible. But actually Ricardo's economy is not a simple macro-model; it is a decentralized economy consisting of an agricultural sector producing corn and industrial sectors manufacturing non-food wage goods and luxuries as well as those to be used for production such as materials, tools and machines. The ratio of fixed (or 'constant' in Marx's terminology) to circulating (or 'variable') capital may differ from sector to sector; therefore, prices and values generally deviate from each other. Land is diversified in quality; land of grade 1 is higher in productivity than that of grade 2 which is, in turn, higher than that of grade 3, and so on. Consequently, there is no simple aggregate production function for agriculture. Moreover, capitalists or entrepreneurs are concerned with the money wage rate, while workers are interested in corn wages, or real wages in terms of some given consumption bundle of wage goods. Finally, the rate of profit of each sector (agriculture and industry) may generally be unequal, but will converge at a certain uniform rate, where competition prevails.

This is the general character of the economy which Ricardo was concerned with. The task of formulating it mathematically is essentially the same as the one undertaken by Walras, that is, to establish a general equilibrium formulation. In fact, in my view,

---

[1] L. Pasinetti, *Growth and Income Distribution*, Cambridge University Press, 1974; P. A. Samuelson, 'The Canonical Classical Model of Political Economy', *Journal of Economic Literature*, 1978, pp. 1415–34; C. Casarosa, 'The "New View" of the Ricardian Theory of Distribution and Economic Growth', in G. A. Caravale (ed.), *The Legacy of Ricardo*, Basil Blackwell, 1985.

there are a number of indications which have led me to believe that Walras took Ricardo's *Principles* as a model for his general equilibrium system. I would say that Samuelson's and Casarosa's one-sector interpretation of Ricardo's growth theory is the most remote from Ricardo – 'myth-making' according to Hollander – although it is simple, looks neat and seems appealing.[2] It is indeed a formidable task to make a mathematical reconstruction of Ricardo's theory of accumulation; it amounts to establishing a theory of dynamic movement of a general equilibrium system. Ricardo's major analytical tools have to be constructed from elements discussed in various chapters of *Principles* and then these have to be used together to generate dynamic motion of the system so as to establish a clear-cut meaningful result. This is why I depart from macro-Ricardians.

We shall adopt the following approach. Movement is traced out by a sequence of short-run equilibria. With the wage fund ξ, the capital stock M and the labourforce N all being given at the commencement of a certain period, say, period 0, there exists a short-run equilibrium correspondingly. The agricultural short-run equilibrium output ζ of period 0 – after subtracting from it the landlords' consumption of corn – becomes the wage-fund of period 1, while the industrial output x – after subtracting from it the workers' and the landlords' consumption of these goods, the part consumed for production during the period, including the wear and tear of capital goods, and the part to be devoted to an expansion of the non-food wage fund – becomes the net investment in capital goods which is added to the existing capital stock M to get the stock of the next period. The labourforce increases during the period and the increment is added to the existing labourforce to make the working population in the next period. In this way all the parameters, ξ, M, N, for the next period are determined; then, a short-run equilibrium will be obtained in the next period in the same way that it was established in the present period.

2 In order to elucidate this process of transition from one period to another in more detail and more exactly, let us assume, as was done in Chapter 2, that industry is decomposable (or near-decomposable) from agriculture by supposing that the industrial use

[2] S. Hollander, 'On Professor Samuelson's Canonical Classical Model of Political Economy', *Journal of Economic Literature*, 1980, pp. 559–74.

of corn is negligible, i.e. the production coefficient h is either 0 or negligible. We also make a similar assumption concerning the use of corn as seed. That is to say, the coefficient $\theta(m_u)$ is also 0 or negligible. These assumptions are not necessary for the following analysis but have the advantage of making it simple. We may then proceed with our analysis on the basis of the short-run equilibrium equation system discussed in Chapter 2. It consists of four sets of equations:[3]

The price equations

$$\pi = (1 + r)w\lambda(m_u) + (\delta + r)p\kappa(m_u), \tag{1}$$

$$p = (1 + r)wl + (\delta + r)pk, \tag{2}$$

where $\lambda(m_u) = \lambda \dfrac{dm_u}{dF_u}(m_u)$ and $\kappa(m_u) = \kappa \dfrac{dm_u}{dF_u}(m_u)$. (1) holds at the marginal intensity m_u of the marginal land u. It has been seen that the wage–profit frontiers are obtained from (1) and (2). One of the prices (π, p), either π or p_G or the price of any other composite-commodity numeraire may be fixed at 1. Throughout this chapter we normalize prices such that $p_G = 1$.

The rent equation

$$\pi F_i(m_i, 1) = [(1 + r)w\lambda + (\delta + r)p\kappa]m_i + \pi R_i(m_i),$$
$$i = 1, \ldots, u, \tag{3}$$

$$R = \sum_1^{u-1} R_i(m_i)T_i^0 + R_u(m_u)T_u, \qquad T_u \leqq T_u^0, \tag{4}$$

where $R_i(m_i)$ is the corn rent per acre of land of grade i. R is of course the total corn rent and $\bar{R}$ is the one from the previous period.

The corn equation, or the wage-fund equation

$$\xi = b_f\omega(\lambda\eta + lx) + c(\bar{R}), \tag{5}$$
where

$$m_1 T_1^0 + m_2 T_2^0 + \cdots + m_{u-1} T_{u-1}^0 + m_u T_u = \eta. \tag{6}$$

It should be noted that equation (5) slightly departs from the corresponding one, (13), of Chapter 2. Although the worker in the present chapter, like the one in Chapter 2, does not save at all, he

---

[3] Below we use the same notation as in Chapter 2.

now buys both food and non-food goods; he, in fact, buys the consumption basket containing food and non-food in the quantities, b_f and b_n, respectively. ω is the number of baskets he buys. Also, note that, whilst in Chapter 2 we have normalized prices such that $\pi = 1$ so that the w there represents the corn wages, we now have prices in terms of gold; the wages w in (1), (2) and (3) are, accordingly, all money wages.

The full employment equations

$$\kappa\eta + kx = M, \tag{7}$$

$$\lambda\eta + lx = N. \tag{8}$$

This completes the system of short-run equilibrium conditions. As has been seen in Chapter 2, with given ξ, M, N, these equations may be solved to give a temporary equilibrium, which turns out to be a state of disequilibrium at the commencement of the next period, because of a change in ξ, M, N. A short-run equilibrium will soon be reestablished since the intensities of cultivation, prices, wages, rent, the rate of profit and output adapt themselves to the new values of the parameters, ξ, M, N. This new equilibrium too lasts only for one period. It is destroyed again because the parameters change during the period.

As for non-food goods, the workers' consumption is given by $\omega b_n N$. The landlords who save the amount $c(R)$ for the consumption of corn in the next period will spend the rest of their income on buying gold (the sole luxury good in the economy); then

$$\pi[R - c(\bar{R})] = d_G,$$

where d_G is the demand for gold. Let D be a vector with components d_G at the Gth place and 0 otherwise. Then capital stock M increases according to

$$\Delta M = x - \omega b_n N - D - \delta\kappa\eta - \delta kx - \omega b_n \Delta N, \tag{9}$$

where the last term represents the increase in the wage fund in the form of industrial products. The right-hand side of (9) represents savings, i.e. the industrial output (x) *minus* workers' consumption $(\omega b_n N)$ *minus* landlords' consumption (D) *minus* depreciation $(\delta\kappa\eta + \delta kx)$ *minus* provisions for the increase in the wage funds in the form of industrial products $(\omega b_n \Delta N)$. Where (9) holds, there is no independent investment function, and savings are automatically invested; thus (9) implies Say's law, as will be discussed, in more detail, in Parts IV and V below. The total amount of corn produced in the current period is available at the beginning of the next period. After subtracting the landlords' consumption $c(R)$ in the next period, the remainder is used as the wage fund of that period. The total output of corn is given by

$$\xi = F_1(m_1, 1)T_1^0 + \cdots + F_{u-1}(m_{u-1}, 1)T_{u-1}^0 + F_u(m_u, 1)T_u. \tag{10}$$

Finally, Ricardo considered that labour is increased or diminished, according to whether real wages are higher or lower than the 'natural price'. He wrote:

> The natural price of labour is that price which is necessary to enable the labourers, one with another, to subsist and to perpetuate their race, without either increase or diminution.
>
> The power of the labourer to support himself, and the family which may be necessary to keep up the number of labourers, does not depend on the quantity of money which he may receive for wages, but on the quantity of food, necessaries, and conveniences become essential to him from habit, which that money will purchase. (p. 93)

Let $b_f \omega^s$ be the amount of food necessary for supporting one worker and his family for one period, and $b_n \omega^s$ the amount of clothing, furniture, and other necessaries needed, per worker, for living one period at the minimum level, then the natural price of labour which I call the subsistence level of wages, may be written as

$$(p_f b_f + p_n b_n)\omega^s,$$

where $p_f(= \pi)$ and $p_n(= p)$ are the prices of food and non-food goods, respectively. Throughout the present chapter we shall use this new notation.

> The natural price of labour, therefore, depends on the price of the food, necessaries, and conveniences required for the support of the labourer and his family. With a rise in the price of food and necessaries, the natural price of labour will rise; with the fall in their price, the natural price of labour will fall. (p. 93)

Ricardo assumed that if $w > (p_f b_f + p_n b_n)\omega^s$, viz. $\omega > \omega^s$, where ω is real wages in terms of the basic consumption bundle, i.e. $w/(p_f b_f + p_n b_n)$, the population will grow, while if $w < (p_f b_f + p_n b_n)\omega^s$, or $\omega < \omega^s$, it will decrease. In his words,

> It is when the market price of labour exceeds its natural price, the condition of the labourer is flourishing and happy, that he has it in his power to command a greater proportion of the necessaries and enjoyments of life, and therefore to rear a healthy numerous family . . .
>
> When the market price of labour is below its natural price, the condition of the labourers is most wretched: then poverty deprives them of those comforts which custom renders absolute necessaries. It is only after their privations have reduced their number, or the demand for labour has increased, that the market price of labour will rise to its natural price, and that the labourer will have the moderate comforts which the natural rate of wages will afford. (p. 94)

We may now write the assumption as:

$\Delta N >, =, < 0$ according to whether

$$w - (p_f b_f + p_n b_n)\omega^s >, =, < 0. \quad (11)$$

The whole set of equations from which Ricardian dynamic movement of the economy through time can be generated has now been given. Equations (1)–(8) constitute a static part which determined a short-run equilibrium in one period. They are then accompanied by a dynamic part consisting of three equations (9), (10), (11) which link a short-run equilibrium in one period with another in the next.

Of course, the time taken to produce the labourforce is much, much longer than that taken to produce corn. Thus the ratio of the economically active population to the total population may fluctuate over time. These fluctuations are ignored by Ricardo, who tacitly assumed the ratio as being constant.

3 Before we proceed to the sequential analysis of temporary equilibria, let us be concerned with describing what constitutes the long-run equilibrium. The long-run equilibrium is, first of all, a stationary state where

$$\xi = \bar{\xi}, \qquad \Delta M = 0, \qquad \Delta N = 0 \quad (12)$$

are all satisfied. Therefore, the real wage rate ω equals the subsistence rate ω^s, so that the money wage rate is set at a level such that

$$w = (p_f b_f + p_n b_n)\omega^s. \quad (13)$$

These w, p_f and p_n are normalized such that

$$p_G = 1, \tag{14}$$

and must fulfil the price equations,

$$p_f = (1 + r)w\lambda(m_u) + (\delta + r)p_n\kappa(m_u), \tag{15}$$

$$p_n = (1 + r)wl + (\delta + r)p_n k. \tag{16}$$

Moreover, we have, in the state of long-run equilibrium, an additional condition,

$$r = 0, \tag{17}$$

which follows, as will be shown later, from (12). Let there be n non-food goods, so that (16) consists of n equations, while p_n represents n prices. Then $n + 4$ equations (13)–(17) include the same number of unknowns, p_f, p_n, w, r, m_u. Once these are determined, other m_i's, $i = 1, \ldots, u - 1$, are also determined, as we have seen in Section 2 of Chapter 2.

According to the m_u thus determined, there are two cases: (i) $m_u > 1$ and (ii) $m_u = 1$. In the first case

$$\eta = m_1 T_1^0 + \cdots + m_u T_u^0.$$

Therefore, η too is determined. We also obtain $R_i(m_i)$ from (3); multiplying it by T_i^0 and summing over $i = 1, \ldots, u$, we are provided with R. Therefore, D is determined.

We now regard M and N, which play the role of parameters in the short-run analysis, as variables. Substituting (8) into (9) and remembering (12), we have equations which determine x. Once x is given, we have, from (7) and (8), the long-run equilibrium values of M and N.

Let us now multiply each equation of (3) by T_i^0 and add them up; we then have, in view of (10) and (4),

$$p_f\xi = (1 + r)w\lambda\eta + (\delta + r)p_n\kappa\eta + p_f R. \tag{18}$$

Considering (17) and (13), we may rewrite this in the form,

$$p_f\xi = p_f b_f \omega^s \lambda\eta + p_n \delta\kappa\eta + p_n b_n \omega^s \lambda\eta + p_f R. \tag{19}$$

Substituting from (8), therefore, we get

$$p_f\xi = p_f b_f \omega^s N - p_f b_f \omega^s lx + p_n \delta\kappa\eta + p_n b_n \omega^s N - p_n b_n \omega^s lx$$
$$+ p_f c(R) + pD \tag{19'}$$

because $p_f[R - c(R)] = pD$. Considering (9) with $\Delta M = 0$ and $\Delta N = 0$, the budget equation (13) and finally the price equation (16) with $r = 0$, we are able to write (19') in the following form:

$$\xi = b_f \omega^s N + c(R).$$

This is the wage fund equation (5) in the state of long-run equilibrium, because $\xi = \bar{\xi}$ in that state. From (22) below, $R = \bar{R}$.

We now finally show that r is 0 in price equations (15) and (16) if all the other equilibrium conditions,

$$\kappa\eta + kx = M, \tag{20}$$

$$\lambda\eta + lx = N, \tag{21}$$

$$\bar{\xi} = b_f \omega^s N + c(\bar{R}), \tag{22}$$

as well as (12), are fulfilled. This is seen in the following way. We shall start with (22). Considering the workers' and the landlords' budget equations and in view of the fact that $\Delta M = 0$ in (9), it, (22), may be put in the form,

$$p_f \bar{\xi} = wN - (p_n x - p_n \delta \kappa \eta - p_n \delta kx) + p_f R.$$

As $\xi = \bar{\xi}$ in the state of long-run equilibrium, we finally get

$$p_f \xi + p_n x = wN + \delta(p_n \kappa \eta + p_n kx) + p_f R. \tag{23}$$

On the other hand, (18) is obtained regardless of the value of r. This is added to (16) postmultiplied by x. Then

$$p_f \xi + p_n x = (1 + r)wN + (\delta + r)(p_n \kappa \eta + p_n kx) + p_f R$$

which may be compared with (23). We then get $r = 0$.

Thus, by regarding M and N as variables, we arrive at a stationary state where the short-run equilibrium conditions are all satisfied. This is what we call long-run equilibrium; it is obviously a special kind of short-run equilibrium where population (the labourforce) and capital are perfectly adjusted so that the economy can remain unchanged indefinitely unless disturbed by an exogenous shock.

In the second case of m_u being determined to be equal to 1, all the lands which are superior to the marginal land u are fully employed, $T_i = T_i^0, i = 1, \ldots, u - 1$, but the marginal land itself may be underemployed. Accordingly, T_u may take on any value that is less than T_u^0. Then η may take on any value such that

$$\eta = m_1 T_1^0 + \cdots + m_{u-1} T_{u-1}^0 + T_u, \qquad T_u \leqq T_u^0,$$

where the first $u - 1$ terms are determinate and the last indeterminate. This would cause M and N to be indeterminate. This means that there are multiple stationary states, all of which satisfy the long-run equilibrium conditions.

The above description of the long-run equilibrium establishes its existence too. We have seen that there is a case where the long-run equilibrium is unique, while there is also a case of multiple equilibria. Since the latter occurs only where m_u is set at 1, it should be considered as the exceptional case. Ricardo seems not to have realized that there could be multiple long-run equilibria at $m_u = 1$. But this should not create any serious trouble. In the case of multiple equilibria, the economy which started its dynamic movement from a non-stationary short-run equilibrium will finally approach one of long-run equilibria. When the economy reaches it, it will settle there forever.

4 How will an economy settled at a short-run equilibrium be set in motion? Where and how will the motion eventually cease to be active? To discuss these problems we need to make a few more preparations. First, a relationship has to be established between money wages with which capitalists are concerned, and real wages in which workers are interested. We shall first show that, when m_u is fixed, ω is an increasing function of w through the origin. Secondly, when m_u is increased, the curve $\omega(w)$ shifts downwards. These are illustrated in Figure 5.

The first relationship is established in the following way. Dividing the price equations of industries (2) above by w, and solving with respect to p_n/w, we obtain

$$\frac{p_n}{w} = (1 + r)l[I - (\delta + r)k]^{-1}. \tag{24}$$

It is evident from this that p_n/w decreases when r does so. On the other hand r decreases whenever w increases, by virtue of the money wage–profit frontier discussed in the last chapter. Taking this result into account it may be seen that, with m_u being constant, the price of corn in terms of money wages, p_f/w, diminishes as r decreases,

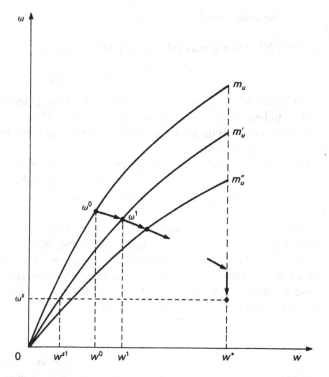

Figure 5

because we obtain

$$\frac{p_f}{w} = (1+r)\lambda(m_u) + (\delta+r)\frac{p_n}{w}\kappa(m_u). \tag{25}$$

from the price equation of agriculture (1). Thus an increase in w gives rise to a decline of all prices (p_f/w, p_n/w), which results in an increase in real wages, $\omega = w/(p_f b_f + p_n b_n)$.

When m_u increases, it may be seen from (24) and (25) that p_n/w is unaffected but p_f/w increases. Therefore, to a higher m_u, there corresponds a lower real wage rate. That is to say, the curve $\omega(w)$ obtained for a given m_u shifts downwards when m_u takes on a higher value.

Next, concerning labour, Ricardo assumed that full employment always exists and that employment in agriculture expands when total labour increases. This means that in the equation,

$$\lambda\Delta\eta + l\Delta x = \Delta N, \tag{26}$$

following from (8) which holds for any period, $\Delta\eta$ is positive wherever $\Delta N > 0$. Let $\Delta N = gN$ and $l\Delta x = g_n lx$, where g is the rate of growth of the labourforce, whilst g_n is the rate of growth of industrial (non-food producing sectors') employment. Then (26) may be written in the form

$$\lambda\Delta\eta + g_n lx = gN.$$

Therefore, $\Delta\eta$ is positive as long as

$$g - g_n \frac{lx}{N} > 0. \tag{27}$$

Ricardo assumed, though he did not clearly say so, that (27) is always fulfilled.

At an early stage of industrialization where the total employment in industry is only 10 per cent of the total labourforce, (27) is satisfied as long as g_n does not exceed ten times the rate of growth of the labourforce. At a subsequent stage, however, where the share of employment of the industrial sectors is one third of the total labourforce, the limit of g_n/g, for which (27) holds, would be 3, while the limit would be only 1.5 for the share of two thirds. These limits asymptotically approach 1 when lx/N tends to 1. Therefore, this assumption seems perfectly acceptable for the early nineteenth-century economy in which Ricardo was interested.

The final assumption (or conjecture) which was implicitly made by Ricardo concerns wage increases. He was interested in the following comparative statics problem. First, substituting from (8), equation (5) may be written in the form,

$$\bar{\xi} = b_f \omega N + c(\bar{R}), \tag{5'}$$

where

$$\omega = w/(p_f b_f + p_n b_n). \tag{5*}$$

These two equations, together with (1), and (2) consisting of n equations, and

$$p_G = 1, \tag{5**}$$

enable us to determine $n + 4$ unknowns, p_f, p_n, w, r, ω, where N is fixed at N^0. Let these values be $p_f^0, p_n^0, w^0, r^0, \omega^0$. In the next period 1, (5) is replaced by

$$\xi = b_f \omega N^1 + c(R), \tag{5''}$$

where ξ is the short-run equilibrium amount of corn produced by the activity in period 0, and which is available in the market at the beginning of period 1, and R is the total amount of rent paid in period 0. Equation (5''), together with the other $n + 3$ equations (5*), (5**), (1) and (2), is enough to determine the short-run equilibrium values, $p_f^1, p_n^1, w^1, r^1, \omega^1$, corresponding to $N = N^1$. These are compared with $p_f^0, p_n^0, w^0, r^0, \omega^0$, respectively. In this comparative statics problem, it is assumed that m_u in (1) takes on the short-run equilibrium value m_u^0, when p_f^0, p_n^0, etc. are determined, while $m_u = m_u^1$, when p_f^1, p_n^1, etc. are derived. In order to determine the value of m_u, other equations of the short-run equilibrium are utilized, as has been seen in Chapter 2.

Concerning this problem, Ricardo took the following proposition for granted. Where $N^1 > N^0$ (with $m_u^1 > m_u^0$)[4], the following are obtained: (i) $w^1 > w^0$ for money wages, as long as w^0 is lower than the maximum money wages w^*, at which $r = 0$ according to the money wage–profit frontier, (ii) the percentage increase in money wages is lower than that of the cost of living, $p_f b_f + p_n b_n$, so that $\omega^1 < \omega^0$ for real wages, (iii) the new money wages thus determined do not exceed the maximum wages, i.e. $w^1 \leqq w^*$, and finally, (iv) the new real wages are higher than the subsistence wages, i.e. $\omega^1 > \omega^s$. Concerning (i) and (ii) Ricardo explicitly wrote, as I have already quoted in Chapter 3: 'As population increases, ... [the labourer] receive[s] more money wages. ... While the price of corn rises to 10 per cent., wages will always rise less than 10 per cent. ...; the condition of the labourer [his real wages] will generally decline' (pp. 101–3). Assumptions (iii) and (iv), however, are not clearly stated in *Principles*, though, for reasons of preciseness, Ricardo should have explicitly stated similar assumptions in his theory of accumulation.

Unfortunately Ricardo accepted these comparative statics properties without any rigorous proof. Though it seems that no one criticizes Ricardo on this, it is, in my view, the weakest point in the classical growth theory. It is very difficult to prove the proposition;

---

[4] We shall discuss, in Section 5 below, how m_u will change when N is increased.

furthermore it might be, as a general rule, an entirely erroneous proposition, because it would seem rather easy to produce counter-examples to it. Nevertheless, Ricardo took it to be economically reasonable. We might also take part (ii) of the proposition as being economically reasonable from the point of view of contemporary wage negotiation. Let ω^0 be the current real wages; when $p_f^0 b_f + p_n^0 b_n$ increases to the level of $p_f^1 b_f + p_n^1 b_n$, the proposition implies that the negotiation will be settled at the new wages $w^1 = (p_f^1 b_f + p_n^1 b_n)\omega^1$, which only enables the workers to enjoy the real wages ω^1 such that $\omega^1 < \omega^0$, in spite of the workers' initial insistence of new money wages of the amount, $(p_f^1 b_f + p_n^1 b_n)\omega^0$. Notwithstanding all these it must be emphasized that the proposition is not a proven one but could, at best, be only a conjecture or a hypothesis.[5]

5 We can now discuss how the economy works through time. Let the values of the parameters at the beginning of period 0 be ζ^0, M^0, N^0. Then $m_u, p_f, p_n, w, \omega, r, \xi, \eta, x, R$ will all take on the short-run equilibrium values, m_u^0, p_f^0, p_n^0, etc., respectively. If real wages ω^0 thus determined are higher than subsistence wages ω^s, then the labourforce will expand, so that $N^1 > N^0$ and more will be employed in the agricultural sector. This means $\Delta\eta > 0$, which implies either (i) $\Delta T_u > 0$, or (ii) $\Delta m_u > 0$, by virtue of the definition of η. In case (i), m_u is kept equal to 1, no other m_i's being affected, so that there will be no change in the price equations; therefore

---

[5] My interpretation of Ricardo's dynamic analysis – as a sequential analysis of short-run equilibria, using the comparative statics method – would be different from the interpretation that would be supported by many contemporary economists. They seem to consider that Ricardo assumed an equation of dynamic wage adjustment,

$$\Delta w = f(\Delta p_f^{-1} b_f + \Delta p_n^{-1} b_n),$$

where $\Delta w = w^1 - w^0$, $\Delta p_f^{-1} = p_f^0 - p_f^{-1}$, and $\Delta p_n^{-1} = p_n^0 - p_n^{-1}$; p_f^i's and p_n^i's, $i = 1, 0, -1$, are the equilibrium prices in the coming, current and last periods, respectively.

If this interpretation were adopted, however, the Ricardian short-run equilibrium system would become a system of overdeterminancy because at the commencement of period 1, the wages w^1 would have already been determined, so that they could not be determined again by the equilibrium conditions of period 1. In particular, with w^1 predetermined, full employment of labour would not be realized in period 1. I, therefore, interpret Ricardo as having assumed the comparative statics proposition mentioned above, implying, as Figure 5 above illustrates, that an increase in m_u establishes new equilibrium wages, w^1, ω^1 such that $w^* \geq w^1 > w^0$ and $\omega^s < \omega^1 < \omega^0$.

p_f, p_n, w, r, and hence ω, will all remain unchanged. Since marginal land yields no rent at these prices, the expansion of cultivation on marginal land does not affect the total value of rent R. Finally, η and x are determined by the full employment equations, (7) and (8), with N^1 and M^1 on their respective right-hand sides. As ω^1 equals ω^0, which is larger than ω^s, we still have $\omega^1 > \omega^s$. Then $N^2 > N^1$; therefore, T_u is increased again. This process continues until T_u finally reaches T_u^0.

Where $T_u = T_u^0$, case (ii) is applicable. Then, $m_u^1 > m_u^0$, and by Ricardo's assumption (or conjecture) concerning wage increases, we will have higher wages in the new period 1. Thus, $w^1 > w^0$, which is followed by $r^1 < r^0$ and $\omega^1 < \omega^0$. It also follows from Figure 5 that, when m_u increases, money wages corresponding to subsistence wages ω^s become larger and nearer to maximum money wages w^*. The real wages ω^1 are determined such that they remain higher than subsistence wages ω^s. Therefore more labour is available at the beginning of period 2: $N^2 > N^1$. This then means $\Delta\eta^2 > 0$, so that $m_u^2 > m_u^1$. Corn will then be produced under more unfavourable conditions; its price will be increased, and the workers' cost of living will rise. As a consequence w will increase: $w^2 > w^1$. In Ricardo's own words,

> In the first place, the price of corn would rise only in proportion to the increased difficulty of growing it on land of a worse quality.
> ... therefore, I think it is clearly demonstrated that a rise in the price of corn, which increases the money wages of the labourer, diminishes the money value of the farmer's profits. (pp. 113–14)

This creates a further fall in real wages and an increase in subsistence money wages. (See Figure 5.) Ricardo wrote: 'each labourer would receive more money wages; but the condition of the labourer, as we have already shewn, would be worse, inasmuch as he would be able to command a less quantity of the produce of the country' (p. 125).

Proceeding in this way for several periods, the economy may start to use land of lower grade, $u + 1$; then $m_{u+1} = 1$ and the dynamic process will be switched to the one of case (i) with new marginal land $u + 1$; we have several periods in which cultivation expands on land $u + 1$, although there is no rent from it. Throughout the whole sequence of short-run equilibria, money wages increase, while real wages decrease. The former will finally reach maximum money wages w^*, whereas the latter may be higher than subsistence wages ω^s. If so, then the population N will grow but money wages will not be increased, because the rate of profit will be negative if w is higher than w^*. In such circumstances, we will observe an increase in m_{u+1}, which will give rise to a decrease in real wages. If they are still above subsistence wages after the decline, there will be another increase in m_{u+1}, and, therefore, another fall in real wages. In this way they will eventually approach the subsistence level. When they reach that level, the economy will be in a stationary state of long-run equilibrium, and classical growth completed.

We have so far taken for granted that a full-employment and full-capacity equilibrium is established in each period. However, in a period in which solutions to (20) and (21) are not non-negative, it is obvious that either full employment of labour or full utilization of capital (or both) is impossible. At this point in time, the Ricardian sequence of short-run equilibria will collapse into a disequilibrium path. Ricardo rules out this possibility, probably by assuming tacitly a strong tendency towards the long-run equilibrium, so that η and x will converge upon the long-run equilibrium values, $\eta^* > 0$ and $x^* > 0$, more or less in monotone and, therefore, η and x will remain positive until they reach η^* and x^*, respectively, once the initial values η^0 and x^0 are assumed to be positive.

6 A comment is now due on the uniform rate of profit which the price equations (1) and (2) assume. In the actual economy the rate of profit usually differs from industry to industry, or, more precisely, from one firm to another. A uniform, general rate of profit would nevertheless be established in the model economy under conditions of perfect competition. If one sector's or firm's rate of profit is, in fact, higher than that of other sectors or firms, it will attract more capital from other sectors or firms where business is in slump and hence the rate of profit lower. If the uniform rate of profit is not established by this sort of reallocation of capital, capital will depart totally from the industries with lesser rates of profit, and hence, they will disappear from the economy. The process of capital movement was described by Ricardo as:[6]

> There is perhaps no manufacturer, however rich, who limits his business to the extent that his own funds alone will allow: he has

---

[6] The following passages are made on an implicit assumption that industries are subject to constant returns to scale. To those where diminishing returns prevail a more careful examination is desirable, which Ricardo has provided for agriculture. See his *Principles*, p. 71.

always some portion of this floating capital, increasing or diminishing according to the activity of the demand for his commodities. (p. 89)

The high profits on capital employed in producing that commodity, will naturally attract capital to that trade; and as soon as the requisite funds are supplied, and the quantity of the commodity is duly increased, its price will fall, and the profits of the trade will conform to the general level. .... It is through the inequality of profits, that capital is moved from one employment to another. (p. 119)

This restless desire on the part of all the employers of stock, to quit a less profitable for a more advantageous business, has a strong tendency to equalize the rate of profit of all, or to fix them in such proportions, as may in the estimation of the parties, compensate for any advantage which one may have, or may appear to have over the other. (pp. 88–9)

The second passage quoted above implies that dual cross adjustment works behind the process of establishing the equal rate of profit. This type of adjustment, originally devised by Ricardo, was to be formulated more exactly by Walras. First, under constant returns to scale, the amount of output x_i is proportional to the amount of capital the industry i can use. (In the case of agriculture where returns are diminishing, the intensity of cultivation is assumed to be constant at a certain level throughout the process of establishing the uniform rate of profit, so that agriculture may also be regarded as if it were a constant-returns industry.) In those industries i whose rate of profit is not the biggest, x_i will decrease, while in the industries j which earn profits at a maximum rate, x_j will increase.

Where output x_i decreases, an excess demand appears, whereas where x_j increases, an excess supply is obtained. This excess demand will give rise to an increase in the prices of the commodity produced by industry i, so that the rate of profit of that industry will improve. Conversely, in industry j where an excess supply is created, the price of the product will diminish; hence the rate of profit will decrease. In Walras' own words,

These entrepreneurs will expand output whenever the selling price of the products exceeds the cost of the productive services involved in their production; and they will reduce their output whenever the cost of the productive services exceeds the selling price. In each market, prices rise whenever demand exceeds supply, and fall whenever supply exceeds demand. (*Elements*, pp. 41–2)

The manufacturers of new capital goods, like those of consumers' goods, expand or contract their output accordingly as the selling price exceeds the cost of production or the cost of production exceeds the selling price. (*Ibid.*, p. 42)

It must be noted that in these passages Walras included normal profits in the cost of production. In this way the maximum rate of profit is decreased and other lower rates of profit are increased; and all these are eventually equalized and become normal.[7]

This duality within the general equilibrium system, i.e. the duality of the price–cost equations and the demand–supply equations, clearly observed in Ricardo and refined by Walras, constitutes the mainstay of the von Neumann system,[8] though it has disappeared from the dominating models of the contemporary general equilibrium school (Hicks, Arrow, Debreu, etc.). Von Neumann emphasizes the role of two rules, the rule of free goods and the rule of profitability in the formation of general equilibrium. The former implies that those goods that are overproduced are free goods and zero prices are charged for them. On the other hand, the latter implies that those processes which do not earn profits at the maximum rate are not actually utilized for production.[9] These rules must hold in equilibrium.

One can easily acknowledge that von Neumann's two rules implicitly assume the Ricardo–Walras dual cross adjustment working behind the scenes. In fact, the former are an extreme form of the latter, where prices and outputs are perfectly adjusted instantaneously. If p_i is decreased and reaches zero, according to the Ricardo–Walras rule of price adjustment, but the excess supply of commodity i is not completely removed, then we obtain a state of affairs where p_i is zero with an excess supply of i being positive. This is von Neumann's rule of free goods. Similarly, if production activity x_j is decreased and reaches zero, according to the

---

[7] This dual cross adjustment is in contrast to the dual direct adjustment, often discussed in the context of the input–output analysis, where excess profits are regulated by changing prices while excess demands by outputs. See my *Walras' Economics*, pp. 59–69, and *The Economic Theory of Modern Society*, Cambridge University Press, 1976, pp. 232–50. Also see P. Flaschel and W. Semmler, 'The Dynamic Equalization of Profit Rates for Input–Output Models with Fixed Capital', in W. Semmler, *Competition, Instability, and Nonlinear Cycles*, Lecture Notes in Economics and Mathematical Systems, Springer-Verlag, 1986, pp. 1–34.

[8] J. von Neumann, 'A Model of General Economic Equilibrium', *Review of Economic Studies*, 1945–6, pp. 1–9.

[9] See my *Theory of Economic Growth*, Oxford University Press, 1969, pp. 95–6.

Ricardo–Walras rule regarding output, but still process j is not profitable (i.e., its rate of profit is less than the maximum one), then we have an equilibrium in which x_j is zero and process j is unprofitable, and thus von Neumann's rule of profitability is obtained.[10] These findings suggest that a modernization of Ricardo's economics in line with von Neumann's article may be a feasible and reasonable project; it could be accomplished in a way more or less similar to the one I have used in my previous works on Marx and Walras.

There is another similarity between Ricardo and Walras. Notwithstanding W. Jaffé's allegation that there is no theory of growth, or dynamic analysis in Walras,[11] we can find the following statements:

> Let us drop the assumption of an indefinite period and imagine, instead, a determinate period of, let us say a day, or better a year, in order to allow for seasonal variations. (*Elements*, p. 378)

> We shall suppose the basic idea of the economic problem (viz. the quantities possessed of capital goods, the utilities of consumers' goods and services, and the utility of additions to net income) to remain fixed. (*Ibid.*, p. 378)

> Moreover, we shall assume not only that the preliminary phase of grouping [*tâtonnement* – M.M.] has been completed with equilibrium established *in principle*, but also that the phase of static equilibrium has actually commenced, so that equilibrium is established *in fact*. (*Ibid.*, p. 378)

At the beginning of the next year, the basic data will be altered, since they are affected by the economic activities of the present period. 'Personal capital [that is labour – M.M.], capital goods proper and money' as well as 'circulating capital' (*Elements*, p. 380)

---

[10] Although Arrow attributes the rules of free goods and profitability to German-speaking economists in the 1930s, Schlesinger, Wald, Zeuthen etc., a careful reader of Walras could find them in his *Elements*. Walras says: 'If, of the two commodities, (A) and (B), one of them ... become unlimited in quantity, that commodity would no longer be scarce and would cease to have value in exchange' (*Elements*, p. 145). Obviously this is the rule of free goods. (Cf. K. J. Arrow and F. H. Hahn, *General Competitive Analysis*, North-Holland, 1971, pp. 8–11; also see my *Walras' Economics*, pp. 12–15.) Also we can find in Walras a passage to the effect of the rule of profitability: 'it is necessary ... to give up producing those capital goods whose cost of production exceeds their selling price' (*Elements*, p. 481).

[11] W. Jaffé, 'Walras's Economics As Others See It', *Journal of Economic Literature*, XVIII, 1980, pp. 528–49; see also M. Morishima, 'W. Jaffé on León Walras: A Comment', *Journal of Economic Literature*, XVIII, pp. 550–8.

will be increased or decreased. Only land capital escapes this change. A new *tâtonnement* will be carried out in the next year and a new equilibrium will be established. This type of sequential equilibrium analysis discussed in Part III of *Elements* is very similar to the Ricardian analysis of growth in Sections 4 and 5 above. Although Walras intended to make a dynamic analysis of economic activities even within the elementary period, one year,[12] he, like Ricardo, used the comparative statics method, in order to develop the dynamics of period analysis on the basis of which he confirmed exactly the same conclusions[13] as Ricardo reached. In this sense Walras is a Ricardian.

7 Instead of formulating, like Walras, a microeconomic version of Ricardo's economics, Samuelson and Casarosa have constructed macroeconomic models in order to generate classical, or Ricardian growth. Although Casarosa claims that his view is 'new', it is evident that Samuelson's model is the prototype of Casarosa's. Except for one aspect of Casarosa's new view which is a significant improvement on Samuelson's original version, their models are essentially the same. This will be seen below together with the final conclusion that both models – especially Samuelson's – have to be rejected because they distort Ricardo's theory immensely.

Let us begin by summarizing Samuelson's article. His model consists of the following six equations to the effect that (1) aggregate output is distributed between consumption and investment; (2) diminishing returns to scale prevails but isoquants are L-shaped; (3) total land rent equals surplus output; (4) marginal output is distributed between wages and profits; (5) population increases or decreases according to whether real wages are higher or lower than subsistence level; and finally (6) the rate of investment is positive or negative according to whether the rate of profit exceeds or falls short of its 'subsistence' level.

In this formulation, it has to be noted that the model does not accommodate the idea of the wage-fund theory which is a most essential element of classical theory. Without it, it is not surprising to see that the model has one degree of freedom, and thus it cannot determine the wage rate. To compensate for this missing wage determination equation Samuelson makes three possible alternative

[12] See *Elements*, p. 380.
[13] *Ibid.*, pp. 390–1.

assumptions concerning wages and examines how the economy works under the respective assumptions. As will be seen below, none of these can unfortunately claim to be Ricardian. It is nothing but Samuelson in the garb of Ricardo. Moreover, it is regrettably inappropriate as an economic theory.

In the first case Samuelson makes an assumption which he calls the polar Ricardian assumption. It assumes that 'population adjusts virtually instantly, so that [the real wage rate] falls or rises immediately to the subsistence wage.'[14] It is impossible to find a document in Ricardo's works which supports this polar assumption, so that it cannot be said to be Ricardian. This historical inaccuracy may, however, be regarded as insignificant, if it is compared with the fact that the phenomena which Ricardo was concerned with will never happen in the economy. Samuelson thus chases a will-o'-the-wisp.

Under the polar assumption it is obvious that there is no population growth because wages are set at subsistence level. With a stationary population, the Ricardian problem will never occur as the land per man remains unchanged forever. Still Samuelson has observed a dynamic process which shows that the economy converges to the classical, long-run stationary state. This sham Ricardian process is a process of adjustment of the amount of capital to the size of the population (or the labourforce); it is nothing to do with Ricardo's problem, that is the adjustment of the population to the existing fixed quantity of land. Samuelson is confused by diagrams and differential equations and misses the point of the economic problem which Ricardo dealt with.

Furthermore he has entirely neglected the following point. Suppose, at the start of the adjustment process, the capital stock (his K_0) is less than the population or the labourforce (his L_0) requires. Then, because of this shortage, the marginal productivity of capital will be higher than the subsistence profit rate. Then the stock of capital will be increased by Samuelson's investment function (6) above. This process will continue until the shortage of capital disappears. It is evident, however, that a part of the existing population will be unemployed due to a lack of capital throughout Samuelson's adjustment process. These unemployed will not be paid and will die instantly by virtue of his assumption. Since the marginal

---

[14] Samuelson, 'A Modern Treatment', p. 1,422.

productivity of capital is large, capital increases, so that the labourforce, which had been adjusted to the amount of capital before its increase, is now in relatively short supply, compared with capital after its increase. The population has to be increased, but real wages are fixed at subsistence level by the polar Ricardian assumption. Thus Samuelson's 'Ricardian' dynamic process inevitably meets a deadlock.

The second device used to determine real wages is that they are adjusted such that the rate of growth of labour equals the rate of growth of capital. This idea too is totally unrelated to Ricardo. It is impossible to find in Ricardo any bibliographical evidence which hints at this type of adjustment in real wages, in spite of Samuelson's vague statement which may mislead the reader and may make him feel that Ricardo might not have been entirely foreign to it.[15] In any case it is extremely difficult to control the real wage rate. How could it be changed such that the rates of growth of capital and labour are equalized with each other?

Thirdly, Samuelson applies the neoclassical rule of shadow prices: if there is an excess supply of one of the factors, then its price is zero. If the rule is applied to capital, its owners will destroy excessive capital goods to avoid zero prices. If it is applied to labour, workers will die because they are not paid at all. Not only unemployed, but also employed workers will, in fact, all die, because they evenly obtain zero wages. The economy thus ceases to exist, capital goods are left unused.[16]

Compared with Samuelson's game in terms of differential equations, Casarosa's is much better. It contains six equations altogether, that is, four ordinary equations and two differential equations. The differential equations are the same as Samuelson's equations (5) and (6). Casarosa has one aggregate production function, corresponding to Samuelson's equation (2) above, but he does not assume L-shaped isoquants. He also has a marginal productivity equation which plays the same role as equation (4) above plays in Samuelson's system. Casarosa, however, replaces equations (1) and (3) above, which are not significant members of Samuelson's system, by two equations which together determine the real wage rate. One is the equation to the effect that the total wage

[15] *Ibid.*, p. 1,422.
[16] *Ibid.*, p. 1,423. Thus the neoclassical price rule should not be applied to labour. This is one of the points of Keynes' *General Theory*.

bill equals the wage rate times the total number of workers since full employment is assumed. The other equation states that the total wage bill equals the available wage fund, i.e. the demand for and supply of the wage fund is equalized.[17]

This system can evidently determine the wage rate: with the wage fund and the total number of workers, or population given, it is obtained by dividing the former by the latter. Therefore, Casarosa, unlike Samuelson, does not need any additional rule of real wage determination. By solving his system of equations in this way he obtains a dynamic path and can show that it approaches the classical long-run equilibrium eventually.

So far so good in the case of Casarosa. But it must be noticed that in his model there is no industry except agriculture. In spite of this the role of land in production, which is the key factor of Ricardo's economics, is implicit, so that the effects created by the limited supply of land are left unexamined. In Ricardo, as has been stated already, if more labourers work on the same land, productivity decreases, so that corn per man, the real wage rate, declines. It is clear that this chain of repercussions does not exist in Casarosa's model (nor in Samuelson's), because he does not succeed in connecting the wage fund (i.e. his stock of capital K) with the output of agriculture (his X). While in Ricardo, the wage fund in year t is the output of corn in year $t-1$, Casarosa instead uses Samuelson's investment function (6) above, which is $\dfrac{dK}{dt}\bigg/ K = F(r - r_s)$ with $F(0) = 0$, $F' > 0$ and $r_s =$ the subsistence rate of profit. The wage fund $K(t)$ obtained by solving this differential equation is not necessarily equal to the output of corn in year $t-1$. Thus Casarosa's dynamic path too is un-Ricardian. I repeat, there is no investment function, like Samuelson's (or Casarosa's) equation (6), in Ricardo's system. Ricardo instead assumed Say's law and, therefore, savings are all automatically invested, as is implied by equation (9) above.

In Samuelson too, the role of land is unclear. In his model, agriculture is not distinguished from industry and the limitedness of land is not explicit in the aggregate production function. It is true that he assumes diminishing returns, but they may not all be attributable to land. They may diminish because of increasing inefficiency in the management of the economy as its scale increases.

---

[17] Casarosa, 'The "New View" of the Ricardian Theory', pp. 46–7.

Still Samuelson attributes total surplus output to land rent as his equation (3) does.[18]

It should be realized that in order to reproduce the Ricardian theory of distribution and economic growth we need an economic model where agriculture is clearly distinguished from industry and land explicitly affects the productivity of agriculture. Even though Ricardo severed technological interdependence between agriculture and industry by assuming that the latter does not buy the former's product as material for producing non-food goods, he connected them with each other by workers' budget since they buy both food and non-food goods. Moreover, industry produces not only non-food consumption goods but also capital goods. The rate of profit is equalized throughout agriculture and industry by competition. These are the characteristics of Ricardo's model, and, therefore, as has been seen before, Ricardian economics must be formulated in the form of a multi-sectoral general equilibrium system. Walras has done this. It is not surprising to see that the macroeconomic formulations presented by Samuelson and Casarosa are unsuccessful, or at least unsatisfactory, in reproducing the essence of Ricardo's theory.[19]

[18] There may be other comments on Samuelson and Casarosa. In their one-commodity models, there is no place for the value theory to which Ricardo devoted a substantial portion of his book, because the price of commodity is always normalized to equal 1. The models have other inadequacies. One of them concerns the fact that a great amount of corn is handed over to landlords as rent, but they can consume only a part of it. However, Samuelson and Casarosa implicitly assume that no one, other than capitalists, invests. Then how can landlords deal with the enormous surplus corn mountain in the one-commodity world?

[19] It is true that Pasinetti constructed a two-sector Ricardian model consisting of agriculture and gold producing industry. (See L. Pasinetti, *Growth and Income Distribution*, pp. 1–28.) Since the only industry produces gold for landlords, non-food wage goods and fixed capital are entirely absent in Pasinetti's model. It is obvious that such a model is not suitable for investigating the problem of 'agriculture versus industry', the main theme of Ricardo's economics. Moreover, like in Casarosa's model, corn X and circulating capital K are unconnected in Pasinetti's. It is Costa who has revised Pasinetti in this respect and has fully developed the idea of the wage fund theory by taking the relationship $K_t = X_{t-1}$ into account. Unfortunately, however, Costa follows Pasinetti in every other aspect. Therefore, the above criticism of the latter entirely applies to the former too. See G. Costa, 'Time in Ricardian Models: Some Critical Observations and Some New Results', in G. A. Caravale (ed.), *The Legacy of Ricardo*, Basil Blackwell, 1985.

6   International trade

1 Ricardo's theory of foreign trade, which he developed in Chapter VII of the *Principles*, is a classic theory of comparative cost. The chapter forms, in conjunction with later ones (XIX, XXII, XXV and XXVIII), the part of the book in which he advocates free trade. It is closely connected with his theory of growth and elucidates, as will be seen later, that diminishing returns due to the limited availability of land can be avoided by abandoning domestic agriculture and importing agricultural products from countries and colonies where land is abundant and agriculture is not subject to diminishing returns. In this way, the price of food is kept low and, therefore, wages are low, so that the rate of profit is maintained at a high level; therefore the accumulation of capital continues at a high speed. Thus, according to the principle of free trade, Ricardo's theory of an international division of labour appeared to guarantee Great Britain's position as the Workshop of the World.

Ricardo's theory has a well-established position in the history of economic theory. Nevertheless, it has been pointed out that his argument is ambiguous and confusing,[1] and, at a number of crucial points, it seems entirely mistaken. For example, he stated:

> It has been my endeavour to shew throughout this work, that the rate of profits can never be increased but by a fall in wages, and that there can be no permanent fall of wages but in consequence of a fall of the necessaries on which wages are expended. If, therefore, by the extension of foreign trade, or by improvements in machinery, the food and necessaries of the labourer can be brought to market at a reduced price, profits will rise. (p. 132)

However, this argument is incorrect. First of all when the wage–profit frontier shifts upwards the rate of profits can be

---

[1] J. S. Chipman, 'A Survey of the Theory of International Trade: Part 1, The Classical Theory', *Econometrica*, Vol. 33, 1965, p. 480.

increased without a fall in wages, and, in fact, this is what happens when a country embarks on international trade. Secondly, the latter half of the quotation should have been stated more carefully, because, regardless of changes in the prices of food and necessaries caused by newly opened foreign trade, the rate of profit will rise, as will be seen later.

Ricardo's following proposition is also mistaken: 'The rate of profits is never increased by a better distribution of labour, by the invention of machinery, by the establishment of roads and canals, or by any means of abridging labour either in the manufacture or in the conveyance of goods' (p. 133). All these to some degree affect the capital (circulating and fixed) or labour input coefficients and may induce an upwards shift in the wage–profit frontier. We may further point out that, even if they do not shift the frontier itself, they may create a fall in wages. Consequently, contrary to Ricardo's conclusion, they will have a positive effect upon the rate of profits.

In the cases cited above, we may note that the production possibilities will be either widened or improved because of access to international trade, or an improvement of technology, causing the frontier to shift upwards. However, throughout the book, Ricardo failed to recognize this mobility and thus derived false conclusions from his wrong supposition. The problem concerns the comparison of two different situations: one in which only domestic trade is allowed, the other in which possibilities of foreign trade are available. In these two circumstances, there is no reason to suppose that the wage–profit frontier will stay at the same place.

2 Ricardo made a similar sort of mistake at the very beginning of the chapter on foreign trade and therefore it affects the whole chapter. Asking whether an extension of foreign trade would increase the rate of profits or not, Ricardo discussed Adam Smith's view which the former summed up to the effect:

> that the great profits which are sometimes made by particular merchants in foreign trade, will elevate the general rate of profits in the country, and that the abstraction of capital from other employments, to partake of the new and beneficial foreign commerce, will raise prices generally, and thereby increase profits. (pp. 128–9)

Contrary to Smith, Ricardo denied the rise of the general rate of profits and described his own position as:[2]

> They who hold this argument agree with me, that the profits of
> different employments have a tendency to conform to one another,
> to advance and recede together. Our variance consists in this: They
> contend, that the equality of profits will be brought about by the
> general rise of profits; and I am of the opinion, that the profits of
> the favoured trade will speedily subside to the general level. (p. 129)

However, we can show, as will be done in the following paragraphs,
that Smith was right in concluding that there would be a general
rise of profits. Thus the chapter begins on the wrong foot and results
in confusion and incomprehensibility.

To show this heuristically, I shall use simple mathematics. Suppose
there are n sectors, and land is assumed to be abundant for
simplicity's sake. Each worker has an L-shaped utility function, so
that he buys baskets containing food and necessaries in appropriate
fixed proportions. Let ω be the number of the baskets which a
worker buys. Let b be the bundle of the wage goods in a single
basket, w the wages of a single worker and p the price row vector.
Under the assumption that the worker does not save, we have the
budget equation of the following form:

$$w = p\omega b. \tag{1}$$

Next, let A be the matrix of physical input coefficients and L the
vector of labour input coefficients. Then, where the economy is
closed, the price–cost equations are put in the form:

$$p = (1 + r)p(A + \omega bL), \tag{2}$$

where r is the rate of profits. We assume, for the sake of simplicity,
$\delta = 1$, so that $A = K$. Let us write the matrix of augmented input
coefficients as

$$M = A + \omega bL$$

---

[2] It has been pointed out by Chipman, 'A Survey', p. 481, that there is a vague
statement in Ricardo's *1815 Essay* to the opposite effect that trade leads to an
increase of the general rate of profits. D. Ricardo, 'An Essay of the Influence of a
Low Price of Corn on the Profits of Stock; Shewing the Inexpediency of Restrictions
on Importation: With Remarks on Mr. Malthus', in *The Works and Correspondence
of David Ricardo* (ed. by P. Sraffa), Vol. IV.

and partition it, for the convenience of exposition, into:

$$M = \begin{pmatrix} m_{11} & \vdots & m_1 \\ \cdots\cdots\cdots & & \\ m_{\cdot 1} & \vdots & M_1 \end{pmatrix}.$$

Let us now suppose that industry 1 (say, agriculture) is exposed to international competition. Let p_1^* be the price of the foreign agricultural produce in terms of the pound sterling. We assume that inputs of commodities $2, \ldots, n$ and labour denoted by $a_{21}', \ldots, a_{n1}'$, l_1' are needed for importing one unit of output 1. Then the rate of profits of the import activity may be calculated at r^* such that

$$p_1^0 = (1 + r^*)(p_1^* + p_2^0 a_{21}' + \cdots + p_n^0 a_{n1}' + \sum \omega p_j^0 b_j l_1'),$$

where p^0 are the closed-economy equilibrium prices which satisfy (2). Suppose now that r^* thus determined is greater than the general rate of profits r^0 determined by (2), then the domestic production of sector 1 would be replaced by the activity of importing output 1. Evaluating this import activity and the production activities of sectors $2, \ldots, n$, at p^0 and r^0, we have

$$p_1^0 > (1 + r^0)(p_1^* + p_2^0 a_{21}' + \cdots + p_n^0 a_{n1}' + \sum \omega p_j^0 b_j l_1') \qquad (3)$$

and

$$p_{(1)}^0 = (1 + r^0)(p_1^0 m_1 + p_{(1)}^0 M_1), \qquad (4)$$

respectively, where $p_{(1)}$ denotes the $(n-1)$-dimensional vector of prices excluding p_1, that is $p_{(1)}^0 = (p_2^0, \ldots, p_n^0)$.

Thus (3) shows that there is room to enlarge the rate of profits in sector 1, while (4) shows that such an enlargement of r^0 gives rise to an increase in $p_{(1)}^0$, with p_1^0 being fixed. This increase in $p_2^0, \ldots, p_n^0$ will raise the cost of importing output 1 in (3). Therefore, r cannot rise as much as originally expected. Nonetheless it is still true that with p_1^0, as well as p_1^*, being given, the r^1 satisfying both (3) and (4) with strict equality is larger than the original general rate of profit r^0 satisfying (2).

This can also be seen alternatively by regarding $p_{(1)}^0$ as given and decreasing p_1^0 slightly. Then both (3) and (4) hold with strict inequality, so that the new general rate r^1 is greater than r^0. It is interesting to see that the former proof of $r^1 > r^0$ is parallel to Ricardo's passage summarizing Adam Smith's argument:[3]

> less capital being necessarily devoted ... to the manufacture of
> cloth, hats, shoes, &. while the demand continues the same, the
> price of these commodities will be so increased, that the ... hatter,
> clothier, and shoemaker, will have an increase of profits, as well
> as the foreign merchant. (p. 129)

A more rigorous mathematical proof of this result may be outlined
as follows. Let $a'_{11} = p_1^*/p_1^0$; then (3) may be written as

$$p_1^0 > (1 + r^0) \sum p_i^0 m'_{i1}, \tag{3'}$$

where $m'_{11} = a'_{11} + \omega b_1 l'_1$, $m'_{21} = a'_{21} + \omega b_2 l'_1$, ..., $m'_{n1} = a'_{n1} + \omega b_n l'_1$.
Let us further define M' as

$$M' = \begin{pmatrix} m'_{11} & \vdots & m_1 \\ \cdots\cdots\cdots \\ m'_{.1} & \vdots & M_1 \end{pmatrix},$$

which is assumed to be an indecomposable matrix.[4] Then (3') and
(4) together may equivalently be written as

$$p^0 \geqq (1 + r^0) p^0 M', \tag{5}$$

where the strict inequality holds for sector 1.

As all elements of M' are non-negative and M' itself is
indecomposable, we find by virtue of the famous Frobenius theorem[5]
that there is a positive eigenvector p and a scalar r^1 such that

$$p = (1 + r^1) p M' \qquad \text{and} \qquad 1 + r^1 > 0.$$

These are the equilibrium price vector and the equilibrium rate of
profits, respectively, which would prevail when food is entirely
imported. (The level of p may be set such that $p_1 = p_1^0$.) We can
show by use of the same theorem that there exists a positive vector
y in association with this r^1 such that

$$y = (1 + r^1) M' y. \tag{6}$$

Now, if (5) is post-multiplied by y, and (6) is pre-multiplied by

---

[3] He refers to Adam Smith, *The Wealth of Nations*, Cannan's edn, Vol. I, p. 95. We
have removed the words 'to the growth of corn' and 'farmer' from the passage
because we are concerned with the case of total replacement of agriculture by
imported food, rather than Ricardo's case where agriculture is partly replaced.

[4] For the definition of indecomposability, see p. 75n above.

[5] See my *Equilibrium, Stability and Growth*, Oxford University Press, 1964, p. 195 ff.

p^0, bearing $p^0 > 0$ and $y > 0$ in mind, we obtain

$$r^1 > r^0,$$

because M' is non-negative and non-zero. Thus the general rate of profits is *increased* when the economy is opened to international trade. This is obviously in contradiction to Ricardo's conjecture. Where $p_1^1 = p_1^0$, we can show $p_i^1 > p_i^0$ for all $i > 1$.

3 Furthermore, Ricardo's theory of comparative advantage is expounded in terms of the labour theory of value:

> England may so circumstanced, that to produce the cloth may require the labour of 100 men for one year; and if she attempted to make the wine, it might require the labour of 120 men for the same time. .... To produce the wine in Portugal, might require only the labour of 80 men for one year, and to produce the cloth in the same country, might require the labour of 90 men for the same time. (p. 135)

He then concluded that it is advantageous for Portugal to export wine in exchange for cloth and for England to export cloth in exchange for wine. This is because Portugal would give wine containing the labour of 80 Portuguese men, for 120/100 units of cloth which contain the labour of 108 ($= 90 \times (120/100)$) Portuguese men, so that she would acquire the surplus labour of 28 men, while England would exchange cloth containing the labour of 100 Englishmen, for 90/80 units of wine containing the labour of 135 ($= 120 \times (90/80)$) Englishmen. This creates the surplus labour of 35 men. From this Ricardo concluded that trade is advantageous for both countries; Portugal exports wine to England, from whom she imports cloth.

This argument, however, can be correct only if the prices of wine and cloth are exactly or approximately proportional to their labour values. Where this proportionality is not obtained, the labour theory of value has nothing to do with determining the comparative advantage between the two countries, as the following numerical example shows. Ricardo's theory has to be rephrased, in terms of the price–cost theory.

The example is constructed on the assumption that England's production coefficients take on the following values: let wine be output 1 and cloth output 2; labour input coefficients are $l_1 = 115$ and $l_2 = 90$, while fixed capital coefficients, are $a_{21} = 0.05$ and

$a_{22} = 0.1$. Then the value equations are:

$$\lambda_1 = 0.05\lambda_2 + 115,$$

$$\lambda_2 = 0.1\lambda_2 + 90$$

so that we obtain $\lambda_1 = 120$ and $\lambda_2 = 100$. These are the same as the labour values assumed by Ricardo in his example.

Next we assume $b_1 = 1/120$ and $b_2 = 0$. Of course, in the actual world, the workers consume cloth but we make $b_2 = 0$ because it simplifies the example. If the reader does not like this assumption, he should retain it and rename the 'cloth' sector as the 'machine' sector. We can easily confirm that, when the number of the baskets a worker consumes, ω, is 1, the rate of profits r is zero and that prices are proportional to labour values. On the other hand, where ω is set at 0.1, we have the following price–cost equations:

$$p_1 = (1 + r)\left(\frac{115}{1200} p_1 + 0.05p_2\right)$$

$$p_2 = (1 + r)\left(\frac{90}{1200} p_1 + 0.1p_2\right).$$

Solving, we get:

$$p_1 = 0.79p_2. \tag{7}$$

In Portugal, we assume for the sake of simplicity, that prices are always proportional to labour values, so that

$$p_1^* = 0.89p_2^*$$

where $0.89 = 80/90$ and p_1^* and p_2^* are prices in Portugal. We then find that a man who buys one unit of cloth at p_2 in England and sends it to Portugal in exchange for wine will bring back 1.125 units of the latter (1.125 is the reciprocal of 0.89). If this person sells the wine at the English price (7), he will definitely lose because

$$1.125 \times 0.79p_2 - p_2 < 0.$$

This means that provided ω is set at 0.1, it is no longer advantageous for England to export cloth to Portugal, although she has comparative advantage in the production of cloth, whenever ω is sufficiently high and close to 1.

Thus, generally speaking the relative price p_1/p_2 in England depends on ω and that in Portugal, p_1^*/p_2^*, on the number of consumption baskets a Portuguese worker consumes, ω^*. Portugal and England have comparative advantages in producing and exporting outputs 1 and 2, respectively if and only if the inequality

$$p_1/p_2 > p_1^*/p_2^*, \tag{8}$$

holds. Ricardo's condition in terms of labour values is only a special condition of this, where both relative prices are independent of ω and ω^* and, therefore, equal to the ratios of labour values of the respective countries.

Ricardo's condition for comparative advantage is stated in terms of labour values in the following form:

$$\lambda_1/\lambda_2 > \lambda_1^*/\lambda_2^*, \tag{9}$$

where λ_1^* and λ_2^* are the values in Portugal. This seems to have been regarded by Bhagwati as the condition for the single-factor economy, which is valid in the case where there are no factors of production (capital goods) other than labour.[6] It is true, however, that throughout the *Principles* Ricardo always assumed that machines were used for the production of commodities. What is important is that they are reproduced, and thus they are not primary factors of production. If his condition (9) is interpreted as being a condition for a single-primary-factor economy with machines reproduced, it is incorrect. According to the Ricardo–Marx theorem discussed in Chapter 1 above, prices are proportional to values only if the proportions in which the capital to support labour and the capital to be invested in machinery, buildings and others combined are the same through all production processes. Therefore, the Ricardian condition (9) generally differs from the true condition (8).

4 Ricardo assumed that factors of production are perfectly mobile within countries, but are immobile between countries. In his own words,

> In one and the same country, profits are, generally speaking, always on the same level; or differ only as the employment of capital may be more or less secure and agreeable. It is not so between different countries. ... [I]f in consequence of the diminished rate of

[6] J. Bhagwati, 'The Pure Theory of International Trade: A Survey', *Surveys of Economic Theory: Growth and Development*, Vol. II, American Economic Association and Royal Economic Society, Macmillan, 1967, pp. 160–1.

> production in the lands of England, ... wages should rise, and profits fall, it would not follow that capital and population would necessarily move from England to Holland, or Spain, or Russia, where profits might be higher. (p. 134)

> Experience, however shews, that the fancied or real insecurity of capital, when not under the immediate control of its owner, together with the natural disinclination which everyman has to quit the country of his birth and connexions, and intrust himself with all his habit fixed, to a strange government and new laws, check the emigration of capital. (p. 136)

In spite of these comments, in the following I shall revise his theory of foreign trade so as to allow for the international movement of workers between countries for the purpose of obtaining better jobs and higher wages. Although more than ten million slaves were transported to America between 1620 and 1776, white migration across the Atlantic in the seventeenth and eighteenth centuries was of a considerably smaller scale. However, the post-Ricardian nineteenth century was an age of large-scale migration. In the twentieth century, as the word 'Gastarbeiter' suggests, workers were sometimes invited, and offered high wages, to fill the gap between the demand for and supply of labour, whereas they were sacked and sent back to their home countries when an excess of supply prevailed in the labour market. Any contemporary longish-run theory of international trade must explicitly take into consideration the mobility of labour between countries.

Capital in the form of money is also highly mobile in the contemporary international world. Certain kinds of physical capital goods, such as dams and atomic power plants are, by their nature, immobile, not only between countries but also within each country. In order to take the immobility of these capital goods into account, we treat the fixed capital goods established in different places as qualitatively different commodities, even though they are physically of the same kind. In the following, the list of commodities is enlarged so as to be consistent with this procedure. With these amendments we now proceed to modernize Ricardo's theory of foreign trade.

5 An international equilibrium may be formulated in von Neumann balanced growth terms. Let us assume there are two countries.[7] Let B and M be output coefficient and augmented input coefficient

---

[7] The model can straightforwardly be extended to the case of more than two countries.

matrices of country I and B^* and M^* those of country II. They may generally be rectangular but not necessarily square. It is also noted that, in order to deal with the inter- or intra-national immobility of some of the capital goods, the list of commodities needs to be extended to treat the same capital goods at different places as different commodities. x and x^*, and ω and ω^*, are output vectors and the numbers of baskets a worker can buy in the two countries, respectively. The price vector and the rate of profits are equalized between the two countries; they are denoted by p and r. It is noted that M depends on ω and M^* on ω^*. We assume, for the sake of simplicity, that workers do not save and capitalists do not consume. Land is abundant, so that rent is zero.

First, let r be the largest of the rates of profit which accrue to production processes of the two countries when prices p prevail. Then we have

$$pB \leqq (1 + r)pM, \tag{10}$$

$$pB^* \leqq (1 + r)pM^*, \tag{11}$$

if the strict inequality '$<$' holds for some i in (10), then the process i's rate of profit is lower than r in country I, so that process i is unprofitable in the same country and is, therefore, not employed. Equation (11) implies the same thing for country II. The rule which determines that unprofitable processes will never be employed, so that their x_i's, or x_i^*'s, are zero, is termed the rule of profitability, under which we have

$$pBx + pB^*x^* = (1 + r)(pMx + pM^*x^*). \tag{12}$$

We are next concerned with an equilibrium state where the two countries are expanding at the same rate, g. In such a state of affairs there are investment demands, gMx and gM^*x^*, from I and II, respectively. Total world demand amounts to $(1 + g)(Mx + M^*x^*)$, which cannot exceed the corresponding supply, $Bx + B^*x^*$. Thus,

$$Bx + B^*x^* \geqq (1 + g)(Mx + M^*x^*). \tag{13}$$

If the jth element of $Bx - (1 + g)Mx$ is positive, then good j will be exported to country II. On the other hand, if it is negative, country I will import good j from II. Thus (13) implies a balance between exports and imports for the commodities for which (13) holds with equality. If we have an excess supply of a commodity, (13) holds

with strict inequality for that commodity. Such a commodity may
be freely disposed, and thus its price is set at zero. This is the rule
of pricing referred to as the rule of free goods. Under it we have

$$p(Bx + B^*x^*) = (1 + g)p(Mx + M^*x^*). \tag{14}$$

We now impose an additional condition

$$p(Bx + B^*x^*) > 0, \tag{15}$$

which implies that the total value of all goods produced in the world
must be positive. Furthermore, we make two reasonable assumptions, attributable to Kemeny, Morgenstern and Thompson,[8] which
imply that every good can be produced by some process, either in
country I or II, and that every process uses some goods as inputs.
It has then been shown by the same authors that the system
constituted by (10)–(15) has solutions such that p is non-negative
and non-zero, x is non-negative and non-zero, and r equals g.

Finally, N and N^* are the numbers of workers available in the
two countries, and $\rho(\omega)$ and $\rho^*(\omega^*)$ the respective rates of growth
of the labourforce; these depend on real wages in the manner that
they are zero at the point of subsistence wages, ω_s and ω_s^*, while
they both are positive and increasing where $\omega > \omega_s$ and $\omega^* > \omega_s^*$.
The activity vectors x and x^* determined by (10)–(15) may be
normalized such that $\sum x_i + \sum x_i^* = 1$, and their absolute level, u,
may be fixed such that the full employment of labour is realized in
the world economy:

$$u(Lx + L^*x^*) = N + N^*. \tag{16}$$

$N - uLx$ gives the migration of workers from country I to II, if it
is positive. If it is negative, $N^* - uL^*x^*$ gives migration in the
opposite direction, that is from II to I. We have the balanced growth
of outputs and the labourforce, where their rates of growth are
equalized.

$$g = \rho(\omega) \qquad \text{and} \qquad g = \rho^*(\omega^*). \tag{17}$$

These equations determine the real wages ω and ω^*, which are
considered as given in the system (10)–(15). We designate the
solutions to the open-economic system (10)–(17) as $p_0, x_0, r_0, g_0, u_0,$
$\omega_0,$ and ω_0^*.

[8] J. G. Kemeny, O. Morgenstern and G. L. Thompson, 'A Generalization of the
von Neumann Model of an Expanding Economy', *Econometrica*, Vol. 24, 1956,
pp. 115–35.

6 These solutions are now compared with the equilibrium state which will be established if the economies of countries I and II are closed. As what we find from the comparison between the open-economy solutions and the closed-economy solutions of country I will *mutatis mutandis* also be valid for country II we are, in the following, concerned only with the first comparison. Let p_C, x_C, r_C, g_C, u_C, ω_C denote the solutions to the following closed von Neumann system of country I:

$$pB \leqq (1+r)pM, \qquad \text{with } pBx = (1+r)pMx, \qquad (18)$$

$$Bx \geqq (1+g)Mx, \qquad \text{with } pBx = (1+g)pMx, \qquad (19)$$

$$pBx > 0, \qquad (20)$$

$$uLx = N, \qquad (21)$$

$$g = \rho(\omega). \qquad (22)$$

We say that the economy is decomposable if there is a proper subset of production processes which uses as inputs only commodities which belong to a proper subset of commodities in order to produce commodities in this subset. For both countries we assume there are no such subsets of commodities, so that each of the two economies is indecomposable, when it is closed. It has already been assumed that for any commodity j there is at least one process i which produces it. Let $J(j)$ be the set of all such processes available in country I, and $J^*(j)$ in country II. If (10) holds with the strict inequality '$<$' for all i in $J(j)$ in the state of the open-economy's growth equilibrium, then there must be at least one i in $J^*(j)$, for which (11) holds with equality in the same state. This is obvious because if (11) holds with strict inequality for all i in $J^*(j)$, the commodity j will not be produced in either of the two countries by the rule of profitability; thus commodity j will be decomposable from the set of commodities which are actually produced.[9] This is in contradiction to our indecomposability assumption. Hence there is a profitable process i in $J^*(j)$ if there is not a profitable process

---

[9] Let S be the set of commodities produced. For the production of any commodity in S, j is not used. Otherwise, j must be produced. Hence there must be at least one profitable process in either of the two countries. This is in contradiction to our null hypothesis that (10) and (11) hold with strict inequality for all i in $J(j)$ and $J^*(j)$. Consequently j is not used for the production of any i in S, as has been asserted in the text. This means that the economy is decomposable.

in $J(j)$; thus, where a commodity j is not produced in country I, it is produced in II.

It is now noted that the augmented input coefficient matrix M depends on the real wages ω. If this is made explicit, then (10) and (19) are written as

$$p_0 B \leq (1 + r_0) p_0 M(\omega_0) \tag{10'}$$

$$B x_C(\omega_0) \geq (1 + g_C(\omega_0)) M(\omega_0) x_C(\omega_0) \tag{19'}$$

respectively, where $g_C(\omega_0)$ represents the equilibrium rate of growth to be established when country I is closed and its wages are fixed at its open-economy equilibrium level, ω_0; $x_C(\omega_0)$ is the corresponding balanced growth activity vector. Those commodities which are unprofitable in the open economy and are produced abroad have to be produced within the country when its economy is closed. Thus some of those i's for which strict inequalities hold for (10') are associated with positive elements of $x_C(\omega_0)$. Hence, post-multiplying (10') by $x_C(\omega_0)$, we get

$$p_0 B x_C(\omega_0) < (1 + r_0) p_0 M(\omega_0) x_C(\omega_0)$$

which should be compared with the result of the premultiplication of (19') by p_0. We finally obtain: $g_C(\omega_0) < r_0$. As $r_C(\omega_0) = g_C(\omega_0)$, where $r_C(\omega_0)$ is the closed-economy equilibrium rate of profit, ω being fixed at ω_0, this results in $r_C(\omega_0) < r_0$; that is to say, the general rate of profit will be lower when country I is closed, than it will be otherwise. Thus foreign trade shifts the wage–profit frontier.

For the open-economy's growth equilibrium, we have

$$r_C(\omega_0) < g_0 = \rho(\omega_0) = \rho^*(\omega_0^*), \tag{17'}$$

whereas we have

$$g_C = \rho(\omega_C) \tag{22'}$$

when the economy is closed. On the other hand, as $M(\omega)$ is an increasing function of ω, we find from (19) that $g_C(\omega)$ is a decreasing function of ω.[10] Therefore, $\omega_C < \omega_0$. This is shown in the following way. If $\omega_C \geq \omega_0$, we will have $g_C = g_C(\omega_C) \leq g_C(\omega_0) = r_C(\omega_0)$ so that from (17') and (22') we will obtain $\rho(\omega_C) < \rho(\omega_0)$. This shows that ρ is a decreasing function of ω, a contradiction. Hence the inequality,

[10] M. Morishima and G. Catephores, *Value, Exploitation and Growth*, McGraw-Hill, 1978, p. 98.

$\omega_C < \omega_0$, is confirmed and this implies $g_C = \rho(\omega_C) < g_0 = \rho(\omega_0)$. Hence $r_C < r_0$.

Thus, when the economy is opened, the general rate of profits, real wages and the rate of growth are all increased. These are the benefits created by foreign trade. Ricardo himself wanted to prove this kind of proposition in the chapter on foreign trade. However, at the very beginning of the chapter he stumbled into insisting the opposite, to the effect that access to a foreign market does not bring about an increase in the general rate of profit. Although our above proposition only describes what will happen in the long run, it accords perfectly with Ricardo's advocacy of free trade: both capitalists and workers benefit from the internationalization of trade.

7 We have so far assumed that land is abundant. We shall now deal with a more realistic case where land is not unlimited in quantity and uniform in quality. Let $T^{(1)}$ be the total area of land of No. 1 quality available in country I, $T^{(2)}$ that of land of No. 2 quality and so on. We follow Ricardo in assuming that only agriculture requires land, and that constant returns to scale prevail in manufacturing industries which do not suffer from the scarcity of land. We deviate, however, from him in assuming that land is not cultivated intensively; if land of No. 1 quality is exhausted, then, rather than ploughing it more deeply, farmers extend cultivation to the land of No. 2 quality. This assumption is made in order to simplify the analysis; it may be avoided by replacing it with a more general assumption that the input coefficients of agriculture, using land of, say, No. 1 quality, are not constant but depend on the degree of intensity of land use.

Suppose there are v kinds of land differing in quality. Using one acre of land No. i quality, we may produce one unit of the agricultural product (corn) by making augmented inputs of $m_1^{(i)}$, where $m_1^{(i)}$ is an n-dimensional vector of augmented input coefficients used to produce corn (commodity 1). There are, of course, v such vectors, $m_1^{(1)}, \ldots, m_1^{(v)}$. Together with other $n-1$ vectors used to produce commodities $2, \ldots, n$, we define the matrix of augmented input coefficients as

$$M = (m_1^{(1)}, \ldots, m_1^{(v)}, m_2, \ldots, m_n).$$

For the marginal land u, we have

$$p_1 = (1 + r)pm_1^{(u)}. \tag{23}$$

For those lands which are superior or inferior to u, we have

$$p_1 = (1 + r)pm_1^{(i)} + p_1 R_i, \qquad i = 1, \ldots, u - 1, \tag{24}$$

and

$$p_1 < (1 + r)pm_1^{(i)}, \qquad i = u + 1, \ldots, v, \tag{25}$$

respectively, where R_i is the rent per acre of land i which is positive. From (23) and (24) we obtain, as the theory of differential rent claims,

$$p_1 R_i = (1 + r)p[m_1^{(u)} - m_1^{(i)}]. \tag{26}$$

Substituting this into (24), we have

$$p_1 = (1 + r)pm_1^{(u)} \qquad \text{for all } i = 1, \ldots, u - 1. \tag{24'}$$

For the processes other than those for agricultural production, we have

$$p_i \leq (1 + r)pm_i, \qquad i = 2, \ldots, n. \tag{27}$$

The price–cost conditions, (24'), (25) and (27), may now be put together in the form:

$$p \leq (1 + r)pM^{(u)}, \tag{28}$$

where

$$M^{(u)} = (m_1^{(u)}, \ldots, m_1^{(u)}, m_1^{(u+1)}, \ldots, m_1^{(v)}, m_2, \ldots, m_n).$$

The rule of profitability is implied by the equation,

$$px = (1 + r)pM^{(u)}x, \tag{29}$$

where x is a non-negative and non-zero column vector consisting of elements, $x_1^{(1)}, \ldots, x_1^{(v)}, x_2, \ldots, x_n$.

Let R be the total amount of rent and c a column vector representing the proportions, $c_1, \ldots, c_n$, in which the landowners spend one unit of rent on various goods. We assume that the landowners propensity to save is zero, so that $pc = p_1$. Where the economy is in a state of balanced growth, we have

$$x \geq (1 + g)Mx + cR.$$

Taking $R = R_i x_1^{(1)} + \cdots + R_{u-1} x^{(u-1)}$ and (26) into account, the above condition for balanced growth can be put in the form:

$$x \geq [(1 + g)M + c(1 + r)p(M^{(u)} - M)/p_1]x.$$

Defining

$$K = M + c\frac{1+r}{1+g}p(M^{(u)} - M)/p_1,$$
(30)

we may rewrite the above condition for balanced growth as

$$x \geqq (1+g)Kx.$$
(31)

Also, we impose the rule of free goods,

$$px = (1+g)pKx$$
(32)

and assume

$$px > 0.$$
(33)

This completes the conditions for the balanced growth equilibrium: (28), (29), (31), (32), (33).

To show the existence of solutions to this system, we replace (28) and (29) by

$$p \leqq (1+r)pK,$$
(28')

$$px = (1+r)pKx,$$
(29')

and consider an auxiliary von Neumann system constituted by (28'), (29'), (31), (32), (33). This system is very similar to the conventional von Neumann system, except that the output matrix K is not constant but depends on p, r, g and u. Nevertheless, it can be shown that, with u given, there exist solutions to this auxiliary system;[11] these solutions depend on u, of course, and also on real wages, ω, because M and, therefore, K depend on it. Thus we obtain

$$p(\omega, u), \qquad x(\omega, u), \qquad r(\omega, u), \qquad g(\omega, u),$$

the last two being equal to each other as in the original von Neumann model. Substituting $r = g$ into (31) and remembering $pc = p_1$, we at once find $pK = pM^{(u)}$. Hence, (28') and (29') imply (28) and (29) respectively. Thus the solutions to the auxiliary system are the solutions to our economy, (28), (29), (31)–(33).

---

[11] This is shown by use of a theorem established in M. Morishima and G. L. Thompson, 'Balanced Growth of Firms in a Competitive Situation with External Economies', *International Economic Review*, Vol. 1, 1960, pp. 129–42.

8 Now, in the same way as before, the level of activity U is decided by

$$ULx(\omega, u) = N, \tag{34}$$

and balanced growth between outputs of commodities and the labour force requires

$$g(\omega, u) = \rho(\omega) \tag{35}$$

which decides the equilibrium real wages, ω. For the determination of u we need some additional conditions. As I shall explain below, one of them is not very realistic, but I have been unable to devise a more suitable substitute. First, assume that $m_1^{(1)}, \ldots, m_1^{(v)}$ are proportional to each other:

$$m_1^{(i)} = h_i m_1^{(1)}, \qquad i = 2, \ldots, v. \tag{36}$$

As $m_1^{(i)}$ is the input vector to be operated on land No. i which is inferior to land No. 1, it must be larger than $m_1^{(1)}$. Therefore, $h_i > 1$. For the same reason $h_j > h_i$ if $j > i$. These are stringent conditions but they are not unreasonable. Secondly, we assume that the landowners spending pattern c is proportional to the farmers' $m_1^{(1)}$; that is,

$$m_1^{(1)} = \gamma c, \tag{37}$$

where the proportionality factor γ is equal to $p m_1^{(1)}/p_1$, because $pc = p_1$. There is no reason why c should satisfy (37); landowners, as distinct from farmers, have no interest in cultivating land, and thus they will never buy agricultural machinery. They are included in $m_1^{(1)}$ but do not appear in c. In the extreme case where no physical inputs are included in $m_1^{(1)}$, this vector consists only of the labour-feeding input coefficients $\omega b l_1^{(1)}$, (37) implies that the workers' consumption vector b is proportional to the landowners c. Although we recognize that (37) is an unreasonable and unrealistic assumption, it is required for the following argument.

Given (36) and (37), we can show that, regardless of p, $K = M^{(u)}$ if $r = g$, as is established in growth equilibrium. The conditions for balanced growth are then reduced to:

$$p \leqq (1 + r)pM^{(u)}, \qquad x \geqq (1 + g)M^{(u)}x,$$

$$px = (1 + r)pM^{(u)}x, \qquad px = (1 + g)pM^{(u)}x,$$

$$px > 0.$$

Bearing in mind the structure of $M^{(u)}$ – its first u columns are identically equal to $m_1^{(u)}$ – it is evident that the sum of $x_1^{(1)}(\omega, u), \ldots, x_1^{(u)}(\omega, u)$, which is designated by $x_1(\omega, u)$, is determined,[12] but its distribution among individual $x_1^{(i)}(\omega, u)$'s, $i = 1, \ldots, u$, remains entirely arbitrary. As long as their sum is equal to the $x_1(\omega, u)$ thus determined, any positive $x_1^{(i)}(\omega, u)$'s, $i = 1, \ldots, u$, will satisfy the above conditions for balanced growth.

Now we can say that u is determined in the following way. It follows from (34) and (35) that the employment of labour increases in a geometrical ratio along the balanced growth path, according to the formula

$$ULx(\omega, u)\alpha^t,$$

where α is the von Neumann growth factor, that is $\alpha = 1 + g(\omega, u)$, whilst the total demand for all kinds of land is

$$Ux_1(\omega, u)\alpha^t.$$

A part of this is the demand for land No. 1, which is $Ux_1^{(1)}(\omega, u)\alpha^t$; the demand for land No. 2 is $Ux_1^{(2)}(\omega, u)\alpha^t$, and so on; finally, the demand for land No. u, which is the marginal land, is given by $Ux_1^{(u)}(\omega, u)\alpha^t$. These demands are limited by the available amounts of the respective kinds of land; we thus have

$$Ux_1^{(1)}(\omega, u)\alpha^t = T^{(1)}, \tag{38.1}$$

$$Ux_1^{(2)}(\omega, u)\alpha^t = T^{(2)}, \tag{38.2}$$

$$\ldots\ldots\ldots\ldots\ldots\ldots,$$

$$Ux_1^{(u)}(\omega, u)\alpha^t \leqq T^{(u)}, \tag{38.u}$$

where, it is noted, the inequality '$\leqq$' may appear in the final condition only. These conditions together imply that u is determined such that the total demand for land satisfies the following condition:

$$T^{(1)} + \cdots + T^{(u-1)} < Ux_1(\omega, u)\alpha^t \leqq T^{(1)} + \cdots + T^{(u)}. \tag{39}$$

When t becomes larger, α^t increases, so that it follows from (38.1), ..., (38.$u-1$) that $x_1^{(1)}(\omega, u), \ldots, x_1^{(u-1)}(\omega, u)$ decreases. This means that $x_1^{(u)}(\omega, u)$ increases, because their sum $x_1(\omega, u)$ is fixed. Where t becomes sufficiently large, the condition (39) will be violated, because the middle term will exceed the sum on the

---

[12] Note that $x_1^{(u+1)}(\omega, u), \ldots, x_1^{(v)}(\omega, u)$ are all zero by the rule of profitability.

right-hand side. Land No. u is no longer the marginal land. The system must be solved for $u + 1$. The new matrix $M^{(u+1)}$ is formed. The new balanced growth inequalities involving $M^{(u+1)}$ should be solved. We then obtain the new solutions: $x(\omega, u + 1)$, $p(\omega, u + 1)$, $r(\omega, u + 1)$, $g(\omega, u + 1)$; therefore, the new U and ω are determined. Needless to say, these new solutions are valid only while t satisfies the following condition of land No. $u + 1$ being the marginal land.

$$T^{(1)} + \cdots + T^{(u)} < Ux_1(\omega, u + 1)\alpha^t \leqq T^{(1)} + \cdots + T^{(u+1)},$$

where α is the new growth factor.

9 We have now a sequence of long-run balanced growth equilibria for $u = 1, 2, 3, \ldots$ If the population, or the labourforce, is very small, because either N or t is small, the demand for land may be so small that the supply of only the best quality land is more than sufficient. In this case $u = 1$, and no land yields rent. This state was described by Ricardo as:

> On the first settling of a country, in which there is an abundance of rich and fertile land, a very small proportion of which is required to be cultivated for the support of the actual population, or indeed can be cultivated with the capital which the population can command, there will be no rent. (p. 69)

At the second state which starts when the labourforce has reached a certain level, it is seen that

> land of the second degree of fertility is taken into cultivation, rent immediately commences on that of the first quality, and the amount of that rent will depend on the difference in the quality of these two portions of land. (p. 70)

Ricardo continued,

> In the same manner it might be shown that when No. 3 is brought into cultivation, the rent of No. 2 must be ten quarters, or the value of ten quarters, whilst the rent of No. 1 would rise to twenty quarters. (p. 71)

Undoubtedly, the sequence of the solutions for $u = 1, 2, 3, \ldots$ perfectly coincides with these passages from the chapter on rent of the *Principles*.

When u increases from u to $u + 1$, the elements of the augmented input coefficients increase from $m_1^{(u)}$ to $m_1^{(u+1)}$. This implies that the wage–profit frontier shifts downwards. As $r(\omega) = g$, the latter will also decline and this downwards shifted growth-rate curve will intersect with the natural rate of growth of the labourforce, $\rho(\omega)$, at a lower level of real wages. Hence the natural rate of growth too will decline. This last creates a falling tendency in the rate of profits because $\rho(\omega) = g = r$, which will continue until ω reaches the subsistence level. At the point of subsistence wages ω_s, the natural growth rate $\rho(\omega)$ takes on the value of zero, so that g and r are also zero; thus the relative quantities of land and population are in a state of harmony. In this manner the closed economy is destined to lose the driving power of growth.

Ricardo's theory of free trade was devised to free a closed country from the fetters of the diminishing returns of land and to revitalize its economy, at least for a considerable time. As has been seen in a previous section, the opening of a country brings about an upwards shift of its wage–profit frontier. When it becomes unprofitable in comparison with agriculture abroad the agricultural sector will cease to exist. By eliminating this sector, the country's general rate of profits will be kept at a higher level. In parallel with this there will also be a higher rate of growth and level of wages. If trade with country II reaches its limits, world trade with m countries will start. As long as we may assume that land is available in a vast quantity in the world economy the diminishing returns of land will not be an effective check on economic growth. The industrial country's real wages are kept high, and its rate of population growth and rate of profits remain positive because of the trade in agricultural products with colonies and less developed countries. The state of balanced growth will continue, over a long period, as long as unused land is available in the world and the international trade regime works effectively and smoothly.

Finally, it should be noted that the switch of balanced growth solutions from those for u to those for $u+1$ is not smooth and immediate. This is because the former are not necessarily on the path of the latter. Prices $p(\omega_u, u)$ and activities $x(\omega_u, u)$ have to be adjusted so as to be equal to the new $p(\omega_{u+1}, u+1)$ and $x(\omega_{u+1}, u+1)$, respectively, where ω_u is the equilibrium real wages for u and ω_{u+1} for $u+1$. Similarly, ω, $\rho(\omega)$, r and g have to be adjusted to ω_{u+1}, $\rho(\omega_{u+1})$, $r(\omega_{u+1})$, and $g(\omega_{u+1})$. Adjustment would take a considerable time during which the economy would be in a state of unbalanced growth. Ricardo did not rigorously discuss the adjustment mechanism. Moreover, he has even no idea of balanced growth and seems to have been satisfied with pointing out the stability of stationary equilibrium. We may now conclude that the essense of Ricardo's economics is contained in his theory of growth. It is based on his marginal theory of rent and coupled with his doctrine of free trade. We may thus say that unmovable and unproducible land and mobile and limitlessly expandable industry are the two main features of his economy.

Part IV

SAY'S LAW

7   Say's law of markets

1 The purpose of the general equilibrium theory (GET) is to construct a system of conditions which are necessary and sufficient to determine all the variables contained in the system. As Walras was the first economist to clearly set forth the idea, he is usually acknowledged as the originator of GE analysis. But the idea of the system-theoretic analysis of the economy can evidently be traced back to Ricardo. Although he did not mathematically spell out what conditions were necessary and sufficient to determine the values of the variables with which he was concerned, we can easily excavate the conditions and reconstruct the whole system of Ricardo's *Principles* as we have done in Chapter 3 above. Indeed, Ricardo is the fore-runner, if not the founder, of the general equilibrium school.

The existence of a state of general equilibrium is, therefore, the most central problem of the GET. The conventional view is that the problem was first examined in a serious way by a number of German-speaking economists in the 1930s. Prior to this, however, Walras himself noted that 'it is possible for these curves [demand and supply curves] to have no point of intersection at all'.[1] This remark by Walras is, at first sight, in obvious contradiction to the Arrow–Debreu proposition that there always exists a GE if demand and supply curves are continuous in price variables. We find, nevertheless, no inconsistency between the two if we carefully examine Walras' and Arrow–Debreu's propositions. Let us distinguish GE into two classes: (1) GE with $D_i = S_i > 0$ for at least one i, where D_i and S_i stand for the demand for and supply of commodity i, and (2) GE with $D_i = S_i = 0$ for all i. They are referred to as the GE of exchange (or essential GE) and the GE of no exchange (or inessential GE) respectively. We may conclude that

---

[1] Walras, *Elements*, p. 108.

Walras and Arrow–Debreu are perfectly consistent with each other because the former only points out possibilities of (2), while the latter asserts that, if there is no GE of the type (1), there should be a GE of the type (2). In cases where GE of (1) exists, we may say that a general equilibrium of exchange, or an essential GE, exists.[2]

This essentiality problem also occurs in the GET of production, the GET of capital formation (or growth) and the GET of money. We say that a GE of production is essential if it is with $x_i > 0$ for some i, where x_i stands for output of commodity i, while it is inessential (or a GE of no production) if $x_i = 0$ for all i. Similarly, a GE of capital formation is said to be essential if $g_i > 0$ for some i, where g_i is the rate of growth of output i, and inessential if $g_i = 0$ for all i. The problem of the essentiality of the GEs has never been pointed out by modern writers (except Walras) in relation to general equilibrium models of exchange, production and capital formation. Hahn was the first writer to attract economists' eyes to the problem with regard to a GE of money; he defines monetary GE as essential if $p_M > 0$, where p_M is the price of money in terms of some numeraire; it is an inessential monetary GE or a barter GE if $p_M = 0$. Like Walras, with regard to a GE of exchange, Hahn points out the possibility of an inessential monetary GE.[3]

Apart from the problem of essentiality, there is the problem of the non-existence of GE. It is absent in the case of the GE systems of exchange and production, while it is present in the GE model of capital formation and may be posed with regard to the monetary GE system too. It is the problem of Say's law which is peculiar to any GE system involving investment and savings. As will be seen later, where Say's law prevails, an essential GE (either GE of capital formation or monetary GE) exists, whereas no GE (neither essential nor inessential) generally exists otherwise. As Walras believed in the truth of the GET he assumed Say's law and was concerned only with those cases where the GE model of capital formation and that of money always have essential solutions.

2 Say's law of markets (or *loi des débouchés*) is often summarized in one sentence as: Supply creates its own demand. It implies that

---

[2] See M. Morishima, *Walras' Economics*, Cambridge University Press, 1977, p. 108.
[3] F. H. Hahn, 'On Some Problems of Proving the Existence of an Equilibrium in a Monetary Economy', in F. H. Hahn and F. P. R. Brechling, *The Theory of Interest Rate*, Macmillan, 1965.

demand and supply are not independent of each other as the demand for output i comes from the supply of other outputs and, conversely, where the latter increases, the created income is spent to obtain some outputs. It has been claimed that no general overproduction is possible under Say's law, in the sense that, if some industries are in the state of overproduction, there must be some other industries which are in the state of underproduction. Secondly, it is sometimes asserted that under Say's law the price level (in terms of money) is left undetermined. A third interpretation of the law proposed by Keynes points out that there is no obstacle to full employment whenever Say's law prevails. The fact that Ricardo ruled out unemployment in his *Principles* (except for the chapter on machinery) may be regarded, from the point of view of Keynes, as an indication that Ricardo implicitly accepted Say's law throughout.

Modern economists such as Lange and Patinkin are usually concerned with Say's law in relationship to monetary GE.[4] In this chapter, however, I shall examine it in the context of the theory of unemployment, by defining Say's law in the same way as Keynes. Goods and services are classified into primary factors, intermediate and capital goods and final products or consumption goods. We assume, for the sake of simplicity, that there are no direct services and that there exists only money and one kind of bond. The subscripts L, I, C, M, B are used to represent primary factors (land and labour), intermediate and capital goods, consumption goods, money and the bond, respectively. Then, according to Walras' law (the sum of the budget equations of each individual and each firm) we get

$$D_L + D_U + D_I + D_C + D_M + D_B \equiv S_L + S_I + S_C + S_M + S_B, \quad (1)$$

where D_L, for example, represents the total demand for primary factors, and S_I the supply of intermediate and capital goods. It is noted that all D's and S's are given in monetary terms. As for D_U and D_I, it is noted that the total demand for intermediate and capital goods is divided into the demand for the replacement of these used up during the period in question and the demand for a net increase in the stock of intermediate and capital goods. These are written as D_U and D_I, respectively, where the subscript U is used because D_U

[4] O. Lange, 'Say's Law: A Restatement and Criticism', in Lange, McIntyre, Yntema (eds), *Studies in Mathematical Economics and Econometrics*, 1942; Don Patinkin, *Money, Interest and Prices*, 2nd edn, Harper and Row, 1965.

is equivalent to Keynes' user-cost. Aggregate net output (Keynes' Y) is obtained by subtracting D_U from the total supply of products $(S_I + S_C)$; D_I is investment I and D_C is consumption C. Then (1) can be put in the form:

$$(D_L - S_L) + (D_M - S_M) + (D_B - S_B) \equiv (Y - C - I). \qquad (2)$$

This is Walras' law in Keynesian terms. It is an identity or a definitional equation which holds regardless of whether the economy is in equilibrium or disequilibrium.[5] Keynes interpreted Say's law as an identity,

$$Y \equiv C + I$$

so that under Say's law the right-hand side of (2) is identically zero. It is a proposition stronger than Walras' law and is satisfied only where the whole of the cost of production is necessarily spent on purchasing the products, either intermediate, capital or consumption goods – meaning that 'the aggregate demand price is equal to the aggregate supply price for all levels of output and employment',[6] or, equivalently, that the sum of the aggregate propensity to consume and the aggregate propensity to invest is always equal to 1.

'A decision to consume or not to consume truly lies within the power of the individual; so does a decision to invest or not invest.'[7] As long as these decisions are made independently by individuals, there is no reason why the sum of the propensities should be one. In fact, in societies which consist of two groups of individuals – those in the first group having propensities to consume which are less than one and making no decision to invest or not to invest at all, while those in the second group (entrepreneurs) being involved everyday in decision-making concerning investment, there is no mechanism whereby a shortage of the propensity to consume is offset by high propensities to invest, so that their sum may be one only by chance. Therefore, Keynes rejected Say's law as implausible, but it was one of Ricardo's main axioms.

As savings S are defined as the excess of income over consumption, $Y - C$, Say's law is alternatively defined as the equivalence of savings

---

[5] An example of identity is: $\log \tan x = \log \sin x - \log \cos x$, which is true for any value of x, so that it has no ability to determine the value of x.

[6] J. M. Keynes, *The General Theory of Employment, Interest and Money*, Macmillan, 1936, p. 22.

[7] *Ibid.*, p. 65.

to investment, $S \equiv I$, that is to say, aggregate investment is equal to aggregate savings for all levels of output and employment.[8] Suppose S and I are decided dependently upon Y and other economic variables. We write $S(Y, \ldots)$ and $I(Y, \ldots)$. Where these are each independently decided by different groups of persons, it is impossible for S to be equal to I at an arbitrary given $Y, \ldots$, unless the investment schedule $I(Y, \ldots)$ is flexibly revised such that the gap between $S(Y, \ldots)$ and $I(Y, \ldots)$ is quickly and smoothly filled up. Thus the flexibility of aggregate investment is a necessary precondition of Say's law; conversely, it is evident that the equality between S and I is assured wherever I is flexible. This means that Say's law is equivalent to the proposition that there are ample opportunities for investment, so that no limit to aggregate investment is set and it flexibly adjusts itself to savings.

One of the most important implications of this definition of Say's law is that under it there is no obstacle to full employment. Let Y_F be the aggregate output produced by employing labour and capital to the full, and S_F the savings out of Y_F. Under the law, investment of the amount S_F is carried out, so that $I \equiv S_F \equiv Y_F - C_F$, where C_F stands for the consumption made by people when they earn income of the amount Y_F. Thus $Y_F \equiv C_F + I$, which means that the full employment aggregate output is purchased either by consumers or by producers. There is neither deficiency of demand nor shortage of supply, so that labour and capital are fully employed. Say's law thus rules out unemployment of labour and capital. Keynes, therefore, concludes that since 'this is not the true law relating the aggregate demand and supply functions, there is a vitally important chapter of economic theory which remains to be written and without which all discussions concerning the volume of aggregate employment are futile'.[9]

It should be noted in this place that the thesis claiming that full employment would prevail under Say's law tacitly assumes that the

---

[8] In discussing the equivalence between savings and investment, Keynes writes: 'The equivalence . . . emerges from the *bilateral* (his italics) character of the transactions between the producer . . . and the consumer or the purchaser of capital equipment' (*ibid.*, pp. 63–5). This should be interpreted as implying *ex-post* savings = *ex-post* investment. However, this *ex-post* equality is entirely different from Say's law $S \equiv I$, which is an *ex-ante* identity. Keynes did not confuse these two, though he failed to write an explicit sentence to this effect.

[9] *Ibid.*, p. 26.

economy is provided with an amount of capital (M) which is enough to employ the whole of the labourforce (N). Where M is set too low and thus this assumption is not fulfilled, full employment is unfeasible. Unemployment which I have called Marxian unemployment elsewhere will appear.[10] In this case capital M will first be accumulated until full employment becomes feasible; the thesis will then become valid and applicable. Thus, after a preliminary period during which a sufficient amount of capital is prepared, the full employment of labour will be realized and maintained under Say's law. Throughout the present and following chapters, wherever the thesis is discussed, it is assumed, though I do not explicitly say so, that M and N are given such that they satisfy the qualification for feasibility of full employment.

3 Ricardo is well known as a strong believer in Say's law of markets. He referred to J. B. Say's *Traité d'Economie Politique* in the preface to his *Principles* and in a footnote he stated that: 'Chap. XV, part i "Des Débouchés", contains, in particular, some very important principles, which I believe were first explained by this distinguished writer.' Ricardo based the most important chapter in the whole of the *Principles*, that is on the 'Effects of Accumulation on Profits and Interest', on Say's law of markets, which he endorsed. Ricardo wrote:

> M. Say has, however, most satisfactorily shewn, that there is no amount of capital which may not be employed in a country, because demand is only limited by production. No man produces, but with a view to consume or sell, and he never sells, but with an intention to purchase some other commodity, which may be immediately useful to him, or which may contribute to future production. By producing, then, he necessarily becomes either the consumer of his own goods, or the purchaser and consumer of the goods of some other person. (p. 290)

> If ten thousand pounds were given to a man having 100,000*l*. per annum, he would not lock it up in a chest, but would either increase his expenses by 10,000*l*.; employ it himself productively, or lend it to some other person for that purpose; in either case, demand would be increased, although it would be for different objects. (p. 291)

> Too much of a particular commodity may be produced, of which

[10] M. Morishima, *The Economics of Industrial Society*, Cambridge University Press, 1984, pp. 188–97.

there may be such a glut in the market, as not to repay the capital
expended on it; but this cannot be the case with respect to all
commodities . . . (p. 292)

It is evident from these quotations that Ricardo saw Say's law
from the viewpoint of aggregate supply and demand $(Y \equiv C + I)$.
As has been discussed, it can also be seen from the point of view of
savings and investment $(S \equiv I)$. To do so we need to analyse the
social structure of the Ricardian economy and to identify the savers
and investors. For this purpose it should first be noted that Ricardo's
society consists of workers, capitalists and landlords. Depending on
the context, capitalists are also frequently referred to as farmers and
manufacturers, so that capitalists are entrepreneurs. The produce of
society is distributed between these three groups in the form of wages,
profits and rents, respectively. People may be divided into the
productive class – those who reproduce another value – and the
unproductive class – those who do not reproduce. One part of the
actual production is distributed under the name of profit to the
productive class, while the other is handed over under the name of
rent to the unproductive class.

Ricardo, therefore, regarded capitalists as the bearers of
reproduction, while the landowners' income, rent, was spent by them
for the purchase of necessities and luxuries and not used for the
long-term purpose of capital accumulation. Using this interpretation,
it is possible to take the view that in most of his theory of
accumulation Ricardo assumed capitalists to have a high propensity
to save, while workers and also landlords to have a propensity to
save which, if not zero, was at most negligible.[11] (Workers could
not save because of the low level of their wage rates; whereas
although the rate of rent was high and their income considerable,
landlords squandered all on luxuries.) Below, we shall consider the
model based on this kind of assumption, the Simple Model.

In the Simple Model capitalists and entrepreneurs (farmers and
manufacturers) are identical, and saving is carried out only by
capitalists, who are at the same time, as entrepreneurs, the investors.
Where savers and investors are one and the same there is no
difference between aggregate savings and investment and for that

---

[11] This is the interpretation reached by Pasinetti, *Growth and Income Distribution*,
Cambridge University Press, 1974, p. 6. See also S. Hollander, *The Economics of
David Ricardo*, Heinemann, 1979, p. 324 ff.

reason I is identically equal to S.[12] However, Ricardo did not confine himself to the Simple Model. In a rather broader sense he did, in fact, believe that all classes of society possess the capacity to save. Landlords in particular are clearly potential savers. Capitalist rentiers, whom he described as 'the monied class', are also regular savers; even workers are accepted as able to save for the first time in a footnote in the third edition of the *Principles*.[13]

When people other than capitalists are able to save, they will find no shortage of willing borrowers since: 'There is perhaps no manufacturer, however rich, who limits his business to the extent that his own funds alone will allow; he has always some portion of this floating capital ...' (p. 89). This must be one of the considerations that led him to conclude, in a later chapter of the *Principles*, that: 'It follows then from these admissions that there is no limit to demand – no limit to the employment of capital while it yields any profit ...' (p. 296). The capitalist, in fact, whose investment exceeds his own savings will finance the excessive part of investment by borrowing money from the non-capitalist savers. In this way, savings made by non-capitalist monied men are transferred to the hands of the capitalists. A limit to aggregate investment is thus set by the savings gathered in the capitalists' (i.e. the entrepreneurs') hands. The entire non-capitalist savings are mobilized for investment, and this together with the savings made by the capitalists sets the limit to aggregate investment; that is, $S \geqq I$.[14]

[12] In order to reach this conclusion it is necessary for us to assume that farmers and manufacturers regularly invest exactly the amount that they themselves have saved. As Marx emphasized, however, such a thing is likely to be technically impossible, if the gradual accumulation of large sums is required prior to the purchase of a particular kind of machine. Furthermore, an appropriate time for investment will be selected. If it is predicted that a wait of several months will bring a considerable drop in the price of the good in which the investment is being made, then investment is likely to be postponed. For this reason, even in Ricardo's model where saver and investor are one and the same, there will be disparity between investment and savings. It must therefore be acknowledged that even in this kind of model Say's law will only operate where investment projects are divisible so that savings are immediately invested. This assumption may have some plausibility as long as investment mainly takes the form of a wage fund, but it is unacceptable where fixed capital is significant.

[13] Ricardo, *Principles*, p. 89, pp. 347–8 and p. 348n.

[14] As is noted by Ricardo, this assumes that the rate of profit is positive; there would be no investment if no industry earned positive profits. Moreover, the rate of interest for borrowing money from non-capitalists would carry out the investment financed by the non-capitalist savings.

On the other hand, as has been stated, Ricardo assumed no shortage of will. He wrote, in a latter to Malthus: 'We agree ... that the effectual demand consists of two elements, the *power* and the *will* to purchase, but I think the will is very seldom wanting when the power exists, – for the desire of accumulation will occasion demand just as a desire to consume, it will only change the objects on which the demand will exercise itself.'[15] If the power to purchase in this sentence is interpreted as Y, and the will to purchase construed as corresponding to $C + I$, then, by the assumption that as long as the power exists the will always exist too, we obtain $Y \leq C + I$, i.e. $S \leq I$. This together with $S \geq I$ shown above, implies $S \equiv I$. By assuming Say's law Ricardo ruled out the problems of under-investment and underconsumption which later became the main concerns of Keynes.

4 Unless Say's law is fulfilled, that is, unless investment I is flexibly adjusted to savings, there exists generally no full-employment-full-capacity equilibrium. This is seen to be true in the one-product-two-factor economy, by using the familiar 'income determination diagram' in the following manner. Where Say's law holds, the $C + I$ curve of the diagram coincides with its 45° line. Consequently, any point of the line can be an equilibrium. This was expressed by Keynes as: there is no obstacle to full employment. Under the law, where full employment actually prevails in the factor markets, the point Y_F on the line, which corresponds to the $Y = F(N_D, K_D)$ at $N_D = N$ and $K_D = K$, is singled out as the actual equilibrium point. On the other hand, where Say's law does not hold, Y_F does not in general coincide with the point of intersection of the $C + I$ curve and the 45° line. Thus Say's law is necessary and sufficient for the full employment thesis.

In this section and the following, it will be seen that the same is true for a model of general equilibrium of capital formation which involves savings and investment. We assume, for the sake of simplicity, a miniature model of a barter economy consisting of one consumption good industry (signified by subscript c) and one capital good industry (subscript k). It is also assumed that no land is used for production in either industry. The production functions of the

---

[15] D. Ricardo, *Letters, The Works and Correspondence of D. Ricardo*, Vol. VI, ed. by P. Sraffa, Cambridge University Press, 1952, p. 133, his italics.

two industries are written as:

$$x_c = F_c(l_c, k_c), \tag{3}$$

$$x_k = F_k(l_k, k_k), \tag{4}$$

respectively, where x stands for output, l for employment of labour and k for employment of capital. Let p_c and p_k be the prices of consumption and capital goods, w the wage rate and q the net returns to capital. The profits π_c and π_k are given as:

$$\pi_c = p_c x_c - \delta p_k k_c - w l_c - q k_c, \tag{5}$$

$$\pi_k = p_k x_k - \delta p_k k_k - w l_k - q k_k, \tag{6}$$

where δ is the rate of depreciation of capital. The variables x_c, k_c, l_c are determined as functions of p_c, p_k, w and q so as to maximize π_c subject to (3). Similarly, x_k, k_k, l_k are functions of p_k, w, q, which maximizes π_k subject to (4).

Let N be the existing amount of labour in the economy and d_c the quantity of consumption goods demanded by workers. After subtracting the amount of money spent for consumption from the workers' income, the remainder is saved in the form of a bond; we thus have the workers' budget equation,

$$wN = p_c d_c + D_B, \tag{7}$$

where D_B is the demand for the bond. Let r be the interest rate of the bond; d_c will obviously be a function of w, p_c and r. On the other hand, the total income of entrepreneurs and capitalists amounts to $\pi_c + \pi_k + q(k_c + k_k)$. Assuming that their personal consumption is negligible, they will buy capital goods of the amount d_k by issuing bonds if their income falls short of the necessary expenditure, $p_k d_k$; hence,

$$p_k d_k - (\pi_c + \pi_k) - q(k_c + k_k) = S_B, \tag{8}$$

where S_B represents the amount of bonds sold. Subtracting (8) from (7) and taking (5) and (6) into account, we can obtain Walras' identity:

$$(D_B - S_B) + w(l_c + l_k - N) \equiv Y - p_c d_c - p_k d_k, \tag{9}$$

where $Y = p_c x_c - \delta p_k k_c + p_k x_k - \delta p_k k_k$. In view of the previous notation of substituting D_L for $w(l_c + l_k)$, S_L for wN, C for $p_c d_c$ and I for $p_k d_k$, it can be easily found that Walras' two laws (2) and (9) are equivalent. (Note that we now assume that money is absent in (2), so that $D_M = S_M = 0$. Also the bond is absent in the past.)

Then we have five equilibrium conditions; the first is for the consumption good,

$$x_c(p_c, p_k, w, q) = d_c(p_c, w, r) \qquad (10)$$

which states, of course, that the supply of the consumption good is equal to its demand; the second for the capital good,

$$x_k(p_k, w, q) = \delta[k_c(p_c, p_k, w, q) + k_k(p_k, w, q)] + d_k, \qquad (11)$$

which states that the output of capital good equals gross investment; the third for labour,

$$N = l_c(p_c, p_k, w, q) + l_k(p_k, w, q), \qquad (12)$$

which implies full employment; the fourth for the use of the capital good,

$$M = k_c(p_c, p_k, w, q) + k_k(p_k, w, q), \qquad (13)$$

where M represents the total amount of capital goods available in the economy; the fifth condition is the supply–demand equation for the bond,

$$S_B = D_B. \qquad (14)$$

In addition to these, the condition,

$$f(q/p_k, d_k) = r, \qquad (15)$$

has to be fulfilled in the state of equilibrium, as f represents the curve which Keynes called the schedule of marginal efficiency of capital. This is the expected rate of the net income accrued from using one unit of capital good for production, so that it depends on its current rate, q/p_k, as well as the amount of capital good to be invested, d_k. Denying Say's law, Keynes assumed that marginal efficiency is a diminishing function of the amount of investment d_k, while the schedule f shifts upwards when the current rate, q/p_k increases. Finally, the consumption good is taken as the numeraire; prices and the wage rate are all normalized such that $p_c = 1$.

5 To examine whether the system of equilibrium conditions (10)–(15) has a solution, let us first investigate under what condition Say's law would prevail. It is easy to answer this question, because, where the marginal efficiency of capital f does not diminish even though the gross investment d_k is increased, f is independent of d_k,

so that there is no condition in the system which restricts d_k of the equation (11). Investment is perfectly flexible, so that (11) is certainly realized. This implies Say's law.

In this case the general equilibrium will be established in the following way. First, omitting d_k from the left-hand side of (15), we may rewrite it in the form:

$$f(q/p_k) = r. \tag{15'}$$

This, together with (10), (12) and (13), forms a four-equation system which has four variables, p_k, w, q and r. (Of course p_c is set at 1 by the normalization.) Therefore, they will be determined. Once p_k, w, q are given, output of the capital good x_k is also given, so that equation (11) has only one variable d_k which is flexibly adjusted to $x_k - \delta M$. Then we have all the five equilibrium conditions except (14). However, this remaining condition for the bond market is necessarily satisfied, by virtue of the Walras' law (9), whenever all the other equilibrium conditions are fulfilled.

What will happen if Say's law is rejected and (15) is restored in place of (15')? The system has five independent equations due to eliminating (14) by Walras' law, and five unknowns, p_k, w, q, r and d_k. This might enable us to conclude that the system has a general equilibrium. For this to be true, however, some preconditions must be satisfied, otherwise, there will not be a general equilibrium solution, and some of the equilibrium conditions will have to be violated. This is the problem of overdeterminacy, peculiar to the world of anti-Say's law.

This is the most important proposition which general equilibrium theorists after Keynes must accept. But, unfortunately, they have so far entirely, or almost entirely, neglected it. I have proposed it in my *Walras' Economics*,[16] but it has not attracted the attention of economists, except for a few such as Negishi, Filippi and Saltari, who have all rejected it.[17] My proposition was unsatisfactory (it

[16] See pp. 121–2 of the book.
[17] T. Negishi, 'M. Morishima, *Walras' Economics*' (in Japanese), *Keizai Kenkyu*, 1980; F. Filippi, 'Morishima's Interpretation of Keynes: Some Comments and Criticism', *Zeitschrift für Nationalökonomie*, 1980; E. Saltari, 'Marginal Notes on a Recent Book by Morishima', *Economic Notes*, Monte dei Paschi di Siena, 1980. Another example is Hahn's recent work on 'The neo-Ricardians' in his *Equilibrium and Macroeconomics*, Blackwell, 1984, pp. 353–84. In this paper, he examines the solvability of the 'Ricardo–Sraffa' model. However, he seems to assume Say's law implicitly. Otherwise, he would confront the problem of 'overdeterminacy' at some stage in his argument.

was too strong), though the message was clear, and I shall correct it in the next section. The proposition does hold, not only for Walras' own rather peculiar general equilibrium system, but also for more usual systems, such as the present one, which most neoclassical economists would accept.

To show that the system (10)–(15) may have no solution, we assume that the workers have no ability to save. Then in (7) D_B is identically zero, and, therefore, d_c is independent of the rate of interest r. Three equations (10), (12) and (13) now contain only three variables p_k, w, q, so that they are determined, say, at p_k^0, w^0, q^0. Substituting these values into the left-hand side of (11), we obtain the full-employment–full-capacity equilibrium value of output of the capital good; that is, $x_k(p_k^0, w^0, q^0)$. On the other hand, r is required to be positive. Then, where we assume that the marginal efficiency of capital diminishes rapidly when the amount of investment d_k is increased, we obtain that d_k satisfying (15) with $p_k = p_k^0$ and $q = q^0$ is very small, however low the rate of interest r may be. Thus we have

$$x_k(p_k^0, w^0, q^0) > d_k(p_k^0, q^0, r) + \delta M,$$

for all possible positive values of r. The equilibrium condition (11) will never be established; we will always have underinvestment. The system of equilibrium conditions (10)–(15) has no set of solutions in the case of f diminishing sharply with respect to d_k. This is completely opposite to the case of Say's law in which f is independent of d_k.

The same result is obtained even if the workers' savings are positive but sufficiently small. The demand for consumption good d_c is then not influenced much by r. Taking r as a parameter, the system (10), (12), (13) may be solved with respect to p_k, w, q; solutions are written as $p_k(r), w(r), q(r)$. As r has not much influence on d_c of (10), these solutions are not much influenced by r, so that $x_k(p_k(r), w(r), q(r))$ is more or less rigid. Therefore, if we additionally assume a rapid decline of the marginal efficiency of capital with respect to d_k, we obtain a similar inequality to the one above:

$$x_k(p_k(r), w(r), q(r)) > d_k(p_k(r), q(r), r) + \delta M,$$

because the left-hand side is more or less rigid, while d_k on the right-hand side is very low for all values of $r > 0$. Thus we always have a lack of effective demand in the capital good market. This shows the impossibility of the full-employment–full-capacity equilibrium.

6 Let us now be concerned with correcting the 'overdeterminacy' thesis on which I insisted in *Walras's Economics*. In the final part of Chapter 7 of the volume, I introduced the marginal efficiency equation (15) (there numbered as (10′)), not as a replacement of, but as an addition to the equation implying equality between the rate of net income from using the capital good in production and the income rate from holding the bond. As this last equals the rate of interest, the equation is written as:

$$q/p_k = r, \tag{15′}$$

which is numbered (10) in the book. I insisted that the system consisting of all of Walras' equilibrium equations (including (15′) above) would yield no solution if the marginal efficiency condition (15) were additionally imposed. Thus, because (15) defined an investment function, I concluded that the introduction of an investment function would give rise to overdeterminacy, and the full-employment–full-capacity equilibrium would generally be impossible.

As I have done in the previous section, I now discard (15′) and replace it with (15). It is then shown that Walras' own system has no solution, provided that the following two conditions are fulfilled: (a) the workers' savings are negligible, so that their demand for the consumption good is almost independent of the rate of interest, and (b) the economy is very depressed and, hence, the investment demand d_k generated by the marginal efficiency condition (15) is very low for all values of the interest rate. It has already been seen in the previous section that the overdeterminacy thesis is true for the usual, now conventional, equilbrium system. It can be shown, as we see below, that this is also true for Walras' own model, though it significantly differs from the conventional one.

Suppose now, as Walras did in his original model, that the technology is given. Then we are provided with a set of constant input coefficients by which consumption and capital goods are connected. We have two sets of equations: (I) the price–cost equations for consumption and capital goods and (II) the supply–demand equations for labour and the productive services of the capital good. The latter equations correspond to (12) and (13) above. However, l_c, l_k, k_c, and k_k of (12) and (13) must be replaced by the products of given input coefficients and the respective outputs, x_c and x_k. As $x_c = d_c$ and the latter only depends on p_c and w, because of the assumption (a) above, we now find that the ultimate variables of the new equations (II) are x_k, p_c and w. In view of $p_c = 1$ due to the normalization, the two equations of (II) determine x_k, w, say at x_k^0, w^0, respectively.

On the other hand, the price–cost equations, which imply entrepreneurial excess profits π_c and π_k being zero in the state of equilibrium, give p_c and p_k as linear functions of w and q (i.e. the sums of w and q multiplied by their respective input coefficients). Since $p_c = 1$, these determine p_k and q. Thus we obtain p_k^0, q^0 at w^0. Substituting these into (15), we find that d_k is given as $d_k(q^0/p_k^0, r)$. Now this is compared with $x_k^0 - \delta M$. Bearing the assumption (b) in mind, we may conclude that in a time of depression d_k does not reach the net amount of the capital good purchased, $x_k^0 - \delta M$, because d_k is small however low r may be.

This result is still valid even though the assumption (a) is relaxed in the right way. Substituting $x_c = d_c$, which is now a function of p_c, w and r, into the supply–demand equations for labour and capital services, we find that they contain three unknowns x_k, w and r, so that, taking r as a parameter, we obtain $x_k(r)$ and $w(r)$. Since the effect of r upon d_c is assumed to be very small, x_k and w are almost constant even though there is a significant change in r. On the other hand we find that p_k and q depend on $w(r)$; thus we obtain $p_k(r)$ and $q(r)$, which in turn give us $d_k(q(r)/p_k(r), r)$. As a change in $w(r)$ is confined in a small range, $p_k(r)$ and $q(r)$ are also fairly constant. Therefore, in depressive circumstances, it is not only possible but also highly likely that we have

$$x_k(r) > d_k(q(r)/p_k(r), r) + \delta M \qquad \text{for all } r.$$

Thus a Walrasian equilibrium is not necessarily realized where Say's law does not prevail. In spite of this possibility, the critics of my *Walras' Economics* such as Negishi, Filippi and Saltari all insist that the replacement of Walras' condition (15′) by Keynes' marginal efficiency condition (15) does not affect the number of equations nor the number of unknowns at all, and that an investment function is implicitly defined by (15). Thus they have an economy in which anti-Say's law prevails with an independent investment function – investment that is independent of savings. They conclude that the economy has a general equilibrium solution because the system contains the same number of independent equations as unknowns. It has nevertheless been shown above that their conclusion is disproved by a counterexample to the effect that the full-employment–full-capacity general equilibrium is impossible when the prospects of investment are depressive. It is indeed very logical that Walras, who wanted to assume the existence of general equilibrium, was led to assume Say's law by replacing (15) with (15′). But it is an unfortunate mistake that, by doing so, he himself closed the door to Keynes. This judgement is also applicable to Ricardo who was fascinated by the *loi des débouchés* but could not entirely see the relationship between unemployment and the law.

If there is a shortage of demand for the capital good, its supply x_k is adjusted, in Walras' system, to the demand $d_k(q(r)/p_k(r), r) + \delta M$. Then the demand for labour and capital of the capital good industry, l_k and k_k, will decrease proportionately, no substitution between labour and capital being possible as the technique is given. Also, a decrease in x_k will create a decrease in x_c by the multiplier effect which, in turn, produces a decrease in the demand for labour and capital for the consumption good industry. In this way we will have unemployment of both labour and capital in Walras' system as soon as Say's law is removed.

We have so far assumed that there is one consumption good, one capital good and no land. But this simplification is not essential for the above argument of 'overdeterminacy'. Of course, Walras assumed many consumption goods, many capital goods and various kinds of land. Even in such economies, the above argument *mutatis mutandis* holds. We may now follow Keynes in concluding that there are two kinds of economics, one accepting Say's law (Ricardo, Walras and many other classical and neoclassical economists) and the other denying it (Sismondi, Malthus, Keynes etc.), in the same way as we have, in geometry, Euclidean and non-Euclidean.

7 Say's law discussed above accords with its definition by Keynes. To the modern reader, however, the law would be more familiar if given the names of Lange and Patinkin. They define it as the 'total demand for commodities (exclusion of money) is *identically* equal to their total supply',[18] where 'commodities' includes not only

---

[18] Lange, 'Say's Law', p. 52, his italics.

consumption and capital goods, but also primary factors of production and the bond. Thus Lange and Patinkin extend the list of commodities which Keynes confined to the physical goods produced (consumption and capital goods) so as to include a bond as well as land and labour. The total demand for and supply of commodities are then given by

$$D_L + D_U + D_I + D_C + D_B \quad \text{and} \quad S_L + S_I + S_C + S_B,$$

respectively. Where supply creates its own demand, they are identically equal to each other. This means $D_M \equiv S_M$ because of Walras's law (1); hence, by (2), it can be said that Say's law prevails if and only if the identity,

$$(Y - C - I) + (S_L - D_L) + (S_B - D_B) \equiv 0, \tag{16}$$

holds. In this system Lange and Patinkin take money as the numeraire, but with the introduction of money the whole system of equations (3)–(15) does not change except for (7) and (8); D_M and S_M must be added on the right-hand sides of (7) and (8), respectively. Lange and Patinkin assume that, with arbitrarily given p_c, six equilibrium conditions (10)–(15), five of which are independent, determine five variables, that is, three relative prices p_k/p_c, w/p_c, q/p_c, one investment variable d_k and the rate of interest r.[19] In making this assumption they neglect the possibility that (10)–(15) may have no solution. This implies that they implicitly assume Say's law in Keynes' sense; that is to say, the demand for the capital good d_k is always available in the economy in an amount which is enough to establish the full employment of the primary factors of production.

The arbitrarily fixed price of the consumption good, p_c, should equate the demand for money to its supply, if it, together with p_k, w, q determined above, constitutes general equilibrium prices. However, under Say's law in the Lange–Patinkin sense (the L–P–Say's law), it should be so however arbitrarily p_c may be fixed, because $D_M \equiv S_M$; therefore, the level of prices is left undetermined. If we make an additional assumption that d_c is homogenous of degree zero in w and p_c,[20] then it can be shown that a change in p_c will not give rise to any change in relative prices p_k/p_c, w/p_c, q/p_c. Thus, after Lange and Patinkin, it has become common knowledge among economists

---

[19] This assumption is valid where Say's law in Keynes' sense (the K–Say's law) prevails.

[20] Note that x_c, x_k, l_c, l_k, k_c and k_k are all homogenous of degree zero in prices.

that, if the L–P–Say's law prevails, relative prices are determined, while the absolute level of prices is completely undetermined. Thus Lange concludes: 'Money is neutral. . . . [I]t is merely a "veil" which can be removed and relative prices can be studied as if the system were based on barter.'[21] 'Say's law precludes any monetary theory. The theory of money must, therefore, start with a rejection of Say's law.'[22]

This common knowledge must be reexamined for the case where Say's law in Keynes' sense (the K–Say's law) does not hold. In this case equations (10)–(15) have no solution, provided that assumptions (a) and (b) of Section 6 are satisfied. It is noted that (a) implies that d_c is homogenous of degree zero in prices w and p_c. Then as x_c, x_k, l_c, l_k, k_c, k_k, d_k and d_c are all homogenous of degree zero in prices, it can be shown that, however radically the price level may be adjusted, we have no price set which establishes equations (10)–(15) simultaneously. In fact, in the manner of Section 6 we can show that those prices, p_k, w, q, with an arbitrary p_c, which satisfy (10), (12), (13) will violate (11), because of (a) and, especially, (b). And we can also show that this holds true for any value of p_c, because of the homogeneity of the functions. Thus the condition of underinvestment cannot be altered by changing the price level, and this result is obtained regardless of whether the L–P–Say's law is satisfied or not.

This shows the irrelevance of the L–P–Say's law to Keynesian unemployment due to underinvestment. We may now summarize our argument in the following manner: (I) Where the K–Say's law prevails, there exists a full-employment–full-capacity equilibrium, as relative prices and the rate of interest are determined. In this case, however, if the L–P–Say's law is additionally assumed, money is neutral and the absolute level of prices is left undetermined. On the other hand, (II) where the K–Say's law does not hold, the impossibility of the full-employment–full-capacity equilibrium becomes possible and such circumstances cannot be altered for the better by adjusting the price level. Thus the L–P–Say's law has nothing to do with establishing the proposition (II).

In what sense is it true that Ricardo assumed Say's law? To answer this question it must be noticed, first, that there is no explicit investment function in his system, and secondly, that throughout

[21] Lange, 'Say's Law', p. 64.
[22] Ibid., p. 66.

the *Principles*, except for Chapter XXXI on machinery which was hastily and carelessly added in the third edition,[23] it is difficult to find a chapter or even passages which discuss the unemployment of labour. This means, he accepted that investment is determined by savings and that there is no difficulty in realizing full employment; this suggests that he implicitly accepted the K–Say's law. On the other hand, concerning money, he was a quantity theorist, believing that the price of money or its reciprocal, the price level, is determined by the quantity of money. In fact, he wrote, 'A circulation can never be so abundant as to overflow; for by diminishing its value, in the same proportion you will increase its quantity, and by increasing its value, diminish its quantity' (p. 352).[24]

Similarly, as will be discussed in a later chapter, Walras, as an elaborator of Ricardo's economics, assumed K–Say's law by regarding the demands for capital goods $k, k', \ldots$ as variables which flexibly adjust themselves to aggregate savings. Also, he considered that the price level is determined by the money equation. The idea of L–P–Say's law is, we must say, very foreign to Walras who derived the law of the quantity theory of money from his monetary equilibrium equation.[25] We may now conclude that if we all agree to say that Ricardo and his followers accepted Say's law, it was not the Say's law as defined by Lange and Patinkin which is now familiar among contemporary economists, but the rather antiquated version of Keynes.

[23] See Chapter VII above.
[24] He also wrote: 'Mr. Buchanan evidently thinks that the whole currency must, necessarily, be brought down to the level of the value of the debased pieces; but, surely, by a diminution of the quantity of the currency, the whole that remains can be elevated to the value of the best pieces.'
[25] Walras, *Elements*, p. 366.

8 Machinery

1 Ricardo added a final chapter on the effects of the introduction of machines to the third edition of the *Principles*. 'On Machinery' is, in essence, related to Schumpeter's problem of innovation, though Ricardo did not use this term. He wrote:

> He, indeed, who made the discovery of the machine, or who first usefully applied it, would enjoy an additional advantage, by making great profits for a time; but, in proportion as the machine came into general use, the price of the commodity produce, would, from the effects of competition, sink to its cost of production, when the capitalist would get the same money profits as before, and he would only participate in the general advantage, as consumer, by being enabled, with the same money revenue, to command an additional quantity of comforts and enjoyments. (p. 387)

Walras gave a more subtle description of the same effects:

> Thus, we pass from the static to the dynamic state. For this purpose, we shall now suppose that the annual production and consumption, which we had hitherto represented as a constant magnitude for every moment of the year under consideration, change from instant to instant along with the basic data of the problem.... Such is the continuous market, which is perpetually tending towards equilibrium without ever actually attaining it, because the market has no other way of approaching equilibrium except by grouping, and, before the goal is reached, it has to renew its efforts and start over again, all the basic data of the problem, e.g. the initial quantities possessed, the utilities of goods and services, the technical coefficients, the excess of income over consumption, the working capital requirements, etc., having changed in the meantime. (Walras, *Elements*, p. 380)

> The diversion of productive services from enterprises that are losing money to profitable enterprises takes place in various ways, the most important being through credit operations, but at best these ways are slow. It can happen and frequently does happen in the

real world, that under some circumstances a selling price will remain for long periods of time above cost of production and continue to rise in spite of increases in output, while under other circumstances, a fall in price, following upon this rise, will suddenly bring the selling price below cost of production and force entrepreneurs to reverse their production policies. (*Ibid.*, pp. 380–1)

Of course, although Schumpeter's innovation is a concept which is much wider than an introduction of new machines (which is discussed by Ricardo) or an exogenous change in technological coefficients and the working capital requirements (mentioned above by Walras), the above passages might have suggested to Schumpeter the idea of the theory of innovations and credit creation, as I discuss in Chapter 9 below. This shows not only that his theory is not entirely new and can be traced back to Walras, and further to Marx and Ricardo, but also how close Ricardo, Marx and Walras were to each other. As a matter of fact, though Walras himself did not write explicitly, it is indeed easy for a contemporary economic theorist to write a Walrasian chapter on machinery on the basis of his exposition in the *Elements* (pp. 380–3). By applying a summary form of his definition of 'technical progress' (p. 383), as distinct from 'economic progress', to his propagation analysis of exogenous shocks, hinted at in the last two passages above, we obtain a Walrasian view of machinery which is very similar to the first passage from Ricardo.

In the first and second editions of the *Principles* Ricardo thought that 'an application of machinery to any branch of production, as should have the effect of saving labour, was a general good' (p. 386), in other words, capitalists, landowners and workers would all be better off if machines were employed; they would all benefit from the general cheapness of commodities resulting from the use of machines. In the third edition, however, he seemed convinced that the substitution of machines for labour would create unemployment and was, therefore, 'very injurious to the interests of the class of labourers' (p. 388); that is to say, the use of machinery does not make the economy Pareto superior.

2 In examining this new proposition, it must first be noted that Ricardo assumed Say's law in the machinery chapter of the third

edition as well as in all the other chapters. In fact, he stated:

> If, by improved machinery, with the employment of the same
> quantity of labour, the quantity of stockings could be quadrupled,
> and the demand for stockings were only doubled, some labourers
> would necessarily be discharged from the stocking trade; but as
> the capital which employed them was still in being, and as it was
> the interest of those who had it to employ it productively, . . . it
> would be employed on the production of some other commodity,
> useful to the society, for which there could not fail to be a demand.
> (p. 387)

This is nothing else but Say's law, which he believed in, as he himself
wrote:

> for *I was, and am*, deeply impressed with the truth of the
> observation of Adam Smith, that 'the desire for food is limited in
> every man, by the narrow capacity of the human stomach, but the
> desire of the conveniences, and ornaments of building, dress,
> equipage and household furniture, seems to have no limit or certain
> boundary'. (p. 387, my italics)

Secondly, Ricardo did not only consider machines in this final
chapter but also in all the others, as when he referred to fixed capital,
he included machines, as well as other capital goods such as
implements, tools and buildings. As he said that the values of gold
and silver 'are subject also to fluctuation, from improvements in the
skill and machinery with which the mines may be worked' (p. 14),
or 'if the shoes and clothing of the labourer, could, by improvements
in machinery, be produced by one fourth of the labour now necessary
to their production, they would probably fall 75 per cent' (p. 16),
Ricardo obviously allowed for machines in his theory of value. There
is no doubt about this once one has read the first chapter.

If so, Ricardo should have deduced similar, consistent results in
both the machinery chapter and the rest of the volume. Nevertheless
he concluded in the former that an introduction of labour saving
machines would create unemployment of labour, while he maintained full employment throughout the latter. This inconsistency
was pointed out by J. R. McCulloch and T. R. Malthus.[1] The present
chapter is a fresh revisit to this point, in which I follow Ricardo in

[1] See *The Works and Correspondence of David Ricardo*, ed. P. Sraffa, Cambridge
University Press (1951–73), Vol. VIII, pp. 381–2 and Vol. IX, pp. 10–11.

adopting a numerical approach. However, since his formulas of accounting are a bit confusing, I shall begin with correcting his numerical example and explain why and where corrections have been made.

First, he imagines a capitalist who carries on the joint business of producing food (corn) and manufactured necessaries, using capital of £20,000, part of which is invested in fixed capital – £7,000, the remainder being employed as circulating capital for the support of labour – £13,000. Profits are 10 per cent, so that the total value of output including profits amounts to £22,000. Thus:

gross produce	fixed capital cost	circulating capital cost	profits
£22,000 =	£7,000 +	£13,000	+ £2,000

The two capital costs are called constant and variable capitals, respectively, if Marx's terminology is used. It is noted that land is implicitly assumed to be abundant, so that it yields no rent. Moreover, Ricardo calculated the gross produce at £15,000, excluding the fixed capital cost of £7,000. The difference between the two gross products, i.e. £22,000 versus £15,000, is not a matter of definition, but arises from incorrect methods of accounting. There exists the produce worth £22,000, a part of which, worth £13,000, is bought by the worker of that business, another part worth £2,000 is bought by the capitalist himself and the remaining part (£7,000) by the workers and capitalists of the industry producing fixed capital goods.

Next, Ricardo supposed that 'the following year the capitalist employs half his men in constructing a machine, and the other half in producing food and necessaries' (p. 389). Ricardo did not say anything about the distribution of fixed capital between the food–necessaries sector (sector I) and the machine sector (sector II). But I simply assume that the capital is divided equally between them. (This implies that the fixed/circulating capital ratio, which is often called the organic composition of capital by Marxist economists, is equal between the two sectors, and therefore, by virtue of the Ricardo–Marx theorem discussed in Chapter 1 above, there is no discrepancy between prices and values; prices are thus proportional to values. This is, however, not essential for the following argument.) Then the following two accounting equations hold for sectors I and

II, respectively:

	gross produce	fixed capital	circulating capital	profits	
Sector I:	£11,000 =	£3,500 +	£6,500	+ £1,000	(1)
Sector II:	£11,000 =	£3,500 +	£6,500	+ £1,000	(2)

For these too, Ricardo stated that, neglecting the fixed capital used, the gross output of the food–necessaries sector is £7,500 (that is the sum of the value of circulating capital, £6,500, and profits, £1,000), and similarly that of the machine sector is £7,500. But the total amount of food and necessaries produced should be £11,000, instead of his £7,500, and that part of the produce which corresponds to the fixed capital cost of £3,500 would be sold to the workers and capitalists of the machine sector. In the same way, the output of the machine sector should be valued at £11,000. After deducting the total profits (£2,000) for the capitalists' consumption from the gross output of food and necessaries, there would remain £9,000 of circulating capital (rather than Ricardo's £5,500[2]), with which the subsequent operations could be carried out. The wage fund would then be reduced from £13,000 to £9,000 (rather than his £5,500) and, consequently, the labour which was employed before would become redundant by £4,000 (= £13,000 − £9,000).[3] Thus the employment of labour is decreased because in the period in which half the workers employed were used for the production of machines, the production of food and necessaries was halved, which resulted in a reduction of the wage fund and therefore the capitalists can only employ a smaller number of workers.

Ricardo did not notice that this conclusion would clearly conflict with his basic assumption of Say's law. As I explained at the beginning of this section, Ricardo assumed the law throughout the book including the chapter on machinery; also, he assumed that machines existed in the preceding chapters. Thus there is no substantial structural change between the model of the original part of the book and that of the newly added chapter; if there is no unemployment in the former, the workers should fully be employed in the latter too. This is especially true because Say's law implies that there is no obstacle to full employment. If so, where did Ricardo

[2] £5,500 = Ricardo gross income (£6,500 + £1,000) − profits (£2,000).
[3] The corresponding figure originally given by Ricardo is £7,500 = £13,000 − £5,500. See *Principles*, p. 389.

stray from the straight and narrow? Where did he admit an obstacle which would make Say's law unworkable, in spite of his superficial support of it, and resulted in a creation of unemployment?

3 Let us begin by pointing out that the state of affairs described by equations (1) and (2) is not an equilibrium. After supplying its own workers and capitalists with £7,500 worth of food and necessaries, sector I still has £3,500 (= £11,000 − £7,500) worth of food and necessaries to be supplied to the workers and capitalists of sector II. Since the demands from sector II amount to £7,500 (= £6,500 + £1,000 of equation (2)), there is (£4,000) of excess demand for food and necessaries (= £7,500 − £3,500). On the other hand, the demand for fixed capital for replacement from sector I is £3,500 and that from sector II is also £3,500, while the supply of machines is £11,000, so that there is an excess supply of machines amounting to £4,000. We have obtained this state of disequilibrium because Ricardo arbitrarily assumed that half the workers were employed in the production of machines. If this distribution of workers does not create an equilibrium, as is the case, the number of labourers working in the machine sector should be adjusted such that there is no excess demand or supply in the market for food and necessaries as well as in that for machines.

What then is the equilibrium distribution of the labourforce? This is the problem of Marx's scheme of reproduction. Since Ricardo's numerical example assumes that capitalists do not save at all, it is a scheme of 'simple' (stationary) reproduction, and the resulting equilibrium is static. Suppose now that total labour (worth £13,000) is distributed between sectors I and II in the ratio 68.2 per cent:31.8 per cent;[4] and that total fixed capital (£7,000) is distributed in the same proportions. Sector I uses £4,773 of fixed capital and £8,864 of circulating capital (for the employment of labour), the total capital used being £13,637, from which 10 per cent profits (£1,364) accrue. Consequently the total gross output of sector I amounts to £15,000. Similarly, sector II employs £2,227 of fixed capital and £4,136 of

---

[4] These figures are obtained in the following way. Let x be the proportion of the output of sector I in the total production and y that of sector II. Then the equilibrium condition for simple reproduction due to Marx, which is referred to below, is written as:

$$x£7,000 = y£13,000 + y£2,000,$$

from which we obtain $x = 68.2$ per cent and $y = 31.8$ per cent, because $y = 1 − x$.

circulating capital and yields profits of £637. Its gross output is £7,000. These are expressed by the following accounting equations in a scheme of simple reproduction:

	gross produce	fixed capital	circulating capital	profits	
Sector I:	£15,000 =	£4,773 +	£8,864	+ £1,364	(3)
Sector II:	£7,000 =	£2,227 +	£4,136	+ £637	(4)

On the right-hand side of these equations, the first terms represent the replacement demands for fixed capital by the two sectors; their sum gives the total demand for machines, because there is no new investment demand. Similarly, the sum of the second terms (£13,000) gives the total demand for circulating capital, while the sum of the third terms (£2,000) represents the total profits. As both workers and capitalists are assumed to spend their whole income on consumption, the total demand for food and necessaries from workers amounts to £15,000 (= £13,000 + £2,000). It is easily seen that the total demand for food and necessaries and that for machines are equal to their supplies (that is, their gross outputs), respectively. Moreover it is seen that fixed capital employed in sector I (£4,773) equals the sum of the circulating capital (£4,136) and the profits (£637) of sector II. This is nothing else but Marx's equilibrium condition of simple reproduction.

Thus, where the labourforce is distributed between the two sectors in the equilibrium proportions, 68.2 per cent:31.8 per cent, the demand for labour after the production of machines will be the same as before such an operation was commenced; thus, it does not cause unemployment. In Ricardo's example unemployment is generated because the labourforce is distributed between the two sectors in the wrong proportions, 50 per cent:50 per cent. There is, however, no reason why it should be so. Where there is an excess supply of one commodity, an excess demand arises from some other commodity. Outputs are then adjusted in order to remove excess demand and supply. When the state of equilibrium is finally brought about, the employment of labour will be as high as it was before, because Say's law is assumed.

4 Attention must be paid to the fact that in his numerical example Ricardo assumed that capitalists consume their whole income;

consequently, there are neither savings nor capital accumulation. The resulting equilibrium is the one of simple reproduction. But the same argument would still *mutatis mutandis* be applied to the economy where capitalists save a part or the whole of their income. We have, in this case, an equilibrium of 'extended' (expanding) reproduction, and the full employment of labour is established, as the demand for labour is adjusted such that it is equal to the supply of labour growing at a rate g determined exogenously.

Let us begin with explaining how an expanding equilibrium is obtained. Although it is possible to follow Marx's own algorithm for obtaining an equilibrium of extended reproduction, ours differs from it, because it is desirable to avoid his very peculiar, unnatural investment function.[5] Let g be 4 per cent. Denoting capitalists' propensity to save by s and their propensity to consume by c, we have $s + c = 1$. Let the total output be distributed between sectors I and II in the proportion, $x : y$, such that $x + y = 1$. The accounting equations, corresponding to (3) and (4), may then be written as:

$$\text{Sector I:} \quad x\pounds22{,}000 = x\pounds7{,}000 + x\pounds13{,}000 + xc\pounds2{,}000$$
$$+ xs\pounds2{,}000 \qquad (5)$$

$$\text{Sector II:} \quad y\pounds22{,}000 = y\pounds7{,}000 + y\pounds13{,}000 + yc\pounds2{,}000$$
$$+ ys\pounds2{,}000 \qquad (6)$$

The amount of output of sector I which remains after the part consumed by capitalists of sectors I and II is removed, is distributed among the workers of the two sectors, so that

$$x\pounds22{,}000 - xc\pounds2{,}000 - yc\pounds2{,}000$$
$$= x\pounds13{,}000(1 + h) + y\pounds13{,}000(1 + h'),$$

where h is the rate of growth of employment in sector I and h' in sector II. If full employment is to prevail, the sum of the increments of employment in the two sectors, $x\pounds13{,}000h + y\pounds13{,}000h'$, equals the increment of the supply of labour, $\pounds13{,}000g$. In view of $x + y = 1$, we have, from the above equation, the equation for sectoral balance,

$$22x = 13(1 + g) + 2c.$$

[5] See my *Marx's Economics*, p. 118.

Next, we additionally require the familiar growth equilibrium condition,

$$sr = g$$

which implies that the economy grows at a rate g equal to the product of the capitalists' propensity to save, s, and the rate of profits on capital, r.[6] This means that, where s and g are given exogenously, the rate of profits is determined such that it fulfils the above condition. We fix s and g at 0.4 and 0.04, respectively, so that the rate of profits takes on the value of 10 per cent, though Ricardo seemed to set it at that value rather arbitrarily. Obviously $c = 0.6$. Substituting these values into the equation for sectoral balance, we find $x = 0.669$ and therefore $y = 0.331$.[7] With these numerical values of x and y, the terms of equations (5) and (6) are seen to take on the following values:

	gross produce	fixed capital	circulating capital	profits	
Sector I:	£14,720 =	£4,683.6 +	£8,698.2 +	£1,338.2	(5')
Sector II:	£7,280 =	£2,316.4 +	£4,301.8 +	£661.8	(6')

where the term of profits of (5') is the sum of the last two terms of (5); the same is true for (6'). These are, needless to say, the cost accounting equations.

Let us finally turn to the supply–demand equations of the two products. First, the supply of sector I's produce (food and necessaries) is worth £14,720 in the market. The demand includes consumption made by capitalists of sector I (£802.9) and that of sector II (£397.1). It also includes workers' demands. As the employment of labour increases at the rate $g = 4$ per cent, wage payments (circulating capitals) are expanded to the amounts £9,046.1 and £4,473.9 in sectors I and II, respectively. They are fully spent on food and necessaries by the workers. It is easily seen that the total sum of the demands is equal to the supply. Thus,

$$£14,720 = £9,046.1 + £4,473.9 + £802.9 + £397.1. \qquad (7)$$

For machines, there is a supply of £7,280 which is compared with replacement demands for machines from sector I (£4,683.6) and

[6] See, for example, my *Equilibrium, Stability and Growth*, Oxford University Press, 1964, p. 151.

[7] More exactly, $x = 0.6690909$ and $y = 0.3309091$.

sector II (£2,316.4) and new investment demands from both sectors. This last provides newly employed workers with machines. Therefore, new investment demands are proportional to replacement investments with a proportionality factor which is equal to the rate of growth of employment, $g = 4$ per cent; these additional demands from sectors I and II are calculated at £187.3 and £92.7, respectively. We find that the total demand for machines is equal to their supply, that is

$$
\begin{array}{ccc}
\text{gross} & \text{replacement} & \text{new} \\
\text{produce} & \text{investment} & \text{investment}
\end{array}
$$
$$£7,280 = £4,683.6 + £2,316.4 + £187.3 + £92.7 \qquad (8)$$

Furthermore, we can show that savings equal investment. As sector I's demand for circulating capital is £9,046.1 and its replacement demand for the same capital is £8,698.2, their difference gives the sector's new investment in circulating capital which is £347.9. This, together with the sector's new investment in fixed capital which is worth £187.3, gives the total new investment made by sector I, which is calculated at £535.2 and equal to the savings made by the capitalists of sector I; similarly for sector II. Thus,

	Capitalists' savings	new investment in:	
		circulating capital	fixed capital
Sector I:	£535.3 =	£347.9	+ £187.3	(9)
Sector II:	£264.7 =	£172.1	+ £92.7	(10)

Four equations (7), (8), (9), (10) establish that the economy is in an equilibrium state of balanced growth, and $h = h' = g$. Since productive activity is growing at the same rate as the labourforce, full employment persists. Thus, contrary to Ricardo, we conclude that, *under Say's law*, the substitution of machinery for human labour is not injurious to the interests of the class of labourers, provided that machines are introduced appropriately. The appropriate magnitude of the machine sector relative to the food–necessaries sector is determined by Marx-like extended reproduction equations. In this sense, Ricardo's machinery chapter and Marx's reproduction schemes are closely related to each other and the latter may be regarded as an extension and an elaboration of the former.

5 Next, Ricardo was concerned with the case of mechanization

undertaken by manufacturers such as clothiers or cotton manufacturers, which resulted in a substitution between fixed and circulating capitals in favour of the former.

> All I wish to prove, is, that the discovery and use of machinery may be attended with a diminution of gross produce; and whenever that is the case, it will be injurious to the labouring class, as some of their number will be thrown out of employment, and population will become redundant, compared with the funds which are to employ it. (p. 390)

As in the previous case, he did not take Say's law into account in his proof and this fact seems responsible for his conclusion, even if his reasoning is correct. Under Say's law, however, the state of things is completely altered and the economy works very differently. Thus, we would still have the full employment of labour.

Let us suppose that those who mechanize their own production processes, like Ricardo's clothier and cotton manufacturer, belong to the food and necessaries producing sector (sector I). Suppose the proportion of fixed to circulating capital of sector I was, for example, 7/13 before the mechanization and is increased to 3 as the result of it. The same ratio of 7/13 also applies to sector II (producing machines), irrespective of the mechanization in sector I. Where the rate of profit is 10 per cent and wage funds of £13,000 are available, the stationary equilibrium to be established before mechanization is given by equations (3) and (4), while (1) and (2) are the accounting equations of the two sectors, with a total capital of £10,000 each. We assume that this is a full employment equilibrium, that is, there are workers whose full employment wages amount to £13,000. After the mechanization, however, the cost accounting equations will be written as:

	gross produce	fixed capital	circulating capital	profits	
Sector I:	£11,000 =	£7,500 +	£2,500	+ £1,000	(11)
Sector II:	£11,000 =	£3,500 +	£6,500	+ £1,000	(12)

It is noted that these two equations satisfy the conditions for the fixed/circulating ratio, 3 for sector I and 7/13 for II, and the rate of profits on the total capital is 10 per cent in both sectors. It is also seen that (11) and (12) fulfil Marx's condition for simple reproduction.

the fixed capital cost of sector I

= the circulating capital cost and the profits of sector II.

Hence (11) and (12) give a stationary equilibrium.

It is seen, however, that the total amount of circulating capital is only £9,000 (= £2,500 + £6,500) which is smaller than the total amount of available wage funds, £13,000. From this, we might be able to say, as Ricardo would have done, that there will be £4,000 of unemployed labour. But this is an argument which neglects Say's law. Where there are unused wage funds of £4,000, farmers and manufacturers can expand their production by 44.4 per cent and sectors I and II each will produce an output of £15,888. Under Say's law, such an expansion of supply creates an expansion of demand. In fact, the accounting equations after the expansion will be obtained by multiplying (11) and (12) by 1.444. We then have a state which satisfies Marx's condition for simple reproduction:

	gross produce	fixed capital	circulating capital	profits	
Sector I:	£15,888 =	£10,833 +	£3,611	+ £1,444	(13)
Sector II:	£15,888 =	£5,055 +	£9,389	+ £1,444	(14)

In this state the outputs are sold in the following way: first, food and necessaries are demanded by workers and capitalists of the two sectors. Workers' and capitalists' demand equals their incomes (wages and profits) which are £13,000 and £2,888, respectively, because we assume their propensity to consume to be 1. Therefore, for sector I total demand (£13,000 + £2,888) equals its supply of food and necessaries which amounts to £15,888. On the other hand, sector II has the replacement demand for fixed capital of £10,833 from sector I, in addition to its own replacement demand of £5,055. Thus demand equals supply for sector II.

These are to be compared with the demands for the produce of the two sectors before the expansion of production, which were calculated as being £11,000 each. Thus the expansion of supply creates an expansion of demand of an exactly equal amount. This is not surprising at all, because it implies Say's law. Ricardo mistakenly concluded that mechanization in one of the sectors would

give rise to the unemployment of labour, because he forgot that
Say's law prevails in his economy.

6 Ricardo finally examined the effect of a change in the consumption
pattern of various goods upon the employment of labour. 'If a
landlord, or a capitalist, expends his revenue in the manner of an
ancient baron, in the support of a great number of retainers, or
menial servants, he will give employment to much more labour, than
if he expended it on fine clothes, or costly furniture; on horses, or
in the purchase of any other luxuries' (p. 393). In obtaining this
result too, he neglected Say's law. It is seen in the following that,
under Say's law, a change in the consumption pattern has no effect
upon the employment of labour. Let commodity 1 be the wage good,
and commodities $2, \ldots, n$ be luxuries or capital goods. To produce
one unit of commodity i, l_i units of labour and a_{ji} units of commodity
j $(j = 2, \ldots, n)$ are used. a_{ji} is zero if j is a luxury good. The wage
rate is denoted by w, the price of commodity i by p_i, and the rate
of profits by r. We take the agricultural product as numeraire, so that

$$p_1 = 1. \tag{15}$$

Finally, c_i represents the quantity of the luxury good i bought by
the capitalists per unit of their income. $c_2, \ldots, c_n$ depend on prices
and the rate of profits and are determined so as to satisfy the
capitalists' budget identity (per unit of profits):

$$\sum p_j c_j(p, r) = 1. \tag{16}$$

Assuming the depreciation rate being 1, the accounting equations
per unit of the respective commodities may be put in the form:

$$p_i = (1 + r)(\sum p_j a_{ji} + w l_i), \qquad i = 1, \ldots, n. \tag{17}$$

Let x_i $(i = 1, \ldots, n)$ be the quantity of commodity i produced, N
the total number of workers available in the economy. It takes one
period to produce agricultural products (food), while production is
assumed to be instantaneous for all other commodities. $\bar{x}_1$ stands
for the product of the agricultural activity in the previous period
and currently available in the market. Then the supply–demand
equations, for commodities and labour, may be put in the following
forms respectively:

$$\bar{x}_1 = w(\sum l_j x_j), \tag{18}$$

$$x_i = \sum a_{ij}x_j + c_i(p, r)\Pi, \qquad i = 2, \ldots, n \qquad (19)$$

$$N = \sum l_j x_j, \qquad (20)$$

where Π is the total profits realized in the current period. In the following we are concerned with the case of w being the same in the present as in the previous periods.

The system consisting of equations (15)–(20) is now solved in the following manner. First, substituting (20) into (18) we obtain full employment wages at $w = \bar{x}_1/N$. If p_1 is eliminated from (17) by use of (15), then n equations (17) determines n unknowns, $p_2, \ldots, p_n$ and r, since w is already determined. As there is no change in w in the current and previous periods, there is also no change in the prices and the rate of profits in the two periods.

Then the total profits realized in the current period may be written as:

$$\Pi = r[(\sum p_j a_{j1} + wl_1)\bar{x}_1 + (\sum p_j a_{j2} + wl_2)x_2 + \cdots$$
$$+ (\sum p_j a_{jn} + wl_n)x_n]. \qquad (21)$$

In agriculture, profits from the activity in the previous period are realized in the current period, because of its one-period production lag, while in the other sectors the realization is instantaneous. Substituting the values of p and r obtained above from (15) and (17) into $c_i(p, r)$ and (21), we obtain the values of the remaining $n + 1$ unknowns $x_1, \ldots, x_n$ and Π which satisfy (19), (20) and (21). We can easily show $\bar{x}_1 = x_1$,[8] so that the equilibrium is stationary.

As is seen at once, this system contains no independent investment function but satisfies Say's law. Where the capitalists' consumption coefficient shifts from $c_i(p, r)$ to $c_i'(p, r)$ such that

$$\sum p_i c_i'(p, r) = 1, \qquad (16')$$

we have a new system consisting of (15), (16'), (17), (18), (19'), (20) and (21), where (19') is:

$$x_i = \sum a_{ij}x_j + c_i'(p, r)\Pi, \qquad i = 2, \ldots, n. \qquad (19')$$

The new system may be solved in exactly the same way as the old one. We thus have a new full employment equilibrium which is also stationary. From this we conclude that the demand for labour will

---

[8] Multiply equations (17) by respective x_i's and add them up and compare the result with the sum of equations (19) multiplied by respective p_i's. We easily obtain $\bar{x}_1 = x_1$ by virtue of (16) and (21).

be as great as before, even if a capitalist diverts his revenue from expenditure on a luxury good to another good.

Ricardo obtained a completely different conclusion, because he not only ignored Say's law but also did not carefully examine how output x_i's are influenced by a shift in the consumption functions, $c_i(p, r)$, $i = 2, \ldots, n$. It seems that he considered them as given, at least in the chapter on machinery. Marx used reproduction schemes to determine the equilibrium scales of industries, whereas Walras used the general equilibrium approach to determine the equilibrium levels of industrial outputs $x_1, \ldots, x_n$. At the time of Ricardo, however, theory was not yet sufficiently developed in this respect. Although it is true that he pursued x_i's repercussions rather carefully, he failed to put the equilibrium supply–demand conditions in the exact form of simultaneous equations. Hence he was unable to see what values output x_i's would eventually take on after a change in the consumption coefficients; he rather assumed all x_i's to be unaffected or to truncate the process of repercussions at a point where the economy was still in the original state of disequilibrium.

Similarly, the system (15)–(21) may enable us to examine the effects of a change in other data on the demand for labour. As we have seen in the preceding section there may be a substitution of machines for labour. If this happens in industry h, that is, a_{kh} increases to a'_{kh}, with l_h decreasing to l'_h, then industry h will employ more machines k and less workers. The new cost–price and supply–demand equations are

$$p_i = (1 + r)(\sum p_j a'_{ji} + w l'_i), \tag{22}$$

$$\bar{x} = w(\sum l'_j x_j), \tag{23}$$

$$x_i = \sum a'_{ij} x_j + c_i(p, r)\Pi, \tag{24}$$

$$N = l'_j x_j, \tag{25}$$

$$\Pi = r[(\sum p_j a'_{j1} + w l'_1)\bar{x}_1 + (\sum p_j a'_{j2} + w l'_2)x_2 + \cdots$$
$$+ (\sum p_j a'_{jn} + w l'_n)x_n], \tag{26}$$

where $a_{ji} = a'_{ji}$ and $l_i = l'_i$ unless $j = k$ and $i = h$. These equations, together with (15) and (16), form a new equilibrium system. Of course, we have full employment in the new state of equilibrium too. Thus, as we have concluded in the preceding section, substitution of machines for labour does not cause any harm to the working class.

7 In the preceding chapter on Say's law, we have seen that the absence of an independent investment function is necessary and sufficient for the law. To reinforce this statement we shall show in the following that the introduction of an *ex-ante* aggregate investment function into the system (15)–(21) above will in general result in an overdeterminacy of the system's variables, such that it violates the full employment of labour which has so far existed. For this purpose we shall rewrite the input–output equations (18) and (19) in terms of the concepts of consumption and investment.

We define the current aggregate net output as

$$Y = p_1\bar{x}_1 + p_2 x_2 + \cdots + p_n x_n - (\sum p_j a_{j1})\bar{x}_1 - (\sum p_j a_{j2})x_2$$
$$- \cdots - (\sum p_j a_{jn})x_n, \tag{27}$$

the workers' consumption of the wage good as

$$C_w = w[l_1\bar{x}_1 + l_2 x_2 + \cdots + l_n x_n] \tag{28}$$

and the capitalists' consumption of luxuries as

$$C_c = (\sum p_j c_j(p,r))\Pi, \tag{29}$$

this being equal to Π because their propensity to consume is 1 as is assumed by (16). We define the investment in circulating capital as

$$I_{cc} = wl_1(x_1 - \bar{x}_1) \tag{30}$$

and that on fixed capital as

$$I_{fc} = (\sum p_j a_{j1})(x_1 - \bar{x}_1). \tag{31}$$

On the other hand, equations (18) and (19) may be put in the form:

$$\bar{x}_1 = w[l_1\bar{x}_1 + l_2 x_2 + \cdots + l_n x_n] + wl_1(x_1 - \bar{x}_1) \tag{32}$$

$$x_i = [a_{i1}\bar{x}_1 + a_{i2}x_2 + \cdots + a_{in}x_n] + a_{i1}(x_1 - \bar{x}_1)$$
$$+ c_i(p,r)\Pi, \quad i = 2, \ldots, n. \tag{33}$$

Multiplying (32) and (33) by p_1 and p_i, respectively, we obtain as their sum, in view of definitions (27)–(31), the following macroeconomic equation:

$$Y = C_w + C_c + I_{cc} + I_{fc}. \tag{34}$$

It should be emphasized that this equation has not so far played a positive role in determining the values of prices and quantities in the system (15)–(21). Once they are determined it will always be satisfied.[9] I_{cc} and I_{fc} are *ex-post* investments, and the system has as yet no *ex-ante* investment function. Aggregate investment is perfectly adaptive in this case.

Independently of this adaptive process of determining I_{cc} and I_{fc} by (30) and (31), there may additionally be an *ex-ante* investment function, describing entrepreneurs' aggregate investment decision making, say,

$$I = f(x_1, \ldots, x_n).$$

Therefore, the equilibrium of the economy requires the equality of *ex-post* to *ex-ante* investment; that is,

$$f(x_1, \ldots, x_n) = I_{cc} + I_{fc}. \tag{35}$$

Since there is no *ex-ante* investment function under Say's law, there is no equilibrium equation (35) in Ricardo's economics. But, once it is introduced by denying the law, we have the problem of overdeterminacy, and thus the full employment of labour is impossible.

The following is an obvious example of this. Suppose entrepreneurs want to make an investment of constant amount A in all circumstances, while workers make no savings but capitalists save in corn. (35) then takes the form,

$$A = I_{cc} + I_{fc}. \tag{35'}$$

Suppose $A > 0$, i.e. $x_1 > \bar{x}_1$; this means that all x_i increase, so that the condition of stationary full employment is violated. On the other hand, where the full employment equilibrium continues to prevail, it is stationary, $\bar{x}_1 = x_1$, so that $I_{cc} = I_{fc} = 0$. Thus (35') is reduced to $A = 0$, but $A > 0$, a contradiction; similarly for negative A. Hence the entrepreneurs' desire to make investment becomes infertile. This dilemma is a phenomenon of overdeterminacy and, where entrepreneurs' intentions are realized, full employment is not achieved. In Ricardo's economics there is no idea of *ex-ante* investment and hence no equality of *ex-post* to *ex-ante* investment. It is, therefore, immune from the dilemma due to overdeterminacy.

Finally, a brief comment, from my point of view, on Hicks' recent

---

[9] In fact, $Y = C_w + C_c$, because $\bar{x}_1 = x_1$ implies $I_{cc} = 0$ and $I_{fc} = 0$. Note that no savings are made by workers and capitalists.

works on Ricardo on machinery.[10] In these he takes explicit account of both the production and service periods of machines, but ignores the problem of inter-industrial repercussions of outputs x_i's generated by the shock of mechanization. It is a one-output macro model. Hicks does not explicitly discuss Say's law. He presumes, I think, that some anti-Say's law prevails, as in Keynes' *General Theory* model; thus mechanization will give rise to the unemployment of labour. This type of analysis based on anti-Say's law, especially if it is multi-sectoralized in an appropriate manner, should be much welcomed and appreciated, because the actual economy does not fulfil Say's law.

Nevertheless, the problem of Say's law is still significant and should be discussed explicitly. No one evidently believes that there can be an economy which satisfies the law rigorously. Even Ricardo would have concurred with this. The point is whether or not a model based on the law can be a reasonable approximation to the reality. From this point of view he would have argued that, in an early stage of capitalism where capitalists and entrepreneurs do not diverge greatly from each other, Say's law would substantially and practically hold true. It would then be reasonable to conjecture that in such an economy full employment would virtually be maintained, irrespective of the degree of mechanization. Where the law almost but not entirely held, unemployment would be created by mechanization but it would not be large. Thus the effect of mechanization upon employment would depend on how closely the actual process of saving and investment approximated Say's law. I believe that the problem of mechanization should be investigated so as to enable us first, to examine what would happen in the idealistic case satisfying Say's law, secondly, to determine how much the actual economy would deviate from the ideal state, and thirdly, to explain the deviations in terms of the degree of approximation of Say's law to the actual saving–investment mechanism. Moreover, in this analysis either a general equilibrium of the Walrasian type, or a Marxian theory of reproduction, or something equivalent to them, has to be explicitly utilized in order to make clear the effects of an introduction of new machines upon the relative magnitudes of industries.

[10] See John Hicks, *A Theory of Economic History*, Oxford University Press, 1969, pp. 168–71; *Capital and Time*, Oxford University Press, 1973, pp. 89–109; *Economic Perspectives*, Oxford University Press, 1977, pp. 184–90.

No one has yet completed such an analysis, while it is observed that the dilemma of overdeterminacy and, therefore, the problem of unemployment becomes more and more serious in the actual economy. A substantial part of unemployment might certainly be due to the fact that the actual economy is diverted from Say's law, because entrepreneurs, on the one hand, and capitalists, on the other, are getting farther apart and are becoming more and more independent of each other.

Part V

THREE PARADIGMS
COMPARED

9 Towards an anti-Say's law regime

1 During the nineteenth century Ricardo occupied a position in the world of economics analogous to that held by Keynes today. A considerable number of economists were still discussing his ideas several decades after his death, and his methods – namely the eliciting of laws and theorems deductively and purely logically on the basis of strict abstract concepts and definitions – continued to prevail among them. His verbal–logical economics and numerical examples were further refined by Marx who developed them into a numerical analysis based on a clearly defined mathematical model, albeit using hypothetical figures. Walras' general equilibrium theory can be seen as innovative of this trend, but it can also be seen as something which attempted to provide what in modern terminology could be called the microfoundations of Ricardian economics.

Marx's commendation of Ricardo's theories as scientific economics is well-known; Walras too, despite his critical stance towards Ricardo, respected him as 'the founder of pure economics in England' and devised three Ricardo-like laws as conclusions to his general equilibrium theory.[1] However, as far as Say's law was concerned both Marx and Walras regarded Ricardo with critical eyes. The fact that most members of the classical school were optimistic regarding the establishment of full employment of labour, despite the categorization of economics as a dismal science, was in part a result of the belief placed in the existence of an automatic regulatory market mechanism, stemming from a fetishistic faith in Adam Smith's invisible hand. However, it was in part also due to the view that because of Say's law the impossibility of general overproduction was guaranteed. For Marx – whose belief in the collapse of the capitalist system led him to reject all bourgeois

---

[1] See Walras, *Elements*, p. 165; Morishima, *Walras's Economics*, pp. 5–6.

doctrines that failed to comprehend the essence of the capitalist mode of production and disregarded the anarchy (or the decentralization) of that machinery of production – the theory of crisis was a highly significant subject. For that reason Say's law (which Marx regarded as 'an established axiom in English political economy') with its denial of the possibility of general overproduction, was a clear object of attack for him.[2]

His main attack was based on a critical analysis of Ricardo's formulation of Say's law, in the form of the statement made by Ricardo himself, 'no man produces, but with a view to consume or sell, and he never sells, but with a view to purchase some other commodity, which may immediately be useful to him, or which may contribute to *future production*' (p. 290) as Marx quoted in *Theories of Surplus Value*.[3] Marx remarked that under conditions of capitalist production no man produces with a view to consuming his own product. He must sell. The sale, however, is in no sense unconditionally to be followed by a purchase. Paying due regard to his perception that commodity exchange establishes a relationship between two producers, mediated but also *interrupted* by money (his well-known formula $C - M \cdots M - C$), he concluded, contrary to Ricardo, that the producer, who initiates a sale, is under no compulsion and may even be well advised (in times of heightened commercial uncertainty) to abstain from following up the sale with a corresponding purchase. A situation may then arise where the aggregate supply of all commodities exceeds the aggregate demand for them because 'the demand for the general commodity, money, exchange-value, is greater than the demand for all particular commodities, in other words, the motive to turn the commodity into money, to realize its exchange-value, prevails over the motive to transform the commodity again into use value'.[4]

If selling (and therefore aggregate supply Y) is cut off from purchase (and therefore aggregate demand $C + I$) then Say's law (i.e. what I have called Say's law in Keynes' sense in the last chapter), which insists not only upon the *ex-post* but also on the *ex-ante* identity of aggregate supply and aggregate demand (the whole concept of what James Mill described as 'the metaphysical

[2] K. Marx, *Theories of Surplus Value*, Part II, Progress Publishers, Moscow, 1968, p. 165, p. 400, p. 468, p. 502.
[3] *Ibid.*, p. 502, his italics.
[4] *Ibid.*, p. 505, his italics.

equilibrium of purchase and sales'), will collapse. Y is no longer identically equal to $C + I$, hence a mathematical identity fails to obtain between S and I. Therefore, in the market for each commodity, with the exception of money and bonds, it is possible for supply to exceed demand and, therefore, for the prices of all commodities to fall. It will happen more frequently that the aggregate supply of all commodities will exceed aggregate demand. The reason for this is that due to the compulsive pursuit of surplus-value, which obviously has no limits of physical satiety, industrial capitalists, in view of their competing mainly through their products, are unable in an anarchic market to form anything but a rather vague idea of the total size of output and demand in their respective sectors, and thus tend to overproduce. At the same time they also tend to restrict aggregate demand by economizing as much as possible on labour and equipment costs, which worsens the effects of overproduction, because the workers' demand for the final commodities will be reduced.

Their tendency to overstep the limits of available demand is strengthened by the fact that industrialists do not directly supply the final consumer, but use a wholesaler, who, for a certain period, will be capable of absorbing excessive output in his stocks. Nor do they need to be dependent on immediate cash sales to cover their needs for short-term working capital, since they can always turn to their bankers for that. Industrialists are, therefore, cushioned against the direct impact of the tailing off of demand at both ends of the circuit of productive capital ($M - C$ (which is divided into LP and $MP) \cdots C' - M'$);[5] a situation that encourages them to force the pace of production to breaking point.

Given the above, Marx may be interpreted as seeing in the denial of Say's law the separation of demand (i.e. investment) from supply (i.e. savings). He also mobilized, in support of his theory of crisis, a very perceptive and thorough dissection of the compound persona of the original capitalist – an individual who combined the various roles of possessor of means of production, manager, entrepreneur and investment-decision-maker – into its constituent parts and

---

[5] In Marx's formal representation of the circuit of capital, M stands for money capital advanced, C for commodity capital (inputs), LP for labour power, MP for means of production, '$\ldots$' for the production process, C' for commodity output (output, gross of surplus-value) and M' for the total value of sales, gross of surplus value. The industrialist may borrow M to expand production, before he recovers M' from sales.

showed how each part was delegated, by a process of historical differentiation, to a separate specialized section of the bourgeoisie. The rise of distinct rentier, entrepreneurial and managerial groups, culminating in a complete separation of ownership and control, leads to a social structure ideally suited to the separation of savings and investment.

It is popularly believed that Marx was examining an economy consisting of two classes, workers and capitalists, but those who read through to the end of Volume III of *Capital* will understand that Marx was considering an economy where two additional personages, the landlord and his capitalist shadow, the farmer, were united with the industrial capitalist in the exploitation of the working class. The presence of merchant capitalists and money capitalists was also mentioned. Thus Marx's world is a multi-social-group economy and, in an economy such as this, those engaging in decision-making in investment and those engaging in decision-making regarding savings are not necessarily one and the same. In order to harmonize their desires and to render them consistent with each other either the interest rate must be subject to flexible adjustment[6] or, failing this, the volume of production Y must be accommodated as a variable to regulate savings, as Keynes believed.

It is noted that this antagonistic determination does not necessarily serve any rational purpose in the allocation of resources. The ultimate regulator for Marx as well was the fluctuating level of income. This is the meaning of his remark that 'crises are always but momentary and forcible solutions of the existing contradictions. They are violent eruptions which for a time restore the disturbed equilibrium.'[7]

Marx, therefore, was able to go beyond the mere rejection of Say's law and isolate at least one of the elements that we consider necessary for an anti-Say's law – the rise of separate social groups, one of which specializes in investment. He may even be said, in view of his insistence on the relatively large degree of independence enjoyed by the industrialist as well as the speculative investor, to have sensed

[6] It is, however, difficult to imagine Marx accepting such a regulatory role for the rate of interest. In his words: 'It is indeed the separation of capitalists into money-capitalists and industrial capitalists that transforms a portion of the profit into interest, that generally creates the category of interest; and it is only the competition between these two kinds of capitalists which creates the rate of interest', Marx, *Capital*, Vol. III, Progress Publishers, Moscow, 1971, p. 370.

[7] *Ibid.*, p. 249.

the need for the second anti-Say's law element: the presence of an independent investment function. Where he may be said to have failed is in the rigorous specification of such a function.[8]

2 In spite of these, Marx could not develop a theory of economics on the basis of anti-Say's law. Rather, he was in a contradictory position. His theory of reproduction is the one which, in terms of mathematical economics, appears as the most advanced and most highly perfected part of his system, but the investment function assumed by Marx in it is *not* independent of S, and is, moreover, identically equal to S. In making up his tables of the two-class reproduction scheme which yields this kind of conclusion, Marx, contrary to his own much richer exposition in *Capital*, Vol. III, on the one hand ruled out the problem of the fragmentation of the capitalist class into differentiated strata, while at the same time he hypothesized that the capitalist, who acquires profit, accumulates a part of it and invests it, according to the formula described below. Here saving is combined with investment, a combination described as the accumulation of capital.

Marx assumed the following, highly singular, activity of accumulation.[9] Capitalists in the capital goods industry (below referred to as Department I) invest $a_1 P_1$, as a part of the profits of Department I, P_1. Ratio a_1 is referred to as the rate of accumulation, and the size of a_1 is exogenously determined. The rate of accumulation by capitalists in the consumption goods industry (Department II) is shown by a_2. But unlike a_1, a_2 is not exogenously determined, being endogenously regulated so as to maintain the balance between the supply of and demand for capital goods. (This implies that there is no excess demand for consumption goods too, because, as will be seen, Say's law in the Keynes sense holds.) In addition to this, Marx assumed that workers did not save, but devoted the whole of their wages to consumption, while capitalists expended the total amount of their income (profits) remaining after investment.

---

[8] The closest Marx has got to a literary formulation of the presence of an independent investment function in the capitalist economy is in his well-known dictum, 'Accumulation for accumulation's sake, production for production's sake: by this formula classical economy expressed the historical mission of the bourgeoisie', Marx, *Capital*, Vol. III, Progress Publishers, Moscow, 1970, p. 595.

[9] Marx, *Capital*, Vol. I, Progress Publishers, Moscow, 1967, p. 514 and Morishima, *Marx's Economics*, p. 118.

For that reason the total demand for consumer goods can be expressed as

$$W_1 + W_2 + (1 - a_1)P_1 + (1 - a_2)P_2.$$

For simplicity's sake let us now assume that the economy consists only of the capital goods and the consumer goods sectors, producing the necessities of life, disregarding the sector concerned with the production of luxuries. We shall also disregard the production period and assume that there will be no investment in variable capital.[10] After subtracting constant capital C_1 and C_2 (which corresponds to Keynes' user costs) from the value of output of Departments I and II respectively, the net value gained remaining will be shown as Y_1 and Y_2. The balance after subtracting the amount of wages in Department I, W_1, from Y_1 will be the amount of profits in that industry P_1; therefore,

$$Y_1 = W_1 + P_1.$$

Similarly,

$$Y_2 = W_2 + P_2.$$

Since aggregate net output is $Y = Y_1 + Y_2$, aggregate savings is

$$S = Y - [W_1 + W_2 + (1 - a_1)P_1 + (1 - a_2)P_2].$$

However, aggregate investment is

$$I = a_1 P_1 + a_2 P_2.$$

Therefore, $S - I = Y_1 + Y_2 - (W_1 + W_2 + P_1 + P_2)$, but given the definition of profits obtained above as P_i, that is the balance obtained after subtracting W_i from Y_i, $S - I$ will always vanish regardless of the value of Y_1 and Y_2. This means that S is identically equal to I for all values of Y.

Thus Marx's reproduction scheme fulfils Say's law in the Keynesian sense. Despite his scathing and justified criticism of the regime of Say's law and his clear intention of extricating himself from its implications, he failed to construct an analytical system founded on anti-Say's law. While he took an important step in the translation from Ricardo to Keynes, he went no more than part of the way along the road.

[10] This is an assumption for the sake of simplicity. As for the case where there is a production lag, see Morishima, *Marx's Economics*, pp. 118 ff.

Marx's reproduction scheme generates balanced growth between the outputs of the two departments. Starting with arbitrary amounts of outputs in the previous year, the economy is seen after one year of unbalanced growth of outputs in the current year to be on the balanced growth path.[11] This rather strange result is a consequence of Marx's peculiar investment assumption, which satisfies Say's law (in Keynes' sense); the result is far from his vision that the capitalistic process of reproduction would reach a deadlock eventually. It must be emphasized that Marx obtained this investment function by assuming that the capitalists' propensity to accumulate capital is exogenously given in Department I while it is endogenously determined in Department II, such that aggregate investment equals aggregate savings. There is no economic rationale for this asymmetry between the attitudes of the capitalists of the two departments concerning accumulation of capital. With this unjustifiable investment function he confined himself to the world of Say's law, in the analysis of a reproduction scheme. Thus the fact that, in spite of his intention and keen desire to get rid of the law, Marx could not formulate a reasonable investment function explains why he had no other option other than to establish a significant part of his economics on a law of which he did not approve.

3 Looked at in this way it is now quite apparent that a separation of the provider of capital (capitalist) from the user of capital (entrepreneur) is imperative if we are to free ourselves from Say's law. It must be said that it is quite natural that the 'English School' which 'fails to distinguish between the role of the capitalist and the role of the entrepreneurs' (Walras, *Elements*, p. 423) should not succeed in separating investment from saving, and it is both surprising and at the same time ironic that Say himself should have devised an extremely pertinent and highly advanced way of comprehending the entrepreneur. At the end of his *Treatise* Say gave something like a glossary of his main concepts. There we read:

> Capitalist: He is the one who owns a capital and who earns a *profit* when he uses it himself, or an interest when he lends it to an entrepreneur who then uses it, and who, from then on, consumes the service of the capital and draws the profits.

[11] Morishima, *Marx's Economics*, p. 120.

> Entrepreneur: ... They are not *capitalists* except when the capital
> or a portion of the capital which they use belongs to themselves;
> they are then simultaneously capitalists and entrepreneurs.[12]

Thus although there are some people who combine the persons
of entrepreneur and capitalist, the two are conceptually independent
of each other; moreover, the entrepreneur is the agent who makes
the decisions regarding investment, as well as the agent who bears
the risk which accompanies the activities of an enterprise. This means
that he is an entrepreneur in the Walras–Schumpeter sense. After
distinguishing three activities necessary to production (research,
application and labour), Say adds:

> It is rare for one person to undertake all three operations. The
> most usual is that someone studies the law of nature. He is the
> scientist. Another person takes advantage of this knowledge in
> order to create useful products. He is the agriculturalist, the
> manufacturer or the merchant, or, to describe them all by a
> collective name, the entrepreneur ...[13]

It is therefore clear that Walras was indebted to Say not just for
the concept of equilibrium but also for the concept of entrepreneur,
but despite this Walras had a low opinion of Say. Walras cited a
passage in Say's *Treatise* which says that the lending of labour, land
and capital is carried out among the possessors of these three items
(i.e. the worker, landowner and capitalist), and wages, interest and
rent are determined as the price of the various loans.[14] He then
added: 'J. B. Say did not fully understand the specific role of
entrepreneur. In fact, this person is absent from his theory' (Walras,
Elements, pp. 425–6). For Walras to have evaluated the whole of
Say's work in this way would, of course, have been unfair, but it is
true that as far as Say's model of the market for the factors of
production is concerned the entrepreneur did not exist – except as
one of the workers. This was described by Walras as Say following
'a certain number of French economists' in regarding 'the
entrepreneur as a worker charged with the special task of managing
a firm' (l.c., p. 222).

[12] J. B. Say, *Traité d'Economie Politique*, 3 vols, Paris, 1826, pp. 272–3, p. 287, his
italics; translation from the French original by Catephores (the co-author of the
original version of this chapter, entitled 'Anti Say's Law versus Say's Law: A
Change in Paradigm' by M. Morishima and G. Catephores).
[13] Say, *Traité d'Economie Politique*, p. 51, G. Catephores' translation.
[14] *Ibid.*, p. 18.

As has been expounded in my *Walras's Economics*, Walras's own model is constructed in the following manner.

> Let us call the holder of land a *landowner*, the holder of personal faculties a *worker* and the holder of capital proper a *capitalist*. In addition, let us designate by the term *entrepreneur* a fourth person, ... whose role it is to lease land from the landowner, hire personal faculties from the labourer and borrow capital from the capitalist, in order to combine the three productive services in agriculture, industry or trade. (Walras, *Elements*, p. 222, his italics)

In the market for consumer goods the entrepreneur appears as the seller of products while the landlord, worker and capitalist appear as the purchasers of products.[15] In the capital goods market 'entrepreneurs who produce new capital goods' (*ibid.*, *p.* 42) sell their products to the entrepreneurs who demand them. These entrepreneurs borrow the sums of money needed to purchase new capital goods from a capitalist, who 'accumulates his savings in money' (*ibid.*, p. 270). With regard to this point it should be observed that Walras noted that 'the demand for new capital goods comes from entrepreneurs who manufacture products and not from capitalists who create savings' (*ibid.*, p. 270). If the volume of production of consumer goods and capital goods is determined in this manner, then the amount of labour, land and capital needed for that production is also determined and the entrepreneur appears in the markets of productive services in order to satisfy his demand for them. 'Here landowners, workers and capitalists appear as sellers, and entrepreneurs as buyers of the various productive services'.[16]

Thus in Walras' system, if investment is decided it will determine the volume of production of capital goods and, as a result, the demand for factors of production in the capital goods industry; hence, the wages, interest and rent to be paid to the relevant individuals by that industry are also determined. This being the case, their demand for consumption goods will be determined too, and, accordingly, the volume of production of consumer goods. The

---

[15] Walras, *Elements*, p. 223.

[16] *Ibid.*, pp. 222–3. This is a point of confusion in Walras. Since entrepreneurs borrow from capitalists the money which they need to purchase capital goods, the capital goods bought with this money are owned not by the capitalist but by the enterprise. Consequently, contrary to the passage in the text, it is not the capitalist who supplies the services of the capital goods; it must be the enterprise itself. Where it is possible for the capital goods to be moved, the entrepreneur is likely to receive an offer for the services of the capital goods from another enterprise. This confusion has been corrected in my *Walras's Economics*, pp. 77–99.

volume of production thus determined creates the demand for consumer goods arising from the wages, interest and rent paid to individuals connected with the consumer goods industry, and thus the total demand for consumer goods, i.e. the total volume of output of the consumption goods industry, is determined. Since the demand for factors of production is in proportion to the volume of production, the total demand for each factor and hence their employment is determined, as long as it does not exceed their supply.

4 Up to this point, the general equilibrium theory of capital formation and credit thus formulated by Walras is in all respects completely Keynesian. Walras' equilibrium formula for the demand and supply of products may be regarded as a microeconomic version of Keynes' theory of income determination analysis, and his analysis of the demand for factors of production is a microeconomic version of Keynes' theory of employment. However, since the demand for capital services and the demand for land and labour determined in this way are not necessarily equal to their respective supplies, Walras regarded the demand for investment, i.e. for new capital goods, as being adjusted flexibly so as to fulfil the various equations for general equilibrium, including those for factors of production. Hence full employment equilibrium is established.

However, this version of Walras' system, which assumes flexible investment, lacks an independent aggregate investment function. Though Walras himself was not aware of this, it satisfies Say's law in the Keynesian sense, in contradiction with his emphasis on the independent role of the entrepreneur in decision-making.[17] This means that, as in an equilibrium regime of perfect competition, prices are flexibly adjusted so as to satisfy the equations for supply and demand at the point of equilibrium. In much the same manner, Walras regarded investment as a flexibly adjustable variable. Thus in the Walrasian system there is no place for entrepreneurs who make investment decisions. There are no independent decision makers but rather market mechanisms which adjust investment to exactly the amount at which a general equilibrium is established.

---

[17] For Walras' system of general equilibrium of capital formation and credit, see his *Elements*, pp. 267–312. For this system the existence of a full-employment equilibrium was rigorously proved under Say's law in my *Equilibrium, Stability and Growth*, pp. 83–92. See also my *Walras's Economics*, pp. 70–122.

Throughout the *Elements* Walras stressed the importance of the
entrepreneur as an independent entity; yet he accepted the perfect
flexibility of investment, turning the entrepreneur quite simply into
a *kuroko*, a scene-shifter,[18] and by doing this he just failed to achieve
what would have been a remarkable success. The shortcoming lies
in Walras' belief in the existence of general equilibrium in any system
– whether it is a general equilibrium of exchange, of production, of
capital formation and credit, or of money and circulation – which
ultimately made him accept the idea of the perfect flexibility of
investment as an instrument for assuring the existence of a general
equilibrium.

Thus, in regard to a general equilibrium of capital formation,
there are two options concerning how to deal with investment: (1)
that of guaranteeing a general full employment equilibrium by
assuming the perfect flexibility of investment, and (2) that of being
satisfied with an underemployment equilibrium by assuming an
independent investment function. Whereas Keynes opted for the
latter, Walras chose the former probably because of his prejudice
in favour of the existence of general equilibrium. In this way, Walras
too was unable to escape from Say's law, and this failure, as has
been seen above, is closely tied up with his turning the entrepreneur
into a mere stage hand, an entity content to receive no income, just
like an auctioneer, who, while adjusting prices, does not receive an
income for what he does.

In line with this, Walras constructed a mathematical model which
he considered as equivalent to his literary one,[19] where he took the
view that capitalists themselves save in the form of capital goods
and the capital goods which they have saved are lent to each industry.
There is a considerable difference, not just in terms of practical
inconvenience as was noticed by Walras, but also in terms of
theoretical significance, between this kind of model and a model
where savings are carried out in the form of money which is then
lent to entrepreneurs so that they may realize their demand for new
capital goods – the kind of model which I have referred to as Walras'

[18] In Kabuki the *kuroko* is an individual dressed in black clothes and wearing a
black headdress who appears on stage to arrange it for example by picking up
clothes discarded by the actors. Their presence is necessary to the play but they
play no role whatsoever in terms of advancing the sequence of events.
[19] Walras, *Elements*, p. 270. He shows no signs of having attempted to prove the
equivalence of the two models, but rather rashly immediately concludes their
equivalence.

literary or first model.[20] The second, or mathematical, model is essentially no different from the classical model where the capitalist both saves and invests. Thus Walras' adherence to his faith in the existence of a general equilibrium meant that his drama of capital formation, though conceived in the light of a magnificent plan and vision, became in the end no more than a farce.

Finally, if Walras, with all his emphasis on independent decision-making by entrepreneurs, had incorporated an investment function into his system, then, as has been said in a previous chapter, general equilibrium would no longer be achieved in that system. Seen in this light we can take the view that Walras' system anticipated Keynes' theory that under anti-Say's law full employment equilibrium cannot in general be achieved. As has already been seen, Say's law was normally discussed with reference to the theory of crisis and the neutrality of money, but Keynes tied it up with unemployment. Seen afresh from this kind of perspective, Walras' economics, which is regarded as providing the microeconomic foundation for Ricardian economics, though it ignores the production lag of agriculture, can also serve to provide the microeconomic foundation for Keynesian economics if an independent investment function is incorporated into it. It would not be at all surprising to find that someone had, on the basis of Walras' theory, begun speculating on an economic theory or conjecture of the Keynesian type. It is ironic to see that the conjecture was not taken up by someone, like Schumpeter who was well acquainted with Walras and respected him, but by Keynes who may not be regarded as having a high appreciation of Walras' thought.

5 In the transition from the regime of Say's law to the one opposing it, there were a number of economists who were critical of the law. Among them most notable would be Wicksell, who, albeit hesitantly, renounced the law and developed, before Schumpeter, a dynamic theory which emphasized the role of the banking sector. Like Lange and Patinkin, however, he was concerned with the law only in its relation to the determination of the price level. He wrote in *Lectures*,

> A general rise in prices is therefore only conceivable on the supposition that the general demand has for some reason become, or is expected to become, greater than the supply. This may sound

[20] See my *Walras's Economics*, p. 73.

paradoxical, because we may have accustomed ourselves, with J. B. Say, to regard goods themselves as reciprocally constituting and limiting the demand for each other. And indeed *ultimately* they do so; here, however, we are concerned with precisely what occurs, *in the first place*, with the middle link in the final exchange of one good against another, which is formed by the demand of money for goods and the supply of goods against money. Any theory of money worthy of the name must be able to show how and why the monetary or pecuniary demand for goods exceeds or falls short of the supply of goods in given conditions.[21]

On the other hand, unlike Keynes, Wicksell never associated Say's law with the problem of the unemployment of labour. In fact, in his analysis of the famous 'cumulative process', Wicksell assumed full employment throughout. In his *Interest and Prices* he wrote: 'all available factors of production will find employment at prices determined by the market situation.'[22] Also, in the *Lectures*:

As a first approximation we are entitled to assume that all production forces are already fully employed, so that the increased monetary demand principally takes the form of rivalry between employers for labour, raw materials and natural facilities, etc., which consequently leads to an increase in their price, . . . (*Lectures*, Vol. II, p. 195)

Moreover, concerning Say's law Wicksell was a bit confused in the analysis of the cumulative process. In some places he renounced the law and wrote:

In order to make a clear distinction between the roles of capitalists and entrepreneurs, we may imagine that the latter work entirely on borrowed money and that they derive this money, not directly from the capitalists, but from a special institution, a bank. (*Interest and Prices*, p. 137)

It lies in the power of the credit institutions, acting in cooperation only with the entrepreneurs, to determine the direction of production and consequently the period of investment of capital, without paying any heed to the actual capitalists, the owners of goods. (*Ibid.*, p. 155)

In other places, however, he seems to support Say's law. In his words: 'An increase in the supply of certain groups of commodities means an increase in the real demand for all other groups of commodities'

---

[21] K. Wicksell, *Lectures on Political Economy*, Vol. II, George Routledge and Sons, 1935, pp. 159–60, his italics.
[22] K. Wicksell, *Interest and Prices*, Macmillan, 1936.

(*ibid.*, p. 105). Furthermore, his assumption 'that all labour and all land, and in its turn all capital, are always seeking employment and are *always* more or less fully employed' (*ibid.*, p. 131, my italics) can be realized, where, and only where, Say's law prevails. It is true that Wicksell neither criticized this sort of association of full employment with Say's law nor provided any justification for his full employment assumption. But from all this we may conclude that, like Marx and Walras, Wicksell was also paradoxically caught between Say's and anti-Say's laws. He is a predecessor of Keynes in the sense that he developed (before both Keynes and Schumpeter) a theory which consolidates real-economic and monetary theories into a unity, but he had no substantial theory of unemployment. In spite of his critical view of Say's law, he was nearer to Ricardo than Walras, because he remained a full employment economist and kept, though in a new Böhm–Bawerk–Wicksell form, a classical wage-fund theory which Walras did not subscribe to.

6 It is generally believed that Schumpeter's hallmarks were the terms 'entrepreneur', 'innovation' and 'new combination'. However, Walras had already emphasized the first of them, as has been seen above, and pointed out the importance of the other two in the context of the progress of an economy. Walras stated: 'a change takes place in the very nature of the coefficients of production as additional technical coefficients are introduced while others are abandoned' (Walras, *Elements*, p. 383). Although he called this *technical progress*, it may be more appropriately called a 'new combination'. Therefore, the aspect of Schumpeter's theory of economic development which is based on these concepts may be considered as a direct extension of Walras' concerns.

It is our view that Schumpeter's greatest contribution lay in his assignment of an explicit role to the banker as the fifth constituent of the equilibrium system. To show this, we need to explain 'capital' which is, according to Schumpeter, 'a fund of purchasing power'.[23] 'Capital is nothing but the lever by which the entrepreneur subjects to his control the concrete goods which he needs, nothing but a means of diverting the factors of production to new uses, or dictating a new direction to production'.[24] 'That form of economic

---

[23] J. A. Schumpeter, *The Theory of Economic Development*, Oxford University Press, 1934, p. 120.
[24] *Ibid.*, p. 116, Schumpeter's italics.

organisation in which the goods necessary for new production are withdrawn from their settled place in the circular flow by the intervention of purchasing power created *ad hoc* is the capitalist economy'.[25] It is the bankers who supply the entrepreneurs with purchasing power by furnishing them with credit. Moreover, since they are not able to create unlimited credit, they have to select from among the investment plans put forward by entrepreneurs those which they regard as desirable or likely to succeed. The direction which the economy will follow will depend on the investment plans which are chosen; therefore, it is the bankers who constitute the selection committees for investment plans. They are the helmsmen of the capitalist economy.

It goes without saying that the savings made by people in society are concentrated in the banks. If the banker should hand over the money just as it is to the investor, then it is savings which regulate investment; although the entrepreneurs will make various investment plans, the investment made must be equal to savings. That is to say investment adapts to savings (and not vice versa), and we will always find that $S = I$. This means that in this case Say's law prevails.

However, this is not how bankers act. Bankers are able to create credit on the basis of the money in their possession (i.e. that they have obtained from savers). While there is a limit to credit creation, as long as they remain inside that limit bankers may advance the required sums to those entrepreneurs whose investment plans are deemed desirable. The total lending is determined both by the quantitative size of each investment plan and by its quality, i.e. the proportion of the proposed investment that the bankers estimate will be successful and therefore they are prepared to advance on. Where credit creation changes flexibly within stipulated limits, the aggregate investment carried out (i.e. effective investment, I) is determined independently of the savings which are available to bankers. Thus when I is decided the investment plans backed up by banks will be carried out; capital goods will be purchased, workers hired and production initiated, with the result that the size of people's savings will change. S will then adjust to I (and not vice versa). This is the way in which Schumpeter's model works; however, this kind of economy is very close to the world of anti-Say's law and in this Schumpeter has come very close to Keynes. For Schumpeter, the people who distinguished investment from saving and guaranteed

[25] *Ibid.*, p. 116.

the independence of investment were the bankers who served as the intermediaries between saving and investment and intervened between them by conducting the flexible creation of credit. Saving is made flexible because of the creation of credit and is adjusted to investment. It is thus seen that 'banker' and 'credit' (rather than, or at least as well as 'entrepreneur' and 'new combination') are inevitably the key words of Schumpeter's economics.

7 What kind of role will bankers play in this process of adaptation? First, if we assume that labour is supplied only in as far as there is a demand for it, then $S_L = D_L$ in (2) of Chapter 7. Furthermore, bearing in mind that $Y - C = S$, (2) can be written

$$S = I + (D_B - S_B) + (D_M - S_M).^{26} \tag{1}$$

In order to simplify our discussion, we will discuss below the case where $D_M = S_M$ prevails initially and assume that individuals do not save in the form of bonds and that the enterprise investment sector holds no money. First of all, where entrepreneurs carry out investment in excess of the sector's net income after the payment of interest, new bonds have to be issued to the value of the excess. Thus it is not until they are able to sell that amount of bonds that entrepreneurs are able to carry out their planned investment. Since it is assumed that individuals do not buy bonds the bond market will be in a state of excess supply.

Let us now assume that the bankers buy up all the excess supply of bonds on the bond market. The equivalent amount of money in the possession of the banking sector thus passes into the hands of the enterprise investment sector through the bond market. The enterprises which have acquired capital in this way will place orders for capital goods, and the capital goods industry will engage in an expansion of production. At the same time, the money received by the investment sector from the banks will be transferred to enterprises in the capital goods industry in payment for capital goods and this money will in turn pass into the hands of those engaged in the capital goods industry. These individuals will consume a part of it and the

[26] Note that the last two parenthesized parts represent the value of excess demand for bonds and money respectively. While these may not initially be 0, they will become 0 after adjustment, hence we get $S = I$, but what changes in this process is not I but S. That is to say, as a result of adjusting the volume of bonds and money held S will change and ultimately become equal to a given, independently determined, I. In this way, under anti-Say's law we get $S = I$.

remainder will either be held in the form of cash or paid into current accounts. (Note that we have assumed that individuals do not save in the form of bonds.) The consumed money passes into the hands of the consumer goods industry and ultimately into the hands of the people involved in the consumer goods industry. They too consume a part and either hold the rest in the form of cash or, if not, put it on current account. That part of the cash placed in a current account, of course, passes into the hands of the banking sector and the remaining cash is held by the private non-banking sector.

Thus the amount of money released by the banks to buy the bonds issued by the entrepreneurs is kept by someone in the economy. This means $D_M = S_M$ in (1). In short, if bankers act on the bond market so as to achieve $D_B = S_B$, then it follows that $D_M = S_M$, and hence $S = I$ from (1). That is to say, as long as there is a balance in the bond market there will also be a balance in the money market and at the same time savings will equal investment.

What then is the limit to the amount of money which can be released by the banks in order to mop up the excess supply on the bond market?[27] The banks hold cash and current accounts as liabilities. They do not know when current accounts might be withdrawn, but the probability of the total sum being withdrawn all at once is very small, therefore the rate of cash reserves held may perhaps be sufficient if it is as low as, say 10 per cent. Thus banks retain as cash in hand only their necessary cash reserve, and all other money held can be advanced to entrepreneurs. The greater the sum advanced by the banks the greater the number of investment plans supported and thus the lower the marginal quality of the investment plans. Thus, at a time when opportunities for investment are restricted, investment plans regarded by bankers as likely to succeed will soon be completely exhausted and the cash reserves held by the banks will be far in excess of the necessary amount. The amount of investment undertaken is related to the extent to which entrepreneurs are able to devise attractive investment plans and the magnitude of the investment projects to which bankers are willing to give favourable considerations. When bankers react negatively,

---

[27] Schumpeter believed that there was the following limitation on the creation of credit. 'If the solvency of the banking system is not to be endangered, the banks can only give credit in such a way that the resulting inflation is really temporary and moreover remains moderate' (*ibid.*, p. 113).

even where there remains good quality investment plans, the aggregate volume of investment which is effective will be small, and when bankers agree to support even a number of poor investment plans the effective volume of investment will for a time be considerable, but any failure of investment will soon rebound on the enterprise or the bank. Since it is the banker, rather than the entrepreneur, who chooses the investment plans which are to be financed, it is the bankers who are the constituent responsible for a decision on effective investment. So, as long as they remain within the limits of credit creation, even where the level of aggregate investment is high, bankers are able to give financial support to that aggregate investment. Savings then adjust themselves to that level of investment.

8 We may now conclude that, after Ricardo, there was a period in the history of economic theory in which economists were still working with models which admitted Say's law; during that period it may be seen that great names such as Marx, Walras and Wicksell were all explicitly critical of the law, but were not able to construct a complete model without it. On the other hand, Ricardo's other instrument, the wage-fund theory, went through changes in that period. It was preserved by Marx, as his use of variable capital evidently shows, while it was extended and modernized into the new wage-fund theory by Wicksell though it was discarded by Walras. If we define the school which admits both Say's law and the wage-fund theory as *classical* and the school which admits only the former, whilst getting rid of the latter, as *neoclassical*, then we may appoint Ricardo and Walras as the representatives of the classical and neoclassical schools, respectively. According to this definition, Marx was classical and Wicksell was more classical than Walras. And from this point of view, Keynes' stance may be characterized as being in contraposition to Ricardo, denying both Say's law and the wage-fund theory.

Where anti-Say's law prevails, savings may deviate from investment. The gap between them is eliminated, according to Keynes, by adjusting savings to investment via the channel of a change in income as this gives rise to a change in savings. This view, however, would not perfectly fit to the recent interpretation of Keynes' theory which regards the *ex-post* equality between S and I as the result of 'rationing' that works so as to remove the excess between S and I and adjust the bigger to the smaller.[28] In contrast, however, Schumpeter's view emphasizing the role of bankers, as has been seen above, would be very amenable to this modern interpretation. Bankers are in charge of rationing in the financial market, so that they control S and I. This anti-Say's law world is a world which has five personae, worker, landowner, capitalist, entrepreneur and banker, as indispensable ingredients.

Finally, a comment on our above definition of the neoclassical school. Evidently, it is entirely different from the usual definition of the term which distinguishes a particular group of economists from the others, according to whether they use marginal concepts and accept the maximum principles.[29] If we adopt this definition, Ricardo would be classified as a neoclassical economist, because marginalism is obvious and essential in his rent-theoretic growth theory, as has been abundantly seen in this book. In my *Marx's Economics*, I have shown that Marx derived two sets of equations which might be interpreted together to imply Walras–Marshall–Hicks' subjective equilibrium conditions.[30] Also, at some stage in the development of his labour theory of value Marx proposed to define value as the minimum time a thing could possibly be produced in.[31] In view of these and the fact that Marx himself spent an enormous amount of effort studying differential calculus, including maxima, minima and Lagrangean multipliers, it is rather difficult to believe that Marx would have been antagonistic to the method of marginalism. Assuming this to be the case, Marx too might be included with the neoclassical economists. Indeed, all sensible economists, after Ricardo, would be neoclassical, if the term is defined in the usual way, notwithstanding the explicit or implicit use of differential calculus. Hahn would agree to and be pleased by this statement but the statement itself implies that the identification of neoclassicism with marginalism is useless for the purpose of distinguishing a group of economists from other economists. All are actually or potentially neoclassical according to this identification.

[28] E. Malinvaud, *The Theory of Unemployment Reconsidered*, Blackwell, 1977.
[29] See, for example, F. H. Hahn, 'The Neo-Ricardian', in his *Equilibrium and Macroeconomics*, Blackwell, 1984, pp. 353–86.
[30] Morishima, *Marx's Economics*, pp. 41–2.
[31] K. Marx, *The Poverty of Philosophy*, New York, 1963, p. 66. See also Morishima and G. Catephores, *Value, Exploitation and Growth*, McGraw-Hill (UK), 1978, pp. 36–58; Morishima, 'Marx in the Light of Modern Economic Theory', *Econometrica*, Vol. 42, 1974, pp. 611–32.

In the following chapters we shall concentrate our attention on Ricardo, Walras and Keynes and construct simple models representing each of their models of economics. We shall examine carefully how the models work and also try to identify the periods in which the respective models fit to the real world most adequately. The problem of congruency between the actual economy and economic theory, it seems, has not been discussed well by either economic historians or historians of economics, though it should be the central subject of their disciplines. It is very unfortunate that none of the major schools of economics has seriously been tested against the reality. Of course, the test is very much more difficult than it is in the natural sciences, because the reality is always in flux. Nevertheless we must say that without it economic theory can at best be only a social philosophy or a social mathematics. However crude or humble it may be, the work of testing should be started.

10   Ricardo, Walras and Keynes

1 Economists are in disarray. They disagree with each other in their theoretical models and policy proposals. Some (the classical and neoclassical economists) believe that full employment and full utilization will be realized in labour and capital markets, respectively, as long as the economy works perfectly, while others (the Keynesians) consider that no mechanism is working in the economy for the establishment of full employment in the factor markets. These contrasting perspectives are based on and derived from their antagonistic premises: Say's law for the Ricardian and Walrasian economics and anti- or non-Say's law for the Keynesian economics. Say's law rules out general overproduction, while anti-Say's law allows for its possibility. Also, on the basis of the wage-fund theory, the classical economists advocate that the real-wage rate should be reduced, if Say's law does not work perfectly so that there remains some positive amount of unemployment to be removed from the market. Keynesian economists, on the other hand, might direct our attention to the fact that labour and capital are complementary, rather than substitutive, so that a decline in the real-wage rate will give rise to a decrease in the demand for the consumption goods but does not create any significant substitution effect between labour and capital in favour of the former. Therefore, it will create a decrease in employment.

These contradictory views still coexist in the general field of economics; economists are divided into their respective camps. In this chapter we compare the three schools: Ricardian, Walrasian and Keynesian by simplifying their models drastically so as to be suitable for a two-industry–two-factor framework and will show how restrictive, and rich in implications, the two premises, Say's law and the wage-fund theory, are. It will be seen that economic theory has developed in such a direction that it frees itself from them.

2 Let us consider an economy consisting of two production sectors: consumption goods and capital goods industries. In the case of the model which I call 'Ricardian', the consumption goods industry is agriculture, and thus the economy is made up of workers, capitalists and landowners. In the case of the 'Walrasian' and 'Keynesian' models, there is no agriculture, and, therefore, no landowner.[1] Price, quantity and production coefficients referring to the consumption goods industry are represented by Greek letters: π is the price of the consumption goods, ξ its output, κ the capital coefficient and λ the labour–input coefficient of the consumption goods industry. p, x, k, l are those for the capital goods industry, respectively. We also assume that one unit of capital goods provides one unit of capital services and represent the price of the last by q.

In the following, price variables are all expressed in terms of consumption goods (say, corn in the Ricardian model or a vitamin compound in the Walrasian and Keynesian models); π is, therefore, always unity; w expresses the real wage rate and p the amount of corn or vitamin with which one can buy a unit of capital goods. Since the Ricardian school assumes that it takes one period (say, a year) to produce consumption goods (corn), the capitalists of that industry must have enough capital to enable them to buy κ units of capital goods (machines) and employ λ units of labour, per unit of output, for one year before the output is actually produced. In the Ricardian model, it is assumed that the capital goods industry pays wages in advance at the beginning of the period, so that the capitalists must have the capital to subsist workers, for which interest is charged; the total amount of capital for the production of one unit of capital goods is: $wl + pk$. It is assumed that capital goods depreciate in both industries at the common rate δ.

For agriculture it is assumed that, inputs of capital and labour, κ and λ, per unit of output depend on the output of corn, ξ. The total cost of output, including depreciation and normal profits (or interest), is denoted by

$$wL(\xi) + p\delta K(\xi) + r[wL(\xi) + pK(\xi)]$$

---

[1] In Walras' own model there are agriculture and landowners, but he neglected the production lag essential to agriculture. He, unlike Ricardo, did not single out agriculture as a sector which played a crucial role in the working of his model; for him, it is merely one of n sectors. Because of this, I exclude it from my Walrasian model and assume, throughout the following, that non-agricultural industries do not use land in any of our three models, Ricardian, Walrasian and Keynesian.

where $K(\xi) = \kappa(\xi)\xi$ and $L(\xi) = \lambda(\xi)\xi$; r represents the normal rate of profit q/p (or the interest rate). The surplus output, which is the difference between the output ξ and the total cost above, is maximized at the point where the following marginal price–cost equation is fulfilled

$$\pi = wL' + pA' + r(wL' + pK'),\tag{1}$$

where $K' = dK/d\xi$, $L' = dL/d\xi$ and $A' = \delta K'$. The Ricardian school attributes the surplus output of agriculture to the landowners as rent; we therefore have the rent equation:

$$\pi\xi = [w\lambda + p\alpha + r(w\lambda + p\kappa)]\xi + \pi R,\tag{1*}$$

where R stands for the total amount of rent and $\alpha = \delta\kappa$.

On the other hand, in the capital goods industry, input coefficients, k, l, a ($= \delta k$), are all constants, because of the assumed constant returns to scale. The price of capital goods is then determined such that it is equal to the average cost. We thus have

$$p = wl + pa + r(wl + pk).\tag{2}$$

In a particular case of $\delta = 1$, all capital goods cease to be serviceable after they have been used once. The above equations, (1) and (2), may then be reduced to

$$\pi = (1 + r)(wL' + pA'),$$

$$p = (1 + r)(wl + pa)$$

which are equations conventionally assumed in a discussion of Marx's 'transformation' problem. At the other extreme where $\delta = 0$, we have

$$\pi = wL' + r(wL' + pK'),$$

$$p = wl + r(wl + pk).$$

As we have already made clear, according to the Ricardian model there is a sharp contrast between the consumption goods and capital goods industries. For the latter we assume that the use of land is negligible and returns to scale constant, so that marginal and average input coefficients are the same. On the other hand, for the consumption goods industry (agriculture), the availability of the most important factor of production, land, is fixed, and hence returns diminish when the scale is expanded. Moreover, where land is cultivated more intensively, we may assume that the proportion of capital and labour does not change but that capital and labour per unit of output increase. We thus have

$$\lambda = f(\xi), \qquad \kappa = \gamma f(\xi), \qquad \text{and hence} \qquad K' = \gamma L',$$

where γ is the constant capital/labour ratio of agriculture which is assumed, throughout the following, to be *greater* than the corresponding ratio of the capital goods industry, $c = k/l$.[2] In the following we write λ and κ as functions of ξ simply as λ and κ.

3 In Walrasian and Keynesian economics the consumption goods industry is not agriculture but a manufacturing industry; furthermore the idea of the wage fund, as will be discussed below, disappears. We shall assume that both consumption and capital goods are produced instantly. (They are subject to constant returns to scale, so that λ, κ, α, as well as l, k, a, are all constant.) Thus no interest is charged on the wage bill in the price determination equations, which are written as:

$$\pi = w\lambda + p\alpha + rp\kappa, \tag{1'}$$

$$p = wl + pa + rpk. \tag{2'}$$

In these equations, as well as in (1) and (2), we may write rp as q; that is the profits or the price to be paid for capital services used.

The demand–supply (or input–output) equation for consumption goods is written in the following form. First, in the case of the Ricardian school which is based on the wage fund theory, let $\bar{\xi}$ be the wage fund from the previous period. In the current period the two industries start production at the levels ξ and x, respectively. Total wages amount to $w(\lambda\xi + lx)$, which workers spend to buy corn. Capitalists do not consume and their total profits are invested. As for the landowners, we assume, for the sake of simplicity, that they do not consume corn; they spend their total income on luxuries which have to be imported since the economy does not produce them. Taking corn as numeraire ($\pi = 1$), the market for corn is cleared if and only if

$$\bar{\xi} = w(\lambda\xi + lx). \tag{3}$$

---

[2] That is to say, the consumption goods industry is always more capital intensive than the capital goods industry. The opposite case where $c \geqq \gamma$ can *mutatis mutandis* be dealt with in a similar way.

In the case of no production lag, as is assumed by Walrasian and Keynesian economists, this is reduced to

$$\xi = w(\lambda\xi + lx). \tag{3'}$$

Thus consumption goods are produced instantly, offered to the market and bought by the workers.

There is a substantial difference in implication between (3) and (3'). In the case of the wage-fund theory (3), an increase in the output of capital goods x gives rise to a decrease in the output of consumption goods, ξ, because they compete for the limited resources of the wage fund $\bar{\xi}$. On the other hand, the investment multiplier theory works in the case of (3'); it is seen that an increase in x would create an expansion of ξ according to the following formula derived from (3'):

$$\xi = \frac{wl}{1 - w\lambda} x.$$

Note that $w\lambda < 1$ from the price–cost equation (1') as π is set at 1. This means that the Walrasian and Keynesian schools replace the classical idea of the wage-fund theory of real wage determination by a theory of interindustrial repercussion between the capital goods and consumption goods industries. As will be seen later, this is one of the most significant structural differences between the Ricardian model, on the one hand, and the Walrasian and Keynesian models, on the other.

As for the savings–investment equation, we have already assumed in (3) and (3') that capitalists do not consume and workers and landowners, who exist in Ricardian economics, do not save, so that total gross savings including depreciation amount to:

$$p(\alpha\xi + ax) + r[w(\lambda\xi + lx) + p(\kappa\xi + kx)]$$

in the Ricardian model, or

$$p(\alpha\xi + ax) + rp(\kappa\xi + kx)$$

in the Walrasian and Keynesian models. Adding (1*) to (2) multiplied by x and taking (3) or (3') into account, it can be shown that savings of the Ricardian model equal investment, $\Delta\bar{\xi} + px$, where $\Delta\bar{\xi} = (\xi - R) - \bar{\xi}$ represents the investment in the wage fund, while px the investment in the capital goods. Landowners who have received rent of the amount R from output ξ are assumed to spend it in the foreign market on luxuries, and the remaining amount of corn, $\xi - R$, is devoted to the wage fund in the next period. On the other hand, in the Walrasian system, there is no wage fund; total investment is only px, which is equal to savings. Thus, in the Ricardian and Walrasian systems, we have the following savings–investment equations, respectively:

$$\Delta \bar{\xi} + px = p(\alpha \xi + ax) + r[w(\lambda \xi + lx) + p(\kappa \xi + kx)], \qquad (4)$$

$$x = (\alpha \xi + ax) + r(\kappa \xi + kx).^3 \qquad (4')$$

It is noted that in these cases, Say's law prevails in Keynes' sense, because there is no independent investment function and (4) or (4') holds wherever (1*), (2), (3) or (1'), (2'), (3'), are established, so that it is not an independent equation. Where, as in Keynes' model, investment decisions are made, say by entrepreneurs, independently of savings, investment x should be given at a particular level i, or as a function of some economic variables, $i(\ldots)$, determined by entrepreneurs. Therefore, we must have, in place of the neoclassical equation (4'), the Keynesian condition:

$$i = x = (\alpha \xi + ax) + r(\kappa \xi + kx). \qquad (4'')$$

The final set of equations consists of the full utilization equation of capital and the full employment equation of labour, both of which can be shown to hold when Say's law holds:

$$\kappa \xi + kx = M, \qquad (5)$$

$$\lambda \xi + lx = N, \qquad (6)$$

where M stands for the total stock of capital and N for the total working population. (We assume that there is a non-negative solution to (5) and (6). If M is too low to establish such a solution, unemployment known as Marxian unemployment will result.) Where Say's law does not prevail, the full-utilization–full-employment equilibrium will not necessarily be realized. In particular, if i is set too low, x will also be low; hence we will have a situation of undercapacity–underemployment production. Thus

$$\kappa \xi + kx \leqq M, \qquad (5')$$

$$\lambda \xi + lx \leqq N. \qquad (6')$$

---

[3] Note that p has been eliminated from both sides of the savings–investment equation.

4 We now have the following three systems. The first is based on the wage-fund theory and Say's law, which we may call the *Ricardian system*:

$$\pi = wL' + pA' + r(wL' + pK'), \atop p = wl + pa + r(wl + pk),$$ the price–cost equations, $\quad$ (1) (2)

$$\xi = w(\lambda\xi + lx),$$ the wage-fund theory, $\quad$ (3)

$$\Delta\overline{\xi} + px = p(\alpha\xi + ax) + r[w(\lambda\xi + lx) + p(\kappa\xi + kx)],$$

$$\text{Say's law,} \quad (4)$$

$$\kappa\xi + kx = M,$$ the full utilization equation, $\quad$ (5)

$$\lambda\xi + lx = N,$$ the full employment equation, $\quad$ (6)

where

$$\Delta\overline{\xi} = (\xi - R) - \overline{\xi},$$

R being determined by the rent equation (1*).

The second system assumes Say's law but no production lag. This is the *Walrasian system*:

$$\pi = w\lambda + p\alpha + rp\kappa, \atop p = wl + pa + rpk,$$ the price–cost equations, $\quad$ (1') (2')

$$\xi = w(\lambda\xi + lx),$$ the multiplier theory, $\quad$ (3')

$$x = (\alpha\xi + ax) + r(\kappa\xi + kx),$$ Say's law, $\quad$ (4')

$$\kappa\xi + kx = M,$$ the full utilization equation, $\quad$ (5)

$$\lambda\xi + lx = N,$$ the full employment equation. $\quad$ (6)

Finally, by negating both premises of the Ricardian school, i.e. the wage-fund theory and Say's law, we obtain the *Keynesian system*:

$$\pi = w\lambda + p\alpha + rp\kappa, \atop p = wl + pa + rpk,$$ the price–cost equations, $\quad$ (1') (2')

$$\xi = w(\lambda\xi + lx),$$ the multiplier theory, $\quad$ (3')

$$i = x = (\alpha\xi + ax) + r(\kappa\xi + kx),$$ the investment function, $\quad$ (4'')

$$\kappa\xi + kx \leqq M,$$ undercapacity, $\quad$ (5')

$$\lambda\xi + lx \leqq N,$$ underemployment. $\quad$ (6')

In this last system strict inequality will prevail in either (5′) or (6′), or both, if the level of investment i is sufficiently low.

In all these three systems, endogenous variables are prices, π, p, w, r, and outputs, ξ, x. As π is set at 1 by normalization, the number of equations exceeds the number of endogenous variables by 1 in the first two systems, but, as will be seen below, one of the equations follows from the rest. In the third system, where (4″) contains two equations, overdetermination arises in order for (5″) and (6″) to hold with equality. This is because, although the second equation of (4″) follows from (1′), (2′) and (3′), the first remains.

Let us now assume that the price–cost equations – (1) and (2), or (1′) and (2′) – and the market-clearing equations – (3) and (4), or (3′) and (4′), or (3′) and (4″) – always hold true, and concentrate our attention upon the factor markets for capital and labour. First, the excess demand for capital is zero if and only if

$$ED_K = [\kappa(\xi/M) + k(x/M) - 1]M \tag{7}$$

vanishes. Eliminating ξ by the use of (3) and taking definitions, $\bar{w} = \bar{\xi}/N$, $\gamma = \kappa/\lambda$ and $c = k/l$ into account, we have

$$ED_K = [\gamma(\bar{w}/w)(N/M) + l(c - \gamma)(x/M) - 1]M. \tag{7'}$$

Assuming that the consumption goods industry is more capital intensive than the capital goods industry ($\gamma > c$) (so that the part in the parentheses of the second term on the right-hand side of the above expression is negative), we find that the equilibrium curve of capital utilization, $ED_K = 0$, traces out a downward sloping curve which starts from the wage rate

$$w = \bar{w}\gamma(N/M) \qquad \text{at } x/M = 0$$

and reaches

$$w = \bar{w}c(N/M) \qquad \text{at } x/M = 1/k, \text{ where } \xi = 0.$$

On a plane measuring w along the vertical axis and x/M along the horizontal axis, the *mm′* curve represents the equilibrium curve (see Figure 6). Keeping x/M constant at a certain level and decreasing (or increasing) w to a level which is lower (or higher) than the equilibrium level on the *mm′* curve, we obviously have an excess demand for (or supply of) capital.

Under the classical wage-fund theory (3), the excess demand for labour may be written as:

$$ED_L = (\lambda \xi + lx) - N = (\bar{w} - w)N/w, \tag{8}$$

where $\bar{w} = \xi/N$, which obviously stands for the availability of consumption goods per worker. If the actual wage rate w equals $\bar{w}$, the excess demand for labour ED_L is zero; thus $\bar{w}$ may be referred to as the full employment level of the wage rate. If w is lower than this, there is an excess demand for labour, but a wage rate above $\bar{w}$ gives rise to an excess supply of labour. From this point of view it is thus seen that unemployment is a consequence of too high a wage rate, whilst a shortage of labour results from too low a wage rate. In view of (8), Figure 6 shows $ED_L = 0$ by a straight horizontal line through $\bar{w}$, i.e. the line nn' that is the curve of the excess demand for labour being zero. The upper (lower) half of the plane divided by nn' is the region where an excess supply of (or demand for) labour prevails.

Let us now denote the region where excess supply prevails for both capital and labour by A, the region where excess demand prevails for capital and excess supply for labour by B, the region where we have excess demand for both capital and labour by C, and finally the region where we have excess supply for capital and excess demand for labour by D. These are divided by the two curves mm' and nn' as Figure 6 illustrates. It is noted that A, B, C, and D are located anticlockwise around the intersection W of the mm' and nn' curves. W is obviously a general equilibrium point where equilibrium is established for both capital and labour.

5 Let us now turn to the Walrasian and Keynesian regimes, which are identical except that in the latter investment is not flexibly adjusted to savings but is regulated according to a certain independently determined investment function. To obtain the full-utilization-of-capital curve we substitute the multiplier formula into (5) or (5′); then

$$ED_K = [\kappa wl/(1 - w\lambda) + k]x - M, \tag{9}$$

from which we can see that the full utilization of capital, $ED_K = 0$, implies that w is zero when x/M is $1/k$ and $w = 1/\lambda$ at $x/M = 0$. (Note that we assume $\gamma > c$.)

On the other hand, in these two regimes the output of consumption goods is proportional to the output of capital goods because of the

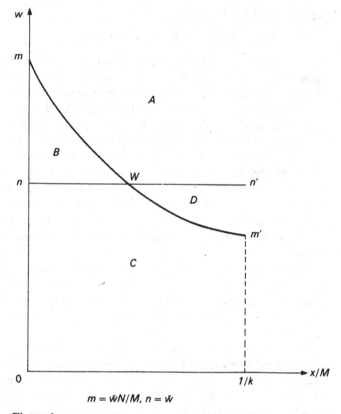

$$m = \bar{w}N/M, \; n = \bar{w}$$

Figure 6

multiplier theory (3'); substituting this relationship into (6) or (6'), we have

$$ED_L = xl/(1 - w\lambda) - N. \tag{10}$$

It is immediately clear that the real wage rate w should be fixed according to the formula,

$$w = (1/\lambda)[1 - (l/N)(x/M)M],$$

in order to be fully employed, i.e., in order to have $ED_L = 0$. Therefore, we have a straight full employment curve which starts at $w = 1/\lambda$ when x/M is set at zero and ends at $w = 0$ when x/M takes

Table 1

	Labour	
	excess supply	excess demand
Capital		
excess supply	A	D
excess demand	B	C

on the value, $(1/l)(N/M)$. Keeping x constant and increasing (or decreasing) w, it is seen from (10) that above (or below) the full employment line there is a region of excess demand for (or supply of) labour.

This full employment line, together with the full-utilization-of-capital curve obtained in the above, produces Figure 7. As in Figure 6, the entire plane is divided into four sections: A, B, C, D. Their location, however, is a complete reverse to that of Figure 6. That is to say, the region C of excess demand for both capital and labour which is nearest to the origin in Figure 6 is located furthest from the origin in Figure 7; similarly, the position of region A (of excess supply of both capital and labour) is reversed between the two figures. However, since regions B and D do not change positions, the four regions, A to D, locate themselves clockwise around the general equilibrium point W in Figure 7, in the Walrasian and Keynesian models.

In these three regimes the economy works in the following manner. First, we are concerned with the Ricardian regime which satisfies Say's law. Given the real wage rate and the output of the capital goods x, the equilibrium output ξ of consumption goods is determined by (3). Hence the marginal input coefficients K', L', A' of agriculture are given in equation (1). It, together with (2), determines the price p of capital goods and the rate of profit r, since the price of consumption goods π is set at 1. Similarly, in the Walrasian regime the price equations (1′) and (2′) determine p and r, wherever the real wage rate is given, and the multiplier theory determines ξ, wherever x is given. Once (1), (2), (3) (or (1′), (2′), (3′)) are satisfied,[4] the savings–investment equation (4) or (4′) is

_____
[4] Note that the rent equation (1*) is obtained by integrating (1) with respect to ξ.

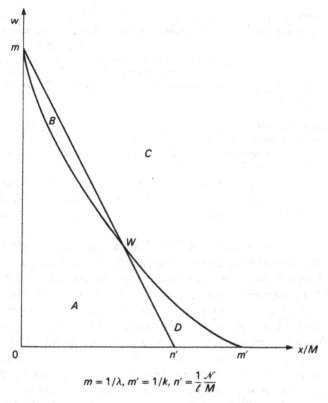

$$m = 1/\lambda, \ m' = 1/k, \ n' = \frac{1}{\ell}\frac{\mathcal{N}}{M}$$

Figure 7

shown to hold identically. This is because of the lack of an independent investment function that is imposed by Say's law. Therefore, in the factor markets of capital and labour we have two variables, w and x – note that ξ is a function of w and x – which adjust themselves such that an equilibrium is established in each factor market. There is no obstacle to realizing the full-utilization–full-employment equilibrium, (5) and (6); temporary equilibrium W will be established.

In the Keynesian system where we have an independent investment function i, the savings–investment equation (4″) is no longer an identity; x must be adjusted to satisfy it. Hence, in two factor markets we only have a single variable w, and the Keynesian regime is a system of overdeterminacy. Either of the two inequalities, (5′), (6′), or both of them, may not be fulfilled with equality. In particular, if x is fixed too low, both (5') and (6') will hold with strict inequality. Thus, in the Keynesian regime the temporary general equilibrium represented by the point W, is generally impossible, regardless of the assumption we make concerning the flexibility or rigidity of the wage rate w. It was Keynes who emphasized the significance of the role played by anti-Say's law in the theory of unemployment.

6 We have so far been concerned with analysing the short-run equilibrium assuming that the existing stocks of capital and labour, M and N, were given. From one period to another, however, capital grows at the rate $(x/M) - \delta$, and labour at the rate ρ. Usually, ρ is considered to be an increasing function of the real wage rate. But we assume that $\rho = \rho^* > 0$ as long as $w > w_s$, while $\rho = \rho_* < 0$ for all $w < w_s$, where ρ^* and ρ_* are constant, and w_s represents the subsistence real wage rate, at which ρ is of course equal to zero. This assumption is crucial for the following proof of convergence of the Ricardian type economy to the long-run stationary equilibrium. In fact, if our ρ function, which I consider approximates the actual population growth curve, was replaced by a more general, smooth S-shaped function, some additional assumption concerning the curvature of the S-shaped function would seem necessary for assuring stability.

Let us first examine the Ricardian model. At the short-run equilibrium point we have $ED_K = 0$ and $ED_L = 0$. The latter implies $w = \bar{w}$. Substituting this into $ED_K = 0$, we obtain

$$\frac{x}{M} = \frac{\gamma(N/M) - 1}{l(\gamma - c)}. \tag{11}$$

(See (7').) We first deal with the case of $\bar{w} > w_s$. If the gross rate of growth of capital, x/M, determined by the above formula is larger (or smaller) than the rate of depreciation of capital *plus* the rate of growth of the labourforce, $\delta + \rho^*$, then capital M grows faster (or slower) than labour N; therefore, x/M diminishes (or increases) according to the formula (11), until it finally reaches $\delta + \rho^*$. (During this process of adjustment of M and N, the short-run full employment wage rate $\bar{w}$ would of course be affected, but as long as $\bar{w}$ remains greater than w_s, there is no change in ρ^* by virtue of our assumption. Thus there is no alteration in the conclusion that the rate of net growth of capital, $(x/M) - \delta$, eventually equals the rate of growth of the labourforce ρ^*.) Similarly, providing $\bar{w} < w_s$, it can be shown that the rate of net growth of capital will approach ρ_*.

After the rates of growth of capital and labour have been equalized, the real wage rate $\bar{w}$ will fluctuate in the following way. Dividing the full utilization and full employment equations in period t by N_{t+1}, and eliminating x_t/N_t from them, we obtain, in view of $N_{t+1} = (1 + \rho^*)N_t$,

$$\frac{\xi_t}{N_{t+1}} = \frac{[(M_t/N_t) - c]\gamma}{(1 + \rho^*)\kappa(\xi_t)(\gamma - c)} \tag{12}$$

where γ and c, as before, are the capital/labour ratios of the consumption and capital goods industries, respectively. Hence,

$$\kappa(z_t N_{t+1})z_t = \frac{[(M_t/N_t) - c]\gamma}{(1 + \rho^*)(\gamma - c)} \tag{13}$$

where $z_t = \xi_t/N_{t+1}$.

On the other hand, if we put $x_t/M_t = \delta + \rho^*$ in equation (11) above, we have

$$\frac{M_t}{N_t} = \frac{c\gamma}{k(\delta + \rho^*)(\gamma - c) + c}, \tag{14}$$

so that M_t/N_t and, hence, the right-hand side of (13) are constant. Taking z and κ along the horizontal and vertical axes respectively, we draw, in Figure 8, the rectangular hyperbola, $\kappa z = H$, where H is the constant given on the right-hand side of (13). Also, taking N_{t+1} as a parameter, a curve of $\kappa(zN_{t+1})$ as a function of z is drawn in the same figure. It is evident that the intersection of this curve with the hyperbola gives the solution to (13) which is $z_t = \xi_t/N_{t+1}$.

As $\rho^* > 0$, N increases through time. In $t + 2$, the curve κ as a function of z shifts upwards because $N_{t+2} > N_{t+1}$. This shift gives rise to a leftwards shift of the intersection of the κ curve and the hyperbola, as is seen in Figure 8, and, therefore, the solution z to (13) declines: $z_{t+1} < z_t$. As Figure 8 shows, this means $\kappa(z_{t+1}N_{t+2}) > \kappa(z_t N_{t+1})$, which in turn means $\xi_{t+1} > \xi_t$.

On the other hand, in view of $K' = \gamma L'$ and $A' = \delta K'$, it follows from (1) that

$$1 = [w_t + p_t\delta\gamma + r_t(w_t + p_t\gamma)]L'.$$

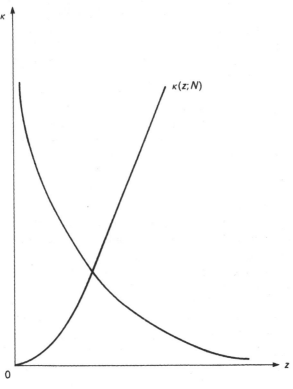

Figure 8

As ξ grows, L' also increases from period to period. This implies that the part in the brackets declines from one period to another. Dividing (1*) for period t by N_{t+1} and taking $K = \gamma L$ and $A = \delta K$, we obtain

$$\frac{\xi_t}{N_{t+1}} - \frac{R_t}{N_{t+1}} = [w_t + p_t \delta \gamma + r_t(w_t + p_t \gamma)] \frac{1}{\gamma} \kappa(\xi_t) \frac{\xi_t}{N_{t+1}}.$$

Since the wage fund of period $t + 1$, $\bar{\xi}_t$, equals output in period t, ξ_t, minus rent, R_t, it is clear that the left-hand side of this equation is the same as $\bar{w}_{t+1} = \bar{\xi}_t/N_{t+1}$ while, on the right-hand side, $\kappa(\xi_t)\xi_t/N_{t+1}$ is constant because of (13) and (14), and the part in the brackets diminishes over time. Hence $\bar{w}_t > \bar{w}_{t+1} > \bar{w}_{t+2} > \cdots$.

In this way, while $\bar{w} > w_s$ the wage rate will decline further and further. In the same way, while $\bar{w} < w_s$, the wage rate continues to rise, because the population declines at a constant rate $\rho_* < 0$. We may thus conclude that the subsistence real wage rate w_s is stable in both directions; if the wage rate is set above (or below) w_s, it declines (or rises) towards it.

At w_s we have $\rho = 0$, so that there is no population growth and the rate of growth of capital x/M equals the rate of depreciation δ. Thus w_s gives a stationary equilibrium, at which $\zeta, \bar{\zeta}, R$ are all constant over time; $\Delta\bar{\zeta}$ no longer appears in the savings–investment equation (4), so that considering (3) and (5) we have

$$\frac{x}{M} = \delta + r\,\frac{\bar{\zeta} + pM}{pM}. \tag{15}$$

As $x/M = \delta$, we have $r = 0$ in the stationary state. It must be noted, however, that this conclusion results from the assumption that capitalists do not consume. Where they consume, we get the following idea of the 'subsistence rate of profit' proposed by Samuelson and Casarosa.[5]

Let Q_s be the total amount of capitalists' consumption at the subsistence level. It is the sum of their food and non-food consumption; that is, $Q_s = \eta_s + py_s$, where η_s and y_s represent capitalists' food and non-food consumption at the subsistence level, respectively. We then have from the savings–investment equation (4)

$$(\Delta\bar{\zeta} - \eta_s) + p(x - y_s) + Q_s$$
$$= p(\alpha\zeta + ax) + r[w(\lambda\zeta + lx) + p(\kappa\zeta + kx)]. \tag{16}$$

Investment in the wage fund and investment in capital goods are now smaller, by η_s and y_s respectively, than in the corresponding case where capitalists do not consume.[6] In the state of stationary equilibrium there is no net investment in the wage fund, so that $\Delta\bar{\zeta} - \eta_s = 0$, and investment in capital goods is equal to depreciation, so that $x - y_s = \alpha\zeta + ax$; hence, equation (16) above reduces to $Q_s = r(\bar{\zeta} + pM)$. Obviously the part in parentheses expresses the total amount of capital including the wage fund. The rate of profit thus

[5] P. A. Samuelson, 'The Canonical Classical Model of Political Economy', *Journal of Economic Literature*, 1978, pp. 1,415–34. C. Casarosa, 'The "New View" of the Ricardian Theory of Distribution and Economic Growth', in G. A. Caravale (ed.), *The Legacy of Ricardo*, Blackwell, 1985, pp. 45–58.
[6] We assume that capitalists can consume 'capital goods'. This *prima facie* unrealistic character of our model can be easily removed by introducing luxury goods.

determined may be called the subsistence rate of profit, at which the rate of net investment is zero. By denoting this profit rate by r_s and the number of capitalists in the economy by n, we have

$$r_s = \frac{Q_s}{n} \frac{n}{\bar{\xi} + pM}.$$

In this expression, the first factor, Q_s/n, represents the per capita subsistence consumption of capitalists, which would be comparable with, but probably higher than, the subsistence wage of workers. The second factor, $(\bar{\xi} + pM)/n$ stands for the total capital per capitalist. Its value is highly flexible; it has an historical tendency to become larger and larger because each capitalist tends to manage an ever growing amount of capital. Thus we may regard the eventual value of r_s as zero, and in such a case the previous conclusion that r is zero in the long-run equilibrium is reconfirmed.[7]

Finally, let us denote the net rate of growth of the aggregate capital (the wage-fund and the stock of capital goods) by g. As $g = [\Delta\bar{\xi} + p(x - \alpha\xi - ax)]/(\bar{\xi} + pM)$, it can easily be shown that (4) implies $g = r$. This is a result which holds regardless of whether the aggregate capital grows in balance or not. It was emphasized by Bruno as the 'fundamental duality relation' in the theory of growth, but is a rather obvious implication of Say's law.[8]

7 The Walrasian economy works through time in the following way. Figure 7 is reproduced in Figure 9, with the addition of the rate-of-growth-of-the-labourforce curve, $\rho\rho'$. We assume ρ is independent of the real wage rate. Note that points m and m' are fixed, but $n' \left(= \frac{1}{l}\frac{N}{M} \right)$ moves leftwards or rightwards according to whether N/M decreases or increases. Because Say's law prevails in the Walrasian economy, the temporary equilibrium W is realized and the capital stock will grow at the rate g^0, while the labourforce at ρ. As $g^0 > \rho$, the labour/capital ratio N/M will decline; so n' moves leftwards and the point of temporary equilibrium (that is the

[7] Subtracting $Q_s = r_s(\bar{\xi} + pM)$ from (16) we obtain the Samuelson–Casarosa equation,

$$I = (r - r_s)(\bar{\xi} + pM),$$

where I signifies the total net investment, $(\Delta\bar{\xi} - \eta_s) + p(x - y_s - \alpha\xi - ax)$.
[8] M. Bruno, 'Fundamental Duality Relation in the Pure Theory of Capital and Growth', *Review of Economic Studies*, 1969, pp. 39–54.

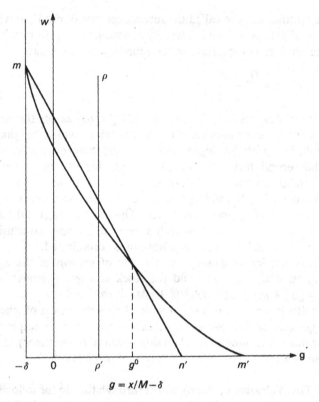

$$g = x/M - \delta$$

Figure 9

intersection of the full employment line mn' and the full utilization curve mm') climbs up the curve. It will finally reach the long-run equilibrium point W^* at which the lines mn', mm' and $\rho\rho'$ all meet each other. (See Figure 10.) Thus the rate of growth of capital stock equals the rate of growth of the labourforce at W^*, so that a proportional growth of capital and labour will be obtained.

In a state of balanced growth between capital and labour, it can be seen that outputs of consumption and capital goods industries, ξ and x, increase proportionately. In both industries, however, returns remain unchanged in spite of the expansion of the scale of production. This is because the limitedness of land is no longer an obstacle to large-scale production. However, some neoclassical economists may want to introduce diminishing returns to scale,

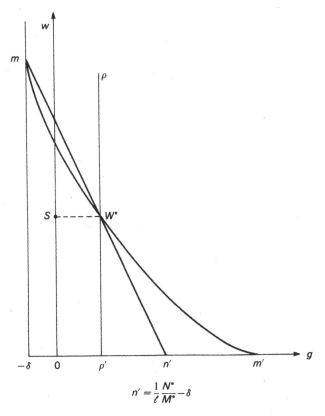

$$n' = \frac{1}{\ell}\frac{N^*}{M^*} - \delta$$

Figure 10

independently of the use of land. For example, if either of the manufacturing industries producing consumption goods or capital goods is subject to diminishing returns, say, because of the scarcity of entrepreneurship, both λ and κ or both k and l will increase as ξ or x is increased. Then in Figure 10 the point m $(= 1/\lambda)$ will be pushed downwards or the point m' $(= (1/k) - \delta)$ will shift leftwards. In either case, the long-run equilibrium point W^* slides down along the natural growth rate line $\rho\rho'$. Finally the wage rate at W^* will reach the subsistence level w_s; then ρ will become zero. This change in ρ will create a movement of the equilibrium point from W^* to S which is the point of the long-run stationary equilibrium on the vertical axis. The point m is further pushed down and m' shifts leftwards, so that the curves mm' and mn' finally cross the vertical axis at S where growth stops: $g = (x/M) - \delta = 0$. Workers are paid subsistence wages, and capitalists earn zero profits. (See Figure 10.)

In this process of quasi-Ricardian economic growth, entrepreneurs, like landowners in the Ricardian system, earn quasi-rent, which constitutes supernormal profits. The normal part of profits is transferred to capitalists and saved by them, while the supernormal part is retained by entrepreneurs who spend it on luxury goods, as landowners do in the Ricardian system. In stationary equilibrium the normal rate of profit will vanish or will be equal to a certain 'subsistence level of profit'. However, entrepreneurs earn a significant amount of quasi-rent and make no savings from it. This implicitly assumed difference in the savings attitude between capitalists and entrepreneurs is too unnatural and implausible for us to make an analogy of the Ricardian tendency towards the stationary equilibrium reasonable in the neoclassical world.

We have so far assumed that no industry requires land. In Walras' own theory of economic progress,[9] however, he assumed that all manufacturing industries use land as well as labour and capital and that the labour and capital coefficients increase when the use of land per unit of output diminishes. He also tacitly assumed that the productive sectors of his economy include agriculture but that it produces output instantly. Being equipped with these assumptions, Walras' three-factor model may be written in the form of our 'Walrasian' system, with the production coefficients of the consumption goods industry, λ, α, κ and those of the capital goods industry, l, a, k, increasing where outputs, ξ and x, respectively expand. Therefore, in the same way as above, though making some necessary alteration to the details, we can generate quasi-Ricardian growth by making the system work through time. The quasi-rent produced during the course of economic progress goes to the landowners in the form of rent, as it went to entrepreneurs in the previous scenario. Thus Walras was not simply a neoclassical economist but, furthermore, very much a Ricardian as far as the theory of economic progress is concerned.

Finally, in the Keynesian economy, temporary equilibrium is not necessarily realized since Say's law does not hold. It is not guaranteed that independently decided investment will be at a level such that

---

[9] Walras, *Elements*, pp. 382–92.

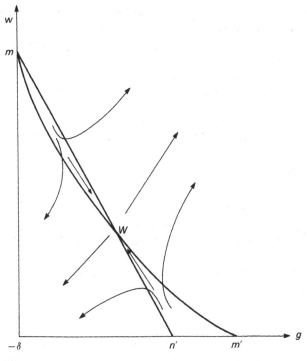

Figure 11

the existing stock of capital is fully utilized. The actual position a of the economy will not coincide with the temporary equilibrium point W. If a is located in the region A in Figure 7, there will be an excess supply in both capital and labour markets. If we assume that the wage rate w decreases or increases according to whether there is an excess supply of or demand for labour, we find that w decreases if a is in A or B and increases if it is in C or D. Investment i may be adjusted such that i is decreased or increased if there is an excess supply of or demand for capital, respectively, so that i/M decreases if a is in A or D and increases if it is in B or C. Being provided with this adjustment assumption, we have a Keynesian phase diagram as Figure 11 illustrates.

It can be easily seen that W is a saddle point. There are two (and only two) streams (one in region B and the other in D) which bring a to W, but at all other points centrifugal forces work. Moreover, the full employment line mn' and hence the temporary equilibrium point W move unless the rate of growth of the labourforce equals that of the capital stock at the actual point a. Therefore, even if a is on one of the two streams converging upon W at some point in time, the actual position a' at the next point in time will not be on a new stream which converges on the new temporary equilibrium. It is thus almost impossible that the actual economy will eventually settle at the long-run equilibrium, a particular temporary equilibrium which reproduces itself once it is established. This is the knife-edge property of the Keynesian economy which has been emphasized by Harrod.[10]

8 We have so far used the concept of the aggregate savings defined as an excess of the aggregate income (or output) over consumption. The aggregate output is obtained by adding (1*) to (2) multiplied by x in the case of the Ricardian economics, or by adding (1') multiplied by ξ to (2) by x in the case of the Walrasian and Keynesian economics. Subtracting from this the total amount of consumption, which is $\bar{\xi} + R = w(\lambda\xi + lx) + R$ in the case of Ricardo, or $\xi = w(\lambda\xi + lx)$ in the case of Walras and Keynes, we obtain the gross savings which are

$$p(\alpha\xi + ax) + r[w(\lambda\xi + lx) + p(\kappa\xi + kx)] \text{ in the Ricardo regime,}$$
$$p(\alpha\xi + ax) + rp(\kappa\xi + kx) \text{ in the Walras and Keynes regimes.} \tag{17}$$

We have said so far that Say's law prevails if the savings thus defined are automatically invested. (In the case of Keynes who denies Say's law, investment is given by an independent investment function; and, by adjusting ξ and x, savings adjust themselves to investment determined in this way, but not vice versa.)

On the other hand, we may alternatively define savings in the following way. Assuming workers and rentiers do not save while capitalists save all the profits accruing to the whole stock of capital they own, $\bar{\xi} + pM$ or pM, then the gross savings are given

$$p(\alpha\xi + ax) + r(\bar{\xi} + pM) \text{ in the Ricardo regime,}$$
$$p(\alpha\xi + ax) + rpM \text{ in the Walras and Keynes regimes,} \tag{18}$$

which are referred to as the notional savings by some economists.

On the basis of this definition we may define a new Say's law which states that the entire notional savings are automatically invested.

Obviously, the two Say's laws are not necessarily equivalent. This is because, if Say's law in the first sense does not hold, M is not necessarily equal to $\kappa\xi + kx$, while $\bar\xi = w(\lambda\xi + lx)$, and Say's law in the second sense may still hold true. Throughout the following we assume that Say's law holds in both senses. It is then clear that under this strong version of Say's law investment equals savings in either sense, (17) or (18), and, therefore, $\kappa\xi + kx$ equals M, irrespective of the other equations of the system being fulfilled or not, so that regardless of the values of other variables, investment is adjusted such that not only is it equal to savings but also it establishes the full utilization of capital. Thus, under Say's law in the strong sense the economy is always located somewhere on the full-utilization-of-capital curve mm' in Figures 6 and 7.

Let us now suppose that there is an excess supply of labour for some reason. For Keynesians, as has been seen, this means that unemployment will be aggravated; the full-employment–full-capacity equilibrium is a saddle point and the wage flexibility and investment adjustment work in an adverse way. For Ricardians and Walrasians who believe Say's law, the picture is completely different. To show this we assume the strong version of Say's law in the following argument, so that the economy is always on the full-capacity curve mm'. As unemployment accompanies it, it must be on the upper half of the curve mm', i.e. on mW in Figures 6 and 7. If we assume that the wages will be decreased wherever there is unemployment,[11] then it is clear that the economy will climb down along the curve mW towards W. In exactly the same way, if there is an excess demand for labour, the economy should be in the lower half of the mm' curve, i.e. on the Wm' segment of the curve. The wages will adjust themselves so as to be higher. Then the economy will approach the equilibrium point W.

This shows that Say's law (of the strong form) plays a powerful role in the stability argument. Those economists such as Ricardians and Walrasians who believe in the regime of Say's law trust the price mechanism, whereas other economists (Keynesians) who reject

[11] Of course, the money wages, rather than the real wages, are adjusted where there is an excess supply or demand in the labour market. Since in our model of real economy money is either eliminated, or its value is taken as constant, the money wages are either absent or change in proportion to the real wages.

the law denounce it. For Keynesians, a reduction of wages in the
time of unemployment implies a decline in the consumption which,
in turn, implies a decrease in the use of capital as well as an increase
in unemployment; an excess supply of capital increased in this way
gives rise to a decrease in investment. Therefore, more
unemployment will result. It would, in any case, be interesting to
see that economists' view of the price mechanism is entirely different
in dependence on whether they subscribe to Say's law of the strong
form.

11 The epoch of Ricardo's economics

1 The actual economy is in a constant state of change; economic theory also changes and develops. This chapter will investigate whether there is some kind of congruity between these phenomena. Obviously, the economy is the basis of people's lives, while economic theory or one's view of the economy belongs to the sphere of ideology. There are two distinct approaches to this congruence problem. Marxists regard ideology as a reflection of underlying basic material conditions, while Max Weber[1] emphasizes the importance of the reverse relationship, from ideology to economy. In our particular case, however, I consider that Weberian relationships are not significant, though I am ready, on the other hand, to accept that it is easy to point out a number of instances where actual economies have been influenced by economic theory. No one can deny that in many western economies the influence of Keynesian doctrines was apparent at least for some time after the War. The Bretton Woods regime of fixed exchange rates which worked from 1950 to 1970 is a well-known example. I shall later point out an economic structural change which was created by Ricardo's economics.

On the other hand, Marxian congruity is essential in this case, because when it is absent economic theory cannot claim to be a science. Unfortunately, the response of theory to the evolution of the economy is slow and delayed, and the epochs which are taken as the subject of investigation by the major economic theories have all so far remained obscure and unidentified; neoclassical (or classical) theorists and Keynesian economists have disputed with each other as if their respective theories are alternative theories of the same type of economy. Without specifying the object precisely

---

[1] M. Weber, *The Protestant Ethic and the Spirit of Capitalism*, George Allen and Unwin, London, 1930.

and accurately, contemporary economists have the unfortunate habit of constructing a *transcendental* model of capitalism (or the free enterprise system) and deriving absolute economic laws or theorems, so that they (or at least many of those who belong to the so-called neoclassical school) believe that their theorems are valid everywhere and forever, as long as capitalism persists. There are even economists who believe that their theorems would be correct and even valid and effective even if the capitalist varieties of economy all died out.

A brave investigation on the identification of the epochs of major economic theories has recently been made by Professor A. K. Dasgupta.[2] He traces the development of economic theory through specific periods, marked by particular historical and socio-economic conditions. Taking the British economy as the standard of reference, he first explains that 'the early phase of the industrial revolution' was the age of the classical theory,[3] by which he means the economics developed and advocated by such economists as Smith, Ricardo and Marx; it is of course a theory of capital accumulation and economic progress. Dasgupta also considers that 'marginalism would appear to be a kind of interlude in the course of the development of economic theory',[4] which is aimed at dealing with the static problem of relative prices and resource allocation. As for the Keynesian era, he says that 'the *General Theory* is the marker of the epoch.'[5] 'Marginalism came when capitalism found itself in what may be called its placid phase,'[6] whilst classical and Keynesian economics are congruent with the progressive and decaying phases of capitalism, respectively.

I have of course no objection to this kind of investigation. But it is very difficult for me to accept his way of handling the problem. First of all, his allotment of epochs to the three major theories, classical, marginal and Keynesian, is very ambiguous. The periodization of marginalism, for example, is not clearly specified; what he obtains almost amounts to a tautological conclusion that marginalism was valid in the period in which it was valid. Also, Dasgupta does not discuss how far back the commencement of the Keynesian epoch can be taken beyond the publication of the *General*

[2] A. K. Dasgupta, *Epochs of Economic Theory*, Basil Blackwell, Oxford, 1985.
[3] *Ibid.*, p. 5.
[4] *Ibid.*, p. 142.
[5] *Ibid.*, p. 8.
[6] *Ibid.*, p. 141.

Theory. Of course no one can provide exact answers to these questions, but we regrettably do not find a hint of the turning points from one economic theory to another, except very vague ones, in Dasgupta's work.

Moreover, as Hollander has already pointed out to Samuelson, there are substantial differences between Smith and Ricardo in their theories of accumulation;[7] there are non-trivial differences between Smith and Ricardo. Like classical theory, marginalist economics can hardly be defined clearly. Moreover, it is very difficult, or indeed almost impossible, to specify a single particular epoch to which the marginalist theory fits. The marginalist revolution (or innovation) is not a revolution due to a drastic change in the object, the actual economy, but a revolution or innovation in methodology. For marginalists it is perfectly legitimate to refurbish the Ricardian theory of accumulation by using concepts of marginalism. In fact Walras constructed his system so that it was amenable to Ricardo's conclusions, and he derived, using the marginalist method, '*the laws of the variation of prices in a progressive [but not static – M.M.] economy*' (his italics), as I have already pointed out. The problem of relative prices and resource allocation which is identified as the theme of marginalist theory by Dasgupta is not specific to any particular epoch; it is a universal problem found in all periods and the originator of this method sees it in a *progressive*, rather than static economy. The significance of the problem only fluctuates from one epoch to another according to circumstances.

In the following, I will, like Dasgupta, be concerned with the problem of the periodization of economic theory. However, there are noticeable differences between us. First, I compare Ricardian, Walrasian and Keynesian theories instead of classical, marginalist and Keynesian economics as Dasgupta did. Secondly, whereas Dasgupta divided epochs 'in terms of questions asked,'[8] I examine the three economic theories selected, asking a certain same question. It would, in fact, be almost meaningless to divide the history of economic theory into epochs according to the questions asked. Such a work would either end in arranging the questions asked in the order that economic theories appeared in history, as in the case of

---

[7] S. Hollander, 'On Professor Samuelson's Canonical Classical Model of Political Economy', *Journal of Economic Literature*, June 1980, p. 560.

[8] Dasgupta, *Epochs of Economic Theory*, p. 5n.

Dasgupta or, in its worst case, would be almost as meaningless as
the work of periodizing, say, economics, physics and psychology in
terms of their entirely different questions into the periods of
economics, the period of physics, etc. In this paper, I will take up
the problem of economic growth and capital accumulation and
examine how economic theory has changed in parallel to the change
in the character of the actual economy. Our Ricardian theory is a
mathematization of Ricardo's *Principles*; Keynesian theory is an
interpretation of Keynes' *General Theory* and Harrod's *Towards a
Dynamic Economics*; our Walrasian theory is a simplification of
Walras' general equilibrium theory of capital formation and is almost
equivalent to a linear-theoretic version of a Solow–Uzawa type
growth model.[9]

2   It goes without saying that the Ricardian model is based on an
economy where (1) agriculture produces a significant proportion of
the national product, so that the wage-fund theory holds and (2)
savers and investors are the same and consequently investment is
identically equal to savings, so that Say's law prevails. This model
naturally fits the economy at an early stage of development, say, in
the case of Britain, in the first half of the nineteenth century. In fact,.
according to historical statistics, the ratio of population engaged in
agriculture (including forestry and fishing) to that engaged in
manufacturing industry (including mining) is, in Britain, 1.21 in
1801, 1.09 in 1811, 0.74 in 1821, but only 0.51 in 1851. It then rapidly
decreases to the level of 0.19 in 1901 and 0.10 in 1951. From this
we may conclude that the first prerequisite of the Ricardian regime,
i.e. the dominance of agriculture, is more or less satisfied in the first
half of the nineteenth century, but that this era was already over in
Britain by the beginning of the twentieth century. The production
lag in agriculture no longer played an important role in the British
economy. It is no wonder that the Ricardian paradigm emphasizing
effects due to the agricultural production lag was replaced by
Walrasian or Keynesian theory constructed upon the assumption
that there is an instantaneous interindustrial multiplier effect from

[9] R. F. Harros, *Towards a Dynamic Economics*, 1948. R. M. Solow, 'A Contribution
to the Theory of Economics Growth', *Quarterly Journal of Economics*, 1956,
pp. 65–94. H. Uzawa, 'On a Two-Sector Model of Economic Growth', *Review of
Economic Studies*, 1961, pp. 40–7.

the manufacturing sector producing capital goods to the other manufacturing sector producing consumption goods.[10]

As for the second prerequisite of Ricardian economics, Say's law, it is very difficult to determine the degree of its applicability to the real world. We shall nevertheless try and determine it in the following way. We begin by classifying investment into two categories: the first is that part of investment which is decided independently of savings and is financed by borrowing money, while the second consists of those items of investment in which capitalists invest exactly the amount that they themselves have saved, and thus it is the category which constitutes the part satisfying Say's law. These two are referred to as the anti-Say's law and Say's law parts respectively. The ratio of the anti-Say's law part to total investment measures the degree of applicability of anti-Say's law index, R, that is

$$R = \frac{\text{anti-Say's law part}}{\text{Total investment}}.$$

Where Say's law is perfectly valid, the anti-Say's law index takes on the value of 0 and when investment is decided entirely independently of savings, the value of the index is 1.

The anti-Say's law part of investment may be further divided between private investment and public investment. If we assume that public investment is subject to anti-Say's law, that is to say, it is autonomously or politically decided, independently of savings, our anti-Say's law index cannot be lower than the ratio of public investment to total investment. This sets a lower bound to R. To obtain this ratio for each year we use the figures listed in the *British Economy Key Statistics 1900–1970*.[11] Dividing the gross fixed capital formation made by the public sector by the total gross domestic fixed capital formation and regarding the ratio obtained as a proxy for the ratio of public investment to total investment, we obtain the figures listed in Table 2, each of which gives a lower bound to the anti-Say's law index of the corresponding year. We note that it could be shown, if appropriate statistics were available, that the true value of the index would be much higher than the lower bound we obtained

[10] Phyllis Deane and W. A. Cole, *British Economic Growth, 1688–1959*, 2nd edn, Cambridge University Press, 1967, p. 142.
[11] *The British Economy Key Statistics, 1900–1970*, ed. by R. F. G. Alford and others, Times Newspapers Ltd, 1973, p. 13.

238   **Ricardo's economics**

Table 2 *Lower bounds to the anti-Say's law index R*

Year	(1) GDFCF	(2) PS	(3) (2) ÷ (1)	(4) NNI	(5) TGE	(6) (5) ÷ (4)
1861				727	72.9	10.0%
1866				846	66.5	7.9
1871				1015	67.8	6.7
1876				1099	74.7	6.8
1881				1117	80.6	7.2
1886				1136	92.2	8.1
1891				1373	93.4	6.8
1896				1484	105.1	7.1
1901	1501	311	20.7%	1727	193.3	11.2
1906	1444	229	15.9	1874	147.0	7.8
1911	1020	182	17.8	2076	167.9	8.1
1921	1289	393	30.5	4460	1188.1	26.2
1926	1512	505	33.4	3914	776.1	19.8
1931	1743	564	32.5	3666	814.2	22.2
1936	2172	583	26.8	4388	829.4	18.9
1951	2632	1294	48.0			
1956	3525	1588	45.0			
1961	4847	1957	40.4			
1966	6100	2789	45.7			
1970	6720	2947	43.8			

Notes: Figures in columns (1) and (2) are in terms of £ million at 1963 prices and those of (4) and (5) are in terms of £ million at current prices.

GDFCF means gross domestic fixed capital formation, PS the part of GDFCF made by the public sector, NNI the net national income and TGE the total gross expenditure of the government.

Sources: The British Economy Key Statistics 1900–1970, Times Newspapers Ltd, 1973, p. 13; B. R. Mitchell and Phyllis Deane, *Abstract of British Historical Statistics,* Cambridge University Press, 1962, p. 367 and p. 396.

because of the existence of private investment following anti-Say's law.

Table 2 shows that our lower bound of anti-Say's law index has a clear upward trend. It is less than 20 per cent for the years from 1900 to 1920 with an average of 18 per cent and between 23 per cent and 33 per cent in period 1921–38, the average being 30 per cent. In the postwar period, 1948–70, it is above 40 per cent throughout, with a peak of nearly 57 per cent and an average of 45 per cent. Viewing these figures it is certain that Say's law can hardly be a good approximation to the savings–investment relationship of the actual world since 1920. For the years before 1900, however, statistics similar to those which enabled us to produce Table 2 are unfortunately unavailable. We have, nevertheless, useful indirect information which would lead us to believe that public investment was not more dominant in the period 1855–99 than in 1900–20. In fact, calculating the ratio of total government expenditure to net national income for each year in the period 1855–99, by using the historical statistics compiled by Mitchell and Deane,[12] and comparing their average, 7.97 per cent with the average for the years 1900–14, 8.74 per cent, we may suppose that the share of public investment in total investment was more or less similar in the two periods, 1855–99 and 1900–14.

On the basis of these observations, we may conclude that Say's law is definitely not a hypothesis which is appropriate for modelling the economy after 1920. But the finding that the lower boundary of anti-Say's law index is relatively low in the years, 1855–99, enables us to make a conjecture to the effect that there may be more room for Say's law in the nineteenth century. If this conjecture is correct – that is, the economy is more or less on the side of Say's law rather than anti-Say's law throughout the nineteenth century – the first half is the age of Ricardian economics, as its two prerequisites are both fulfilled to some degree, while the period of 1855–1920 may be considered as the age of Walrasian economics. In this period, agriculture has already been reduced to an insignificant part of the economy and, if our conjecture is right, the savings–investment relationship is still on the side of Say's law, although the law itself cannot claim 100 per cent validity even at the beginning of the nineteenth century. The years after 1920 definitely belong to the era of Keynesian economics. We may thus say that the succession of Ricardian, Walrasian, and Keynesian models in the history of economic thought corresponds to the historical transformation of the British economy, although no one can deny that any of these models is a drastic abstraction and exaggeration of the characteristics of the reality.

3 None of the three theories above have been concerned with analysing the historical process of transition from one epoch to

---

[12] B. R. Mitchell and Phyllis Deane, *Abstract of British Historical Statistics*, Cambridge University Press, 1962.

another. Hypothetically speaking, it is conceivable that the transition from a Ricardian to a Walrasian regime would be caused by a trigger effect due to the invention of new production techniques. A new industry producing new consumption goods enters the Ricardian economy and replaces the old industry of agriculture. The rule of profitability works; the latter industry whose rate of profit is lower than that of the new industry closes down.

The actual historical transition, however, did not happen in this manner. It was neither purely economic or technological; it would have been influenced by many other elements – political, ideological and even accidental. In the case of the transition from the economy of Ricardo to that of Walras it is well-known that the success of Ricardian theory greatly contributed to the decline of the Ricardian-type economy. *Principles* opposed the Corn Laws. The revision of the Corn Laws was the hottest topic in politics in 1813–15, just before the publication of the first edition of the book in 1817.[13] Although Ricardo himself died in 1823, what he advocated in *Principles* was finally realized in 1846 when the Corn Laws were repealed. (A small, temporary tariff was retained till 1849.) Then agriculture declined drastically in Britain in the second half of the nineteenth century. The Ricardian model emphasizing the agricultural sector became unrealistic and was replaced by the Walrasian model ignoring the production lag specific to agriculture.

To show this we must first be concerned with estimating the output of agriculture of the relevant years. First of all, output statistics for corn (wheat, barley, oats) are available, in terms of bushels, for Great Britain only from 1884 and from 1847 (in terms of hundredweight) for Ireland.[14] Secondly, statistics of crop acreage for wheat, barley and oats are available only for the years since 1867 for Great Britain and since 1847 (except 1848) for Ireland.[15]

From these we obtain the outputs per acre for wheat, barley and oats for the years 1884–93. Their ten year averages are 29 bushels

[13] Ricardo himself published a pamphlet entitled 'An Essay on the Influence of a Low Price of Corn on the Profits of Stock, shewing the Inexpediency of Restrictions on Importation: with Remarks on Mr. Malthus' two Last Publications: "An Inquiry into the Nature and Progress of Men"; and "The Grounds of an Opinion on the Policy of Rewriting the Importation of Foreign Corn" ' in 1815. The *Principles* may be regarded as a book-scale amplification of the pamphlet with revisions and reconstructions.
[14] B. R. Mitchell and Phyllis Deane, *ibid.*, pp. 86–9.
[15] *Ibid.*, pp. 78–81.

for wheat, 33 bushels for barley and 37.8 bushels for oats. These are multiplied by the actual acreage of crops for the years 1867–83 to obtain outputs of wheat, barley and oats in Great Britain, which are then added to the Irish outputs of the respective grains in the respective years. Thus we obtain the estimates of the UK outputs for the years 1867–83. (In converting the Irish output into bushels we use the conversion ratios: 1.81 bushels per hundredweight for wheat, 2.08 bushels for barley and 2.80 bushels for oats.)[16]

In order to obtain the estimates for the years 1840–66, we follow the following procedure adopted by Deane and Cole.[17] First, assuming that seed-corn was equal to 15 per cent of the gross produce,[18] we have for each year, the formula:

the UK output $\times (1 - 0.15)$ + imports $-$ exports

which gives the total consumption of wheat (or barley or oats).[19] By dividing it by the population of the UK for the respective year, we finally obtain consumption per person of wheat (or barley, or oats). However, the UK output statistics are not available for the years 1840–66, while we know that the average consumption of wheat per person for the ten years, 1867–76, is 5.3 bushels; the figures similarly calculated for barley and oats are 2.8 and 5.2 bushels, respectively. We then estimate the UK output, O_t, for the year t ($t = 1840, \ldots, 1866$) by the following formula:

$0.85\ O_t =$ the population of year t *times* the average consumption per person obtained above *plus* exports *minus* imports.

The UK output series for the years since 1840 obtained in this way are summarized in Table 3. On the basis of these we may make the following observations. First we find that 5 per cent of the wheat production, 7 per cent of the barley production and 36 per cent of the oats production in the UK were produced in Ireland in 1867. Assuming that Ireland's shares of outputs of wheat, barley and oats in the UK production had been the same in the years 1840–5 as they were in 1867, we find, by using the conversion ratios of hundredweight into bushels mentioned above, that the aggregate

---

[16] *Ibid.*, p. 90.

[17] Phyllis Deane and W. A. Cole, *British Economic Growth, 1688–1959*, pp. 64–5.

[18] Deane and Cole assumed that it was 10 per cent; but they acknowledged that 'this proportion was probably a trifle low.' See *ibid.*, p. 65.

[19] See B. R. Mitchell and Phyllis Deane, *ibid.*, pp. 98–9, for the statistics of the imports of main grains and exports and reexports of wheat, 1840–1938.

corn output in Great Britain, 1840–5, is estimated at 38,836,000 quarters which compares with the Deane and Cole estimates for England and Wales, 21,102,000 qrs for 1800 and 27,873,000 qrs for 1820.[20] In view of the fact that our estimate includes the products of Scotland, it may be regarded as a reasonable figure which may be smoothly connected with the Deane–Cole estimates.

Secondly the table shows that the production of wheat drastically diminished after the repeal of the Corn Laws in 1846. It was 89 per cent of the 1846 production in the period 1847–9, 82 per cent in 1850–4. The corresponding percentages for periods 1855–9, 60–4, 65–9, 70–4, and 75–9 are 88 per cent, 74 per cent, 76 per cent, 70 per cent, 63 per cent, respectively. It eventually diminished to 33 per cent in the period 1900–4. In the case of barley the downward trend is less dramatic but still obvious. Barley production in the period 1900–4 is 76 per cent of its 1846 production. The production of oats does not trace out a similar downwards movement. It goes down to a level of 96 per cent of the 1846 production in 1865–79 but swings back to a level of 104 per cent in the period of 1900–4.

This decline of agriculture was paralleled by the expansion of the manufacturing industries so that agriculture's share in total gross national income which had been 36 per cent in 1811 was reduced to 22 per cent in 1841 and rapidly diminished to the level of 10 per cent in 1881 and 6 per cent in 1901.[21] Thus, in the last decades of the nineteenth century, British agriculture declined into a minor sector which can safely be neglected with regard to its relative magnitude. In this way, the British economy succeeded in virtually dismembering its agricultural sector as Ricardo advocated. This is a remarkable example of a Max Weber congruence (in a wider sense); that is, an adaptation of economy to ideology (economic theory).

4 About the effectiveness of the Corn Laws and consequences of its repeal there are various views. Engels, for example, said:

> The corn law of 1815 was passed to prohibit the importation of corn so long as the price was less than eighty shillings a quarter. This law was naturally a failure and it has had to be changed on several occasions. But this has not alleviated the agricultural distress. The only consequence of the corn laws was this; if there had been no such import restrictions, and if foreign corn had been

[20] Phyllis Deane and W. A. Cole, *British Economic Growth*.
[21] B. R. Mitchell and Phyllis Deane, *ibid.*, p. 366.

freely admitted, then the sickness afflicting English farming would soon have become acute and would have come to a head as an agricultural crisis. In fact the corn laws have turned 'agricultural distress' into a chronic illness which continually presses severely upon the unfortunate farm workers.[22]

Marx, on the other hand, noticed that the repeal of the Corn Laws had given rise to a transformation of British agriculture with land being more efficiently utilized. Marx wrote:

> When after the abolition of the Corn Laws, cultivation in England became still more intensive, a great deal of former wheat land was devoted to other purposes, particularly cattle pastures, while the fertile land best suited for wheat was drained and otherwise improved. The capital for wheat cultivation was thus concentrated in a more limited area.[23]

This is supplemented by the following comments:

> When the English corn duties were abolished in 1846, ... the landowning aristocracy ... became richer than ever. How did this occur? Very simple. In the first place, the farmers were now compelled by contract to invest £12 per acre annually instead of £8. And secondly, the landlords, being strongly represented in the Lower House too, granted themselves a large government subsidy for drainage projects and other permanent improvement on their land.[24]

As the above passage was written in 1844 and published in the following year, Engels made no comment on the effect of the repeal of the laws, though the passage might be interpreted as implying that he would have agreed to the view that the repeal turned the 'chronic illness' into an acute one. In the preface to the 1892 edition of *The Condition of the Working Class in England*, he acknowledged that the free trade policies pursued following the 1846 repeal had stimulated industry immensely. Marx evidently was ambivalent; on the one hand, he condemned the repeal of the laws because it invited countermeasures by the landowning aristocracy which neutralized its effects, while on the other hand, he acknowledged that it was powerful enough to force farmers to rationalize their business as well as making their use of land more efficient.

---

[22] F. Engels, *The Condition of the Working Class in England*, Basil Blackwell, 1958, pp. 295–6.
[23] K. Marx, *Capital*, Vol. III, Progress Publishers, Moscow, 1966, p. 680.
[24] *Ibid.*, p. 725.

Table 3 *The output and import of wheat, barley and oats: United Kingdom, 1840–1904* (in million bushels)*

Year	Output			Imports		
	Wheat	Barley	Oats	Wheat	Barley	Oats
1840–45	152.0	85.7	163.1	15.0	3.1	2.5
1846	155.8	89.0	164.2	17.0	2.8	6.1
1847–49	138.4	82.3	158.3	30.6	7.8	10.1
1850–54	127.9	83.6	158.1	37.4	5.7	8.3
1855–59	136.8	82.1	159.1	34.4	9.2	11.4
1860–64	114.8	80.9	160.4	62.3	13.1	15.6
1865–69	118.4	79.5	159.8	61.6	15.6	23.5
1870–74	108.1	84.7	157.6	80.9	21.4	31.7
1875–79	97.8	91.3	156.8	107.9	24.7	35.2
1880–84	85.0	83.4	161.8	128.3	27.6	36.9
1885–89	73.8	76.2	159.3	130.6	34.1	42.4
1890–94	64.6	75.9	171.7	152.6	42.6	41.4
1895–99	59.0	74.5	166.7	162.4	44.4	45.0
1900–04	50.6	67.2	170.8	182.5	49.0	49.7

* Calculated from the data contained in B. R. Mitchell and Phyllis Deane, *Abstracts of British Historical Statistics*, Cambridge University Press, 1962, according to the method described in the text.

Morton points out that the effect of the repeal was the opposite to that expected. 'There was no fall in prices [of wheat], in fact the average for the five years 1851–5 was 56s. against 54s. 9d. in the five years 1841–5.'[25] As will be seen later, however, this was only a very short-run appraisal of the effects on prices. The long-run picture is completely different, the five year average for wheat was, for example, 42s. 5d. in the period 1880–4. It was only 27s. 4d. (half of the 1841–5 price) in 1900–4.[26]

5 It is true, as Marx pointed out, that, at the time of the repeal of the Corn Laws, the landowning aristocracy exercised their political power in order to defend themselves. Therefore, the output series in Table 3 as well as the historical price series for wheat, barley and oats reflect mixed effects of various shifts in politics. In addition to these, there are other elements and events which should be taken

[25] A. L. Morton, *A People's History of England*, Lawrence and Wishart, 1984, p. 404.
[26] B. R. Mitchell and Phyllis Deane, *ibid.*, p. 489.

into account in an examination of the effects of the 1846 repeal. For example, a machine for pipe making, invented in 1845, stimulated farms to a further expansion in their size, because it made land drainage possible on a large scale. Also, more machinery was introduced into agriculture. These evidently strengthened UK farms considerably. On the other hand, the construction of railways and improvements in shipping and transportation made foreign produce more easily accessible and resulted in making the British market more competitive. Moreover, there are stochastic and exogenous elements such as several years of bad harvests and the Crimean War which hit the import of wheat from Russia. We must also point out that the threat of foreign competition led British farms to introduce a number of improved techniques. In spite of all these it is still true that the production of wheat greatly suffered after 1846, in comparison with the production of barley and oats.

The Corn Laws regulated exports and imports of not only wheat, barley and oats, but also rye, peas and beans. Under the 1815 laws, foreign corn could be imported without paying any duty when and only when the prices were at or above 80s. for wheat, 53s. for rye, peas and beans, 40s. for barley, and 27s. for oats. It is, therefore, not surprising that after the repeal of the laws Great Britain became increasingly dependent upon foreign grain.

Columns 5, 6, 7 of Table 3 list the average imports of wheat (including wheat meal and flour), barley and oats, for the periods specified in column 1. Table 4 produced from Table 3 shows that the ratio of imports of wheat to its home production was generally much greater than the corresponding ratio for barley as well as that for oats. It may thus be said that wheat produced in the UK was exposed to more rigorous international competition than that encountered by barley and oats. The table shows that after 1875 domestic wheat production was reduced to such a low level that it had only a minor share in the British wheat trade. Therefore, while Morton confines himself to a short-period analysis comparing the average money price of wheat in the period 1851–5 with the one of 1841–5, we should extend the analysis so as to cover those years in which the British wheat producers were really struggling with foreign competitors. Moreover, an investigation into the movement of the relative prices of wheat, barley and oats is required, because the degree of foreign penetration varies greatly between the three markets. It is then naturally to be expected that the price of wheat

Table 4 *The import/output ratio:
United Kingdom 1841–1904** (%)

Year	Wheat	Barley	Oats
1840–45	10	4	2
1846	11	3	4
1847–49	22	10	6
1850–54	29	7	5
1855–59	25	11	7
1860–64	54	16	10
1865–69	52	20	15
1870–74	75	25	20
1875–79	110	27	23
1880–84	151	33	23
1885–89	177	45	27
1890–94	236	56	24
1895–99	275	60	27
1900–04	361	73	29

* Calculated from Table 3.

Table 5 *The relative prices of wheat, barley and oats**

Year	Relative price		
	Wheat/barley	Wheat/oats	Barley/oats
1841–45	1.76	2.66	1.51
1851–55	1.73	2.41	1.39
1860–64	1.45	2.21	1.52
1870–74	1.45	2.24	1.54
1880–84	1.33	1.95	1.47
1890–94	1.11	1.57	1.41
1900–04	1.13	1.53	1.35

* Calculated from B. R. Mitchell and Phyllis Deane, *Abstract of British Historical Statistics*, pp. 488–9.

in terms of barley (or oats) should decline through time, since the wheat market has been more dominated by cheap foreign products than the barley (or oats) market; and this conjecture is clearly supported by the historical statistics as is seen in Table 5. Thus the production of wheat became very unfavourable for British farmers in the last decades of the nineteenth century, and its output diminished to 33 per cent of the 1846 level production at the beginning of the twentieth century.

6 Where prices of grains decline, real wages will be increased unless money wages fall more sharply. Real wages in terms of corn, however, will fluctuate greatly, reflecting the year-to-year fluctuations of the price of corn which are of considerable magnitude. To avoid such an oversensitive change in real wages we use the Rousseaux price indices of total agricultural products which are much steadier than the price indices of grain.[27] The base year of the Rousseaux indices is 1885; we adjust them such that the index for 1840 is 100. The indices of average money wages (not allowing for unemployment) are available, as Part B series, in the Mitchell and Deane volume.[28] By dividing the latter by the former we obtain the indices of the real wages in terms of total agricultural products. As for the wage indices before 1850, Part A series of the volume contains those for Great Britain only for several years at intervals, but Parts A and B have three overlapping years (1850, 1855 and 1860), the figures for which suggest that as there are no major discrepancies between the two series they may be smoothly connected.[29] For the years for which Part A indices are not available we estimate the values by applying the method of interpolation to the A series. These are also divided by the corresponding Rousseaux indices. Table 6 summarizes the results in the form of periodwise averages.

In the years during which the Corn Laws prevailed, the price of grain was more or less stable. It showed some downwards rigidity and it had a tendency to rise, because of the diminishing returns of land which arose when corn output was expanded. It would, therefore, be expected that real wages in terms of grain (or agricultural products) would not show a rising trend whilst the Corn Laws applied, 1815–45, while in the post-1846 years, real wages would increase dramatically because the price of grain would become lower and lower, thanks to the cheap price of imported grain. This is confirmed by Table 6. In the pre-1846 period, except for the years

[27] The Rousseaux price indices are given by B. R. Mitchell and Phyllis Deane, *ibid.*, pp. 471–3.

[28] *Ibid.*, pp. 343–4. Part A gives figures for selected years prior to 1860 whereas Part B gives a full series from 1850 onwards.

[29] *Ibid.*, p. 343. The figures for A and B series are 100 and 100 for 1850, 117 and 116 for 1855 and 115 and 114 for 1860, respectively.

Table 6 *Index of real wages* (1840 = 100)*

Year	Real wages	Year	Real wages
1816–19	96	1860–64	142
1820–24	120	1865–69	154
1825–29	113	1870–74	169
1830–34	116	1875–79	183
1835–39	109	1880–84	197
1840–45	112	1885–89	247
1846	117	1890–94	265
1847–49	126	1895–99	305
1850–54	141	1900–04	290
1855–59	132		

* Calculated from the data contained in B. R. Mitchell and Phyllis Deane, *Abstract of British Historical Statistics*, according to the method described in the text.

1816–19, real wages were declining, with some ups and downs, from the level of 120 for 1820–4 to the 1840–5 value of 112. Throughout the post-1846 period, however, the index of the real wages traced out an explosively expanding curve. Starting from the 1846 value of 117, it finally reached the level of 300 at the end of the nineteenth century. The table clearly shows that the repeal of the Corn Laws released the British economy from the limit set by agriculture.

According to the Ricardian doctrines, the rate of growth of population will decrease where the real wages diminish. No mechanism, therefore, worked to regulate the population in the post-Corn-Laws period, because real wages were steadily expanding. An increase in population was followed by an increase in imports of food. The domestically produced corn became more and more insignificant in the British market, so that the diminishing returns, with respect to land, of the British farms had a negligible effect on the price of grain. Output decreased steadily until the beginning of the twentieth century, though it started to rise again afterwards, especially in the war period, 1914–18, because of the difficulties in importing food. Thus, vicious cycles persisted between food prices, real wages, population growth and import of food.

In modelling the British economy after 1880, the 'Walrasian' model, as has been defined in the previous chapter, would be preferable to the Ricardian model. Of course, as has been seen in the Introduction, Walras supported all three laws of economic progress due to Ricardo. Walras derived them from his own model of the general equilibrium of capital formation by aggregating it into a semi-macroeconomic model with a smaller number of sectors and making reasonable assumptions on the values of various elasticities of demand and supply. His own model includes agriculture but he neglected its production lag. This means that Walras treated agriculture and industry alike, assuming that they both used land alike. In deriving our 'Walrasian' model we keep Ricardo's assumption that no manufacturing industries use land, as well as Walras' assumption that agriculture and industry are alike. This combination of assumptions is reasonable only where agriculture is of negligible magnitude; otherwise we would have a self-contradictory type of agriculture which does not use land.

Thus in our 'Walrasian' model it is assumed that the economy is entirely freed from diminishing returns due to the elimination of agriculture. This model is very similar to the so-called neoclassical growth model, which, I think, fits in with the stage that British economic development reached in the period 1880–1920. Walras himself is a Ricardian, but the 'Walrasian' model modified in the manner as described above is 'neoclassical'. The British economy was opened as Ricardo advocated. Then it was transformed into a 'Walrasian type' economy, to which the Ricardian model was no longer applicable. This is a remarkable example of a decline of an economist's doctrine being caused by its own achievements. The historians of economic thought have later made a similar observation with regard to Keynes.

7 Finally, a comment on the development of economic theory. From a logical, but not historical, point of view, Böhm-Bawerk's and Wicksell's volumes which were published after Walras may adequately be regarded as a generalization of Ricardo.[30] They generalized the wage-fund theory into the new wage-fund theory by assuming that it takes time to produce any commodity. This line of thought later has developed into von Neumann's growth theory.[31]

[30] E. von Böhm-Bawerk, *Positive Theorie des Kapitales*, Gustav Fischer Verlag, Jena, 1888, and J. G. K. Wicksell, *Über Wert, Kapital und Rente*, Gustav Fischer Verlag, Jena, 1893.
[31] J. von Neumann, 'A Model of General Economic Equilibrium', *Review of Economic Studies*, Vol. 13, 1945–6, pp. 1–9.

The existence of a production lag is not limited to agriculture; some period of time is needed to produce non-food consumer goods as well as producer goods. The production period may differ from one commodity to another, but production processes of longer duration may be divided into a sequence of 'standardized' processes of unit duration. For this purpose we need to enlarge our list of commodities to include intermediate products which appear as outputs at the end of some standardized process and appear again as inputs at the commencement of some other processes at a later stage. By formulating technology in this way we may distinguish between capital goods at different stages of wear and tear; that is to say, a brand-new capital good k is qualitatively different from a one-period old capital good k which, in turn, differs from a two-period old good k, and so forth. If a process uses an n-period old capital good k at the beginning of the current period, then the $(n + 1)$-period old capital good of the same kind is left over (or 'produced as a joint output', according to von Neumann's terminology) for future production at the end of the same process.

This is the Wicksell–von Neumann description of technology which enables us to formulate the theory of production as a problem of choice of technique. We may allow for all alternative methods of producing the same commodities in different lengths of time. We may also allow for all alternative ways of using capital goods. Producers choose, from among these, the production processes they use, the length of sequence of which determines the period of production of the commodity they produce. This choice of technique also determines the life-time of the capital goods they employ.[32] Capital goods k will be obsolete and discarded at the age a wherever the processes using k of the age a as inputs are all unprofitable. In this neo-Austrian theory[33] (or von Böhm-Bawerk–Wicksell–von Neumann theory) the economy is, at the beginning of the current period, provided with stocks of commodities which are the results of production in the previous period. These stocks are the funds for production in the current period; the wage-fund theory is thus extended to include not only stocks of wage goods but also stocks of all fixed and circulating capital goods. Unlike the original wage-fund theory, the production period is not a technologically

[32] See my *Theory of Economic Growth*, Oxford University Press, 1964, pp. 89–114.
[33] The neo-Austrian capital theory is formulated differently by Sir John Hicks, in his *Capital and Time*, Oxford University Press, 1973.

determined constant, but is a variable to be economically determined by the choice of technique. Similarly, the life-time of each durable capital good is economically determined and may differ from, and be shorter than, its technologically fixed physical life-time. The life of capital goods is terminated, at some point of time, as a consequence of an economic decision.

Thus the Wicksell–von Neumann system consists of segmenting technology into standardized elementary processes sufficiently short that each procedure may be considered almost instantaneous, though many processes may take place in succession. Thus as a limiting Wicksell–von Neumann system with an elementary production period of negligible length, we obtain a Walrasian system with an enormous number of sectors. However, even if we insert a Wicksell–von Neumann interlude between the Ricardian and 'Walrasian' stages, it is evident that the process of industrialization (or the transition from the Ricardian to the 'Walrasian' economy) has not yet been explained satisfactorily, because Wicksell–von Neumann economics is substantially the same as Ricardo's (it is a logical generalization and refinement of the latter). Thus, there are essentially only two stages, 'Ricardian' and 'Walrasian', and the transition is seen as nothing other than a sudden and instantaneous jump from the old platform onto a new stage. There is no dynamic theory yet that successfully explains how one regime emerges from another. We now have, at best, only a sequence of economic theories – a sequence of snapshots each explaining the economy at a different stage. None of them deals with an economy's transition from one epoch to another.

Finally, the new wage fund theory may be considered not just as a generalization but as a correction of Ricardo's theory, which contained the inconsistency pointed out in Chapter 1 above. Ricardo's cost equation for non-agricultural industry includes interest payment for the wage fund it uses, despite his assumption of instantaneous production in the industry. This definition of cost conflicts with his treatment of non-wage goods which assumes that they are produced and sold instantly. In this case there is no need to charge interest on the wage fund. The Wicksell–von Neumann theory, if formulated in such a form as enables it to be applied to a state of unbalanced growth, permits us to rewrite Ricardo's economics so as to avoid this inconsistency; we then obtain a Ricardo–von Neumann model.

Index

Agriculture
  diminishing return, 126
  production function of, 30, 36–8
Alford, R. F. G., 237
Anti-Say's law, 5, 14, 55, 185, 203, 209
  index, 237
Arrow, K. J., 2, 10, 13, 93, 98, 119–20,
  149–50

Banker, 202–6
Bhagwati, J., 133
Böhm-Bawerk, E. von, 96, 202, 249
Brechling, F. P. R., 150
Bruno, M., 225

Capital
  circulating (or variable), 171
  fixed (or constant), 156n, 171
    see also Ricardo–Marx theorem
  marginal efficiency of, 159, 161
Capital coefficient matrix, 59
  augmented, 27–8, 31, 78
  its decomposability, 59–60, 74–6
Caravale, G. A., 12, 67, 103, 125, 224
Casarosa, C., 12–13, 103–4, 121–5,
  224–5
Catephores, G., 99, 138, 196
Chipman, J. S., 126, 128
Class
  productive, 155
  unproductive, 155
Classical school, 207
Cole, W. A., 241–2
Comparative advantage (or cost), 5,
  131–2
  theory of, 126, 131
Congruity between economy and
  economics, 233
Corn law, 240
  its repeal, 242–8

Costa, G., 12, 125

Dasgupta, A. K., 8, 234–6
Deane, Phyllis, 238–48
Debreu, G., 2, 10, 13, 93, 98, 119, 149–50
Dual adjustment rule
  cross, 81–7, 119
  direct, 119

Equilibrium
  long-run conditions, 108–10
Equilibrium curve
  for capital utilization, 216–17, 219
  for labour employment, 217–19
Engels, F., 242–3
Entrepreneur, 196–7, 202–6, 227
Exploitation rate, 69, 90, 95

Filippi, F., 160, 163
Flaschel, P., 119n
Free goods
  rule of, 87, 119, 136
Frobenius, G., 27, 130

Hahn, F. H., 2, 13, 120, 150, 160, 207
Harrod, R., 230, 236
  knife-edge property, 230
Hatori, T., 4
Hicks, J. R., 7, 13, 19n, 28, 52, 70–5,
  83–4, 119, 184–5, 250
  his wage profit frontier, 71, 75
Hollander, S., 52–3, 104, 155, 235

Indecomposability, 130
Innovation, 168–9
Input coefficient matrix
  augmented, 27–8, 31, 78
Investment
  anti-Say's law part, 237
  Say's law part, 237

Jaffé, W., 1–2, 8, 120

Kemeny, J. G., 136
Kemeny–Morgenstern–Thompson
 condition, 136
Keynes, J. M., 6, 11, 14, 54–5, 151–3,
 157–65, 189, 194, 198–208,
 228–31, 236, 249

Labour
 heterogeneous labour, 99
 market price of, 108
 natural price of, 107–8
Labour theory of value, 9–10, 17, 29,
 48, 59–60, 131
 marginal, 19, 29, 31–3, 48, 50, 55, 100
Labour value
 determination equation, 21
 Marxian and Ricardian, 100
Landowner
 his consumption and savings, 52–3
Land theory of value, 29
Lange, O., 151, 164–6, 200
Leontief, W. W., 27
Lexis, W., 3
Loria, A., 3

McCullock, J. R., 170
McIntyre, F., 151
Malinvaud, E., 201
Malthus, T. R., 157, 164, 170
Marginal
 labour theory of value, *see* labour
  theory of value
 productivity theory, 6, 30, 36
Marginalism, 8–9
Marshall, A., 10, 207
Marx, K., 1–5, 8, 10–13, 18–24, 33–5,
 39, 49, 55, 72, 81, 89–92, 97–8,
 154–6, 171–7, 189–93, 202, 206–7,
 243
 reproduction scheme, 55, 193–5
  extended, 55, 175–7
  simple, 173–4, 179
 Fundamental Marxian theorem
  (FMT), 9, 13, 18, 70, 87–8, 95
 generalized (GFMT), 81, 87–8
 Roemer's (RFMT), 89
 with land, 92–3, 96–8
 strong generalized (SGFMT), 92
Menger, C., 96
Mill, J. S., 51
Mitchell, B. R., 238–42, 244, 246–8

Monied class, 156
Morgenstern, O., 136
Morishima, M., 1, 4, 14, 19n, 55, 61–3,
 70, 85–9, 94, 119, 130, 138, 150,
 160, 175, 193–7, 200–1, 250
Morton, A. L., 244
Multiplier theory, 213, 215

Negishi, T., 38, 160, 163
Neoclassical school, 207
Neumann, J. von, 52–3, 104, 134, 155,
 249–51
 joint production, 85–8
 system, 119
Numeraire, 21, 61

Overdeterminacy thesis
 neoclassical case, 159–62
 Walras' case, 163–4, 184–5

Pareto superior, 169
Pasinetti, L. L., 12, 50–3, 67, 103, 125,
 155
Patinkin, D., 151, 164–5, 200
Petri, F., 81, 88–9
Price of labour
 market, 107–8
 natural, 107
Price–cost equation, 21, 163
Profit
 subsistence rate of, 224–5, 227
 supernormal, 227
Profitability
 rule, 86–7, 119, 135
Purchase
 power to, 157
 will to, 157

Rent
 absolute, 33–5, 39
 differential, 36–49
Ricardo, D.
 his general equilibrium system, 46
 growth, 103–25
  quasi-Ricardian, 227
 international trade, 126–46
 interpretation of
  macroeconomic, 121
  microeconomic, 121
 machinery, 168–86
 marginalism, 17–35
 modernized version of his foreign
  trade theory, 134

Ricardo, D. (*cont.*).
 polar Ricardian, 122–3
 Say's law, 149–67
 simple model, 155–6
 wages and profit, 59–100
Ricardo–Marx theorem (on
 proportionality of values and
 prices), 12, 19–23, 49, 51, 66–75,
 133, 171
Robinson, Joan, 72
Roemer, J. E., 81, 88–9, 92
Rousseaux price index, 247

Saddle point, 229
Saltari, E., 160, 163
Samuelson, P. A., 9, 13, 17–18, 19n,
 28–9, 31–3, 59, 72–3, 81–3, 97,
 103–4, 121–5, 224–5, 235
 thesis of incompatibility of falling
 profit and falling real wage, 9, 72–3
Savings
 landowners', *see* landowner
 notional, 230
Say, J. B., 195–6
Say's law, 5, 11, 14, 54–5, 149–67, 169,
 172–4, 177–9, 180–4, 209
 Keynes sense, 151–2, 165–7, 190,
 195–8, 214
 Lange–Patinkin sense, 164–7, 200
 strong, 231–2
Schlesinger, K., 120
Schumpeter, J. A., 29, 31, 33, 81, 96–8,
 168–9, 196, 200–7
Semmler, W., 119n
Sismondi, J. C. L. S., 164
Smith, A., 8, 17, 127, 130, 170, 189
Solow, R. M., 236
Sraffa, P., 9, 13, 19, 28, 60–8, 74–5,
 128, 157
 distribution line, 66, 69
Standard
 commodity, 61
 composition, 64
 employment, 64
 net output, 64
 ratio, 64

Standard (*cont.*).
 system, 64
Stiglitz, J., 97

Technique
 choice of, 250–1
Thompson, G. L., 136, 141
Tosato, D. A., 12, 67–8, 70, 74
Two-sector–two-factor model
 Keynesian, 215
 Ricardian, 215
 Walrasian, 215

Uzawa, H., 236

Wage fund theory, 12, 20, 45, 104,
 121–4, 156n, 202, 210–15, 236, 249
 new, 206–9, 249–51
Wage–profit frontier, 9, 13–14, 19, 22,
 25–8, 59, 62–6, 72, 105, 111, 127
 real, 22, 80, 144
 money, 22, 78–80
Wage rate
 subsistence level, 107–10, 114–16,
 121–2, 145
 real, 22
Wald, A., 120
Walras, L., 1–14, 18, 33, 37–8, 43–6,
 51–61, 84, 103–4, 118–21, 149–50,
 160–4, 167–9, 206–9, 228–31,
 235–6, 248–9
 laws of price change in a progressive
 economy, 1
 theory of capital formation
 literary model, 199–200
 mathematical model, 199–200
 tâtonnement process, 84
Walras' law, 152, 158, 160, 165
Weber, M., 233
Wicksell, J. G. K., 200–1, 208, 249–51
 cumulative process, 201
Wieser, F. von, 96

Yntema, Th., 151

Zeuthen, F., 120

Printed in the United States
By Bookmasters